AF823983

Serious Managers Guide to Agentic AI Leadership

From Adoption to Alignment:
Frameworks for Leading AI Teams
with Clarity, Trust, and Accountability.

Claude Louis-Charles, PhD

The moral rights of the author have been asserted

Copyrights 2026

All rights reserved

No part of this publication may be reproduced, stored in a retrieval system, or transmitted in any form or by any means, without the prior permission in writing of the publisher, nor be otherwise circulated in any form of binding or cover other than that in which it is published and without a similar condition, including this condition being imposed on the subsequent purchaser.

Cybersoft Publishing LLC

Fort Washington, MD 20744

Drclaude.net

First Edition Dec 2024

Contents

1 Introduction

Why Agentic AI Leadership Is the Defining Skill of Our Era

Eighty-eight percent of organizations now use AI in at least one business function; that is the current reality, not a prediction or a trend to watch. Nearly three-quarters of CEOs say they are now the primary decision makers on AI adoption, and roughly half believe their jobs are on the line if AI does not pay off. Companies are doubling their AI spending as agentic AI autonomous systems that can act, make decisions, and orchestrate complex processes without human intervention at every step moves from experiment to expectation.

So here is the question every serious manager needs to answer: Are you leading AI in your organization, or is AI simply happening to you?

This is not a question about whether you can code. It is not a test of your technical fluency or your ability to recite large language model architectures. It is a fundamentally human question about leadership: about the mindsets, decisions, communications, relationships, and responsibilities that determine whether AI creates lasting value in your organization or quietly erodes what made it work.

The gap between those two outcomes is leadership. Specifically, AI leadership.

The Adoption Paradox

Here is the paradox that prompted this book. AI is everywhere, and yet most of the gains it should deliver remain unrealized. Industry data consistently shows that only around four in ten organizations report any measurable business impact from AI, and nearly two-thirds have not yet begun scaling AI across the enterprise; they are still experimenting, still running pilots, still discovering that deploying a tool and transforming a business are two entirely different challenges.

A second layer of complexity compounds the first. Almost half of workers in major economies report using AI tools without proper authorization or in ways that conflict with organizational guidelines. More than half admit to putting less effort into their work because AI can fill the gap. And the majority avoid disclosing when they have used AI to complete a task. AI arrived in organizations before governance has caught up, and trust is eroding quietly, even while efficiency metrics look promising on paper.

This is the leadership crisis hiding inside the AI boom. Organizations have adopted AI at scale, but most have not developed the leadership infrastructure to use it effectively. Technology is not the bottleneck. Leaders are.

That is not criticism; it is an invitation.

The organizations that will gain the most from AI are not necessarily those with the largest data science teams or the most aggressive AI investment portfolios. They are the ones whose managers at every level and in every function have developed the judgment, the framework, and the habits of mind to lead through an era of continuous AI disruption. They are the ones where leadership keeps pace with technology, rather than being permanently one step behind it.

That gap between adoption and leadership is what this book closes.

Diagram 0.1: The AI Leadership Gap

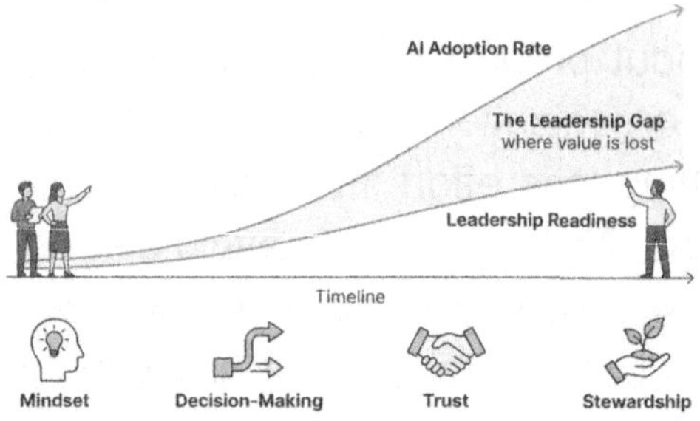

Concluding that 'e on AI was can are able to enct leadership all four pillars and team in the book.

What This Book Is

Serious Managers' Guide to AI Leadership is a practical, authoritative guide for managers who are serious about leading in the AI era. Not just tolerate AI. Not just delegating it and leading it with clear eyes, a strong framework, and the confidence that comes from understanding both what AI can do and, critically, what only you can do.

This book serves two audiences, and they are not as different as they might appear.

If you are a C-suite executive or vice president, you are navigating strategic decisions about AI investment, organizational alignment, and competitive positioning. You need frameworks that work at altitude tools for setting direction, building alignment across a leadership team, governing AI responsibly, and ensuring that what you announce in the boardroom lands in the operating model. You need operational clarity about what it means to be accountable for AI in your organization, not just supportive of it.

If you are a mid-level manager, a department head, or a team leader, you are making AI real. You are involved in daily work that includes evaluating tools, coaching teams, managing AI-informed processes, and translating the organization's AI strategy into actionable solutions that work on Monday morning. You need the same conceptual rigor as the executives above you, applied to the ground-level decisions you make every day, including those for which no one has yet given you a playbook.

Both of you will find this book written for you, because effective AI leadership is neither purely top-down nor bottom-up. It is in continuous dialogue. The executive who sets strategy without understanding how AI lands at the team level will find their initiatives stalling in implementation. The manager who executes without engaging the strategic frame will find themselves reacting to changes rather than shaping them.

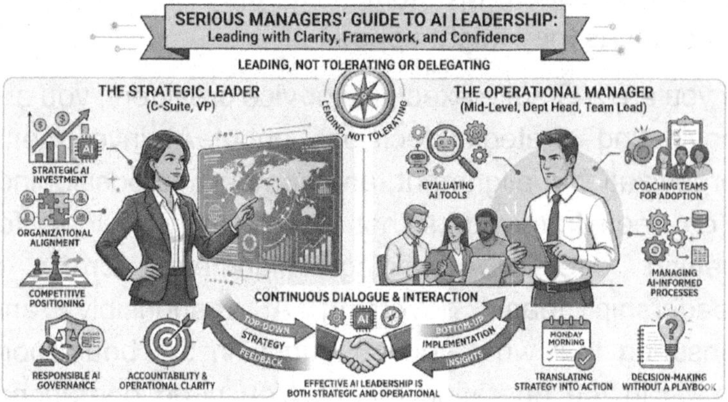

The tone you will encounter throughout these pages is authoritative without being academic, and practical without being simplistic. When we introduce a named framework, we will let you know. When we arrive at a key takeaway, you will know it. And when a chapter ends, you will have something concrete to do, not just something abstract to think about.

This book does not require you to love AI. It does not ask you to be an enthusiast. It asks only that you be serious about your role, your team, and the responsibility that comes with every significant leadership decision. If you bring that seriousness, the frameworks in this book will meet you where you are.

What This Book Is Not

A few boundaries worth drawing, because there are a lot of AI books competing for your attention.

This is not a technical manual. You will not learn to build models, engineer prompts for production systems, or evaluate the architecture of AI infrastructure. Those skills belong to a different kind of reader. What you will develop is the ability to ask the right questions of the people who do those things and to make decisions that go beyond what any technical expert can do for you.

This is not a collection of AI use cases. You will not find lists of the top fifty ways to use ChatGPT in your function. Use cases are useful, but they solve for today. This book builds the judgment infrastructure that lets you evaluate any use case, current or future, and make mission-aligned decisions about when to deploy, pause, or push back.

This is not an ethics manifesto or a regulation guide. AI ethics and regulation are real and important, and this book engages them seriously, especially in the stewardship chapter. But moralizing is not leading. You will find no lectures here, only practical frameworks for making responsible decisions under real constraints, with real teams, in real time.

And this is not a book that assumes AI is already working smoothly in your organization. It assumes you are somewhere in the messy middle: past the initial excitement, perhaps frustrated by the gap between what AI promised and what it has delivered, and trying to figure out what serious leadership looks like in this environment. You are in exactly the right place.

Three Frameworks That Run Through Everything

This book is built around three original frameworks that appear progressively across the chapters and come together in the final integration. They are not metaphors or conceptual gestures; each one is a working tool with a specific decision-support function.

The first is the AI-CLEAR AI Leadership Model. AI-CLEAR is a five-dimensional self-assessment framework that measures the leader, not the organization, not the technology, but you. The five dimensions are Curiosity, Leverage, Empowerment, Accountability, and Readiness. Together, they map the full behavioral profile of an effective AI leader. AI-CLEAR is introduced in Chapter 2 and serves as the human backbone in every subsequent chapter.

The second is the Serious Decision Spectrum. As AI generates more recommendations, alerts, and automated outputs, one of the most consequential leadership skills is knowing how much authority to give the machine on any given decision. The Serious Decision Spectrum is a two-axis framework of data density crossed with human stakes that gives you a reliable method for calibrating that authority. It prevents two equally dangerous errors: under-automating low-stakes, data-rich decisions, and over-automating high-stakes decisions that require human judgment and values. The Spectrum is introduced in Chapter 3.

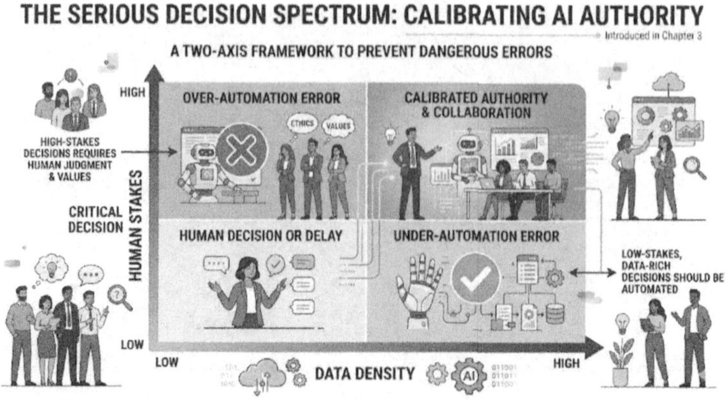

The third is the Trust Architecture. Trust is the invisible infrastructure of every AI initiative, and it is far more complex than most leaders appreciate. The Trust Architecture maps four distinct trust relationships with your AI systems, your team, external stakeholders, and yourself, and provides a quarterly audit process to maintain each one. It is introduced in Chapter 5 and informs the stewardship work of Chapter 8.

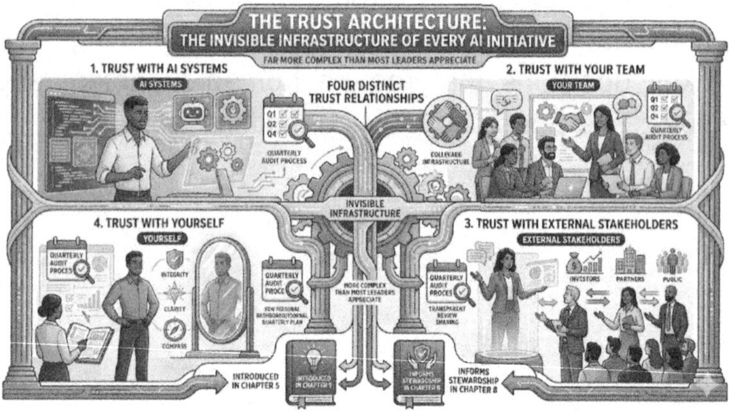

All three frameworks are synthesized together in Chapter 9, which gives you an integrated view of how they operate as a system, the Serious AI Leader's Compass.

The Journey Ahead

Nine chapters. One clear progression.

We begin where every AI leader must begin understanding the landscape. Chapter 1 is your AI primer, a practical, jargon-light grounding in what AI is, how it works at the level that matters for leadership, and what the current state of enterprise AI adoption means for your organization. We pay particular attention to agentic AI because the shift from AI-as-tool to AI-as-autonomous-actor changes the leadership equation in ways that most management frameworks have yet to catch up with. You do not need to become a technologist. You need to stop being a bystander to technology decisions.

Chapter 2 moves from the landscape to the leader. Before you change your organization, you need to examine your thinking. We explore the mindset shifts that distinguish AI-native leaders from those who are simply AI-adjacent, and we introduce the AI-CLEAR model as your primary self-assessment tool. The most underrated leadership skill right now is discernment: knowing when not to use AI is as important as knowing how to use it well.

Chapter 3 enters the decision-making arena. AI has permanently altered the texture of decisions, how fast they can be made, how much data can be incorporated, and where the real risk of error lies. We introduce the Serious Decision Spectrum, a framework for calibrating human authority versus AI authority across different types of organizational decisions. The goal is not to resist AI-assisted decisions or to embrace them uncritically, but to be deliberate about where each decision belongs on the spectrum.

Chapter 4 turns to communication, the leadership skill that connects everything else. Leaders who cannot translate AI's capabilities into compelling, honest, human-centered narratives will struggle to build the support, culture, and accountability structures that enable AI initiatives to succeed. This chapter teaches you to be the bridge between technical possibility and organizational reality.

Chapter 5 is about trust, the most undervalued leadership currency in the AI era. We introduce Trust Architecture: a four-layer model that maps the distinct trust relationships every AI leader must actively maintain. This is where the widespread pattern of unauthorized AI use and avoidance gets resolved not through better policy alone, but through better leadership.

Chapter 6 focuses on executive alignment, the single most powerful predictor of AI success, and the one that receives the least structured attention. Alignment is different from support, as any experienced AI leader will tell you. Support is easy to get in a meeting and hard to sustain through the first major setback. Alignment is structural, operational, and expensive to build, and worth every investment. This chapter gives you the tools to build it deliberately.

Chapter 7 addresses one of the most urgent and underexamined questions in AI leadership: how do you build the team that can lead alongside AI? This is not just about hiring data scientists or running prompt engineering workshops. It is about workforce readiness at scale, equipping middle managers to navigate AI-driven change, creating psychological safety for teams uncertain about their futures, developing credible, rather than cosmetic, reskilling pathways, and rethinking what you look for when you hire. The organizations that will succeed with AI are those that invest as seriously in their people as they do in their platforms.

Chapter 8 explores stewardship: the leader's responsibility for AI systems, data, people, and outcomes. This is where ethics and governance stop being abstract principles and become practical obligations of leadership. It is also where we address what, for many managers, is the most human question in AI leadership: what is your responsibility to the people whose work is being transformed by the technology you are deploying? Responsible by design is not a compliance posture; it is a leadership posture.

Chapter 9 brings everything together. We introduce the Serious AI Leader's Compass. This integrating framework shows how all seven core concepts (mindsets, decision-making, communication, trust, alignment, team building, and stewardship) operate as a system rather than a checklist. We also deliver a 90-day action plan and a leadership maturity assessment so that this book closes not with a sense of completion but with a clear path forward.

How to Use This Book

Serious Managers' Guide to AI Leadership is designed to be read in sequence, because each chapter builds on the one before it. The frameworks are cumulative. The Serious Decision Spectrum is richer if you have already worked through the mindset chapter, and the Trust Architecture is easier to apply if you understand the communication chapter that precedes it. If you jump to a specific chapter because an immediate problem demands it, you will still find value. But the book's full return comes from the journey.

At the end of each chapter, you will find a concrete action set, not a list of aspirational behaviors, but specific decisions, artifacts, and conversations you can take into your work this week. These are not optional extras. They are the mechanism by which the frameworks in this book become leadership habits rather than intellectual exercises.

You will also encounter a manager's checklist in each chapter, a rapid self-assessment against the behaviors that define excellence in that domain. Use it honestly.

The gaps are not embarrassments; they are the most valuable output of the book. Leadership development always begins with an accurate picture of where you stand.

If you are reading this as part of a leadership team, consider aligning one chapter per session and using the checklist as a structured discussion tool. The questions it raises about decision authority, trust, alignment, and responsibility are exactly the conversations AI leadership teams need to have but rarely do.

One final thought on pacing. AI is moving faster than any book can keep up with in real time. Some contexts you encounter here will evolve by the time you read it, not because the research was careless, but because the technology and its organizational consequences are advancing at a pace without modern precedent. That is a leadership reality you need to hold. The frameworks in this book are designed to remain useful even as the specific tools, models, and regulatory landscape shift beneath them. You are not building expertise in any AI system. You are building the judgment to lead through whatever AI becomes next.

A Note on Language

AI leadership literature has a language problem. It oscillates between breathless hype AI as the greatest revolution since the printing press and dark warnings AI as an existential threat, a job destroyer, an algorithmic oppressor. Neither posture is useful to a manager who has a team meeting on Tuesday.

This book uses plain language. When we introduce technical concepts, we define them clearly and move on; we do not dwell on them. When we introduce a framework, we name it and explain why it is named that way, because names matter: a named framework is one you can recall under pressure, share with a colleague, and apply without re-reading the book.

We use 'AI' broadly to mean the full spectrum of machine learning, large language models, generative systems, and autonomous agents that are currently reshaping enterprise work. When a distinction matters, and sometimes it does, we will be specific. When it does not, we will not impose unnecessary precision on you.

We also use 'leader' and 'manager' deliberately. Not everyone with the title of manager leads, and not everyone who leads has a formal title. If you are in this book, you are a leader in the relevant sense: someone whose decisions shape the work of others, and who bears responsibility for the quality of those decisions. That is the audience this book was written for.

A Note Before You Begin

The serious manager is not the one who knows the most about AI. The serious manager is the one who has built the judgment, the relationships, and the organizational infrastructure to lead well, no matter what AI looks like next year.

You are not the first manager to navigate an unprecedented technology transition. Leaders who managed the shift from paper to digital workflows, from local computing to cloud infrastructure, from telephone-based sales to digital CRM, all of them faced the same fundamental question you are facing now: how do I lead effectively through a transformation I cannot fully predict? The answer has never been mastery of the technology. It has always been mastery of leadership.

What this era adds is urgency and compounding complexity. The pace of AI evolution means that the window for leadership development is not indefinite. Organizations that build AI leadership capability now will compound that advantage year over year. Those who defer it, waiting until technology is more stable, waiting for clearer regulation, waiting until the ROI is more obvious, will find themselves further behind with each passing quarter.

This book builds leadership capability that compounds. The frameworks are durable. The mindsets are transferable. The habits are actionable from the first chapter.

You do not need to have everything figured out. You need to begin.

That is what this book is for. Let's begin

2 What Every Leader Actually Needs to Know About Intelligent Machines

When the Machine Outpaces the Meeting

The quarterly business review had been running for forty minutes when the Chief Operating Officer asked a straightforward question: which of the AI initiatives currently underway were producing measurable returns, and which were consuming budget without a credible path to impact? The room went quiet. Three vice presidents looked at their slides. The Chief Information Officer shifted in her seat. The head of the AI Center of Excellence, a title coined 18 months earlier to signal organizational seriousness, began explaining the difference between proof-of-concept deployments and production-ready systems, between model accuracy and business value. The COO, who had approved more than $4 million in AI-related expenditure in the prior fiscal year, nodded slowly and said: "I need to understand this at a level where I can actually hold someone accountable."

That exchange happens in boardrooms and executive suites every week. It is not a technology failure. It is a leadership vocabulary failure. The COO in that room was not unintelligent. He was not averse to technology. He had no conceptual scaffolding onto which the information being presented could attach. When you lack the vocabulary of AI, you cannot ask precise questions. When you cannot ask precise questions, you cannot generate precise accountability. And when you cannot generate precise accountability, you are not leading; you are ratifying.

This chapter exists to solve that problem. It is not a technical manual. You will not leave here able to build a model or audit a neural network. What you will leave with is the conceptual architecture that effective AI leadership requires: an accurate mental model of what these systems are, how they work at the level that matters for decisions, where they fail, and what the current state of enterprise adoption reveals about your competitive environment. Every subsequent chapter in this book builds on what this chapter establishes. The leaders who invest time here will find the rest of the book easier to apply and harder to dismiss.

Why Getting This Right Is a Leadership Obligation

The gap between AI deployment and AI value is one of the defining business challenges of this decade. Organizations of every size and sector are spending on tools, talent, infrastructure, and consultants who arrive with frameworks and depart before the real work begins. And yet, when you look at the pattern of impact across enterprise AI adoption, a consistent and troubling picture emerges: high deployment rates coexist with low realized returns. The technology is available. The capability is real. The leadership clarity needed to deploy it with precision, at scale, and with organizational alignment remains scarce.

That scarcity is where serious managers have their greatest opportunity. Technical capability in AI is becoming commoditized. You can buy models, rent infrastructure, and hire prompt engineers. What cannot be purchased off the shelf is the judgment to know which AI applications are mission-aligned, the authority to enforce governance across organizational silos, the credibility to explain decisions made with algorithmic input to a regulator, a board, or a worried employee. These are leadership functions. They require a leader who understands enough to ask the right questions, evaluate the right answers, and make decisions that the organization can stand behind.

The stakes extend beyond organizational performance. As AI systems move from narrow task execution toward more autonomous behavior, executing multi-step workflows, interacting with external systems, and making consequential decisions within defined parameters, the nature of leadership oversight changes qualitatively. The leader who governed a spell-checker faces a different challenge when governing a system that can initiate procurement actions or restructure customer communications at scale without human review of each output. Understanding this shift before it arrives is not optional. It separates principals in the AI conversation from passengers.

The AI Taxonomy Every Leader Must Own

Precision of language is a leadership tool. In AI conversations with vendors, with technical teams, with boards, imprecise terminology is exploited, sometimes deliberately, more often through accumulated misunderstanding. A vendor who uses "AI" to describe a rules-based system and another who uses it to describe a system capable of genuine generalization are both technically correct and practically misleading. The leader who cannot distinguish between these two things will make poor purchasing decisions, set unrealistic expectations, and struggle to evaluate progress against commitments. What follows is not a glossary; it is a mental model. These distinctions matter not as vocabulary tests but as decision tools.

Machine Learning: Pattern Recognition at Scale

Machine learning is the foundational layer of most AI systems you will encounter in enterprise contexts. At its core, machine learning is a method by which a computer system learns to perform tasks by identifying patterns in large amounts of historical data, rather than by following a set of rules explicitly written by a programmer. This distinction is important. Traditional software operates on explicit logic: if X, then Y. Machine learning systems derive their own logic from exposure to examples. Show a machine learning model tens of thousands of images labeled "fraud" and "not fraud," and it will learn to make that distinction on new examples it has never seen.

The leadership implication is immediate: machine learning outputs are only as reliable as the data on which they were trained. If your historical fraud-detection data reflects biased enforcement practices, your model will learn and replicate those biases. If your training data does not include edge cases common in certain customer segments, the model will fail precisely where those segments interact with your business. The question "what does your training data look like?" is one of the most powerful a leader can ask of any AI system, and the discomfort it sometimes generates is usually informative.

What unites all machine learning sub-fields for leadership purposes is a single principle: these systems optimize for what they are measured on. A model optimized to minimize customer service call duration will not spontaneously optimize for customer satisfaction unless that metric is explicitly included. This dynamic, where systems optimize for the proxy rather than the underlying goal, is one of the most consistent sources of AI project failure, and it is entirely a leadership-and-governance problem, not a technical one.

The AI Hierarchy: From Machine Learning to Agentic Systems.

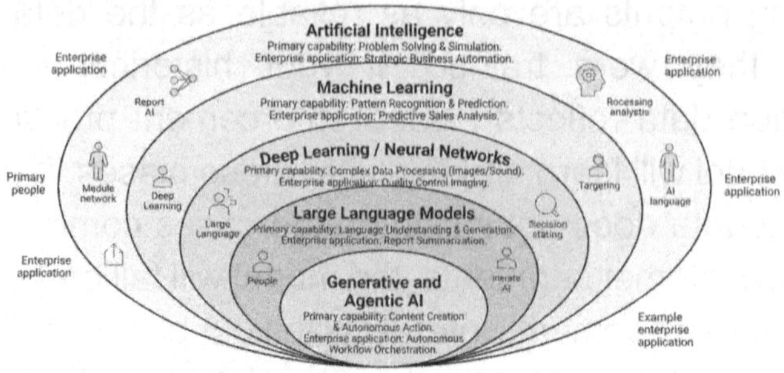

The AI hierarchy: from Machine Learning to Agentic systems, insights and connectivity.

Deep Learning, Neural Networks, and the Black Box Problem

Deep learning is a branch of machine learning that uses artificial neural network computational architectures loosely inspired by the structure of biological brains, with many processing layers that allow the system to learn increasingly abstract representations of data. Deep learning is the engine behind image recognition, speech-to-text, real-time translation, and the large language models that power today's generative AI tools. The "deep" in deep learning refers to the depth of these layered networks, which can contain hundreds of millions or billions of parameters.

The leadership challenge specific to deep learning is known as the black-box problem. Unlike a decision tree or a regression model, where the logic connecting inputs to outputs can be examined and explained, deep neural networks perform their computation through interactions among billions of parameters in ways that even their creators cannot fully interpret. The network arrives at an answer, often a very good answer, through a process that resists simple explanation. For a leader, this creates a specific accountability challenge: how do you justify, defend, or contest a consequential decision when the system that informed it cannot explain why it made the decision it did?

The answer is not to avoid deep learning systems; they are too capable and too prevalent for that to be a realistic strategy. The answer is to build explainability requirements into procurement and deployment decisions, to establish clear human-in-the-loop checkpoints for decisions above certain stakes thresholds, and to maintain institutional knowledge of which human judgments were being replaced or supplemented, and why. These are not technical decisions. They are governance decisions that require the leader to be present and deliberate, not deferential. When AI accountability matters in regulated industries, in customer-facing decisions, and in employment contexts, "the algorithm decided" is not an acceptable answer for a regulator, a court, or a workforce.

Natural Language Processing and the Breakthrough of Large Language Models

Natural language processing, or NLP, is the branch of AI concerned with enabling computers to understand, generate, and reason about human language. For most of its history, NLP was effective at narrow tasks, keyword extraction, sentiment classification, and named entity recognition, but was brittle and limited in its ability to handle the full range of human linguistic expression. The breakthrough came with the development of transformer architecture and, subsequently, large language models, or LLMs. These systems, trained on vast quantities of text drawn from books, articles, websites, and code, learned to predict and generate language with a fluency and apparent coherence that was qualitatively different from anything that had preceded them.

The practical significance for enterprise leaders is substantial. LLMs can draft, summarize, translate, explain, classify, and respond across an enormous range of language tasks without task-specific training. They can answer questions about documents, generate first drafts of communications, extract structured information from unstructured text, and assist with coding. The breadth of their capability means that almost every knowledge-work function in your organization has at least one workflow where LLMs are already useful or imminently deployable. The constraint is no longer capability; it is judgment about where to deploy, what safeguards to apply, and whether deployment produces the workflow-level impact that justified the investment.

What leaders must understand about LLMs is that their apparent fluency does not equate to accuracy, reliability, or reasoning. An LLM generates text by predicting what token is most likely to follow the previous sequence, based on patterns learned from training data. This process produces text that is coherent and often correct, but it can also produce text that is confidently, fluently wrong. This failure mode, known as hallucination, is not a bug that will be eliminated in the next version. It is a structural characteristic of these systems. Managing it is a governance and workflow design challenge, not a wait-for-the-technology-to-improve challenge.

Generative AI: From Content to Reasoning

Generative AI is the category of AI systems capable of producing original content, text, images, code, audio, video, and synthetic data rather than merely classifying or predicting. LLMs are the most prominent form of generative AI, but the category also includes image generation systems, audio synthesis tools, and multimodal models that work fluidly across different content types. Generative AI has seen one of the quickest commercial adoptions in business history. Within two years of the public release of conversational LLM interfaces, a substantial majority of large organizations reported using generative AI in at least one business function.

The leadership significance of generative AI goes beyond content creation. The same capability that allows a model to write a product description can also be applied to synthesizing research, generating code to automate workflows, constructing data analysis pipelines, and critically reasoning through multi-step problems in ways that approximate human analytical work. This is not science fiction. Executives whose organizations have deployed generative AI in analytical roles are already experiencing the productivity implications: the speed at which first-draft analysis can be produced, the breadth of scenarios that can be modeled, and the reduction in the time between a question and a structured answer. The competitive implications for organizations that master this workflow integration are significant. The question for a leader is not whether to engage with generative AI, but whether your organization has the governance infrastructure to capture its value without absorbing its risks.

Agentic AI: The Leadership Frontier

Every concept covered so far- machine learning, deep learning, large language models, and generative AI- describes systems that respond. You provide an input, the system produces an output, and the exchange concludes. Agentic AI is different in kind, not merely in degree. An AI agent is a system that perceives its environment, forms goals, takes actions toward those goals, observes the results of those actions, and adjusts its approach accordingly over multiple steps, without requiring human input at each stage. This autonomy is the defining characteristic. And for leaders, it is the characteristic that changes governance from a compliance exercise into a genuine strategic responsibility.

Diagram 1.2: Agentic AI vs. Reactive AI: The Shift in Autonomy

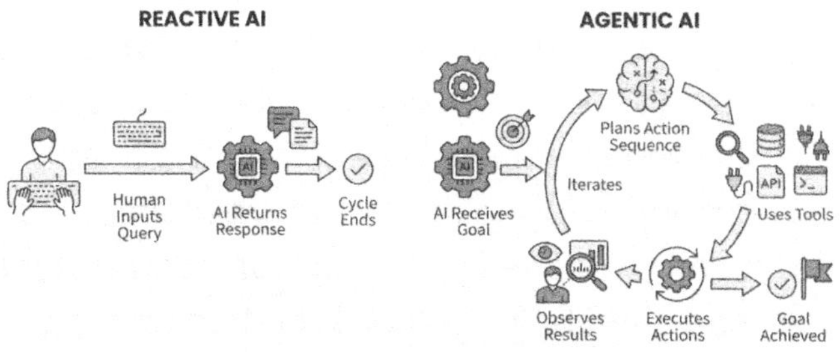

From Passive Response to Proactive Execution: Enabling End-to-End Task Autonomy

What Makes an AI Agent

To describe an AI system as "agentic," four capabilities typically need to be present, at least partially. First, goal-directedness: the system has an objective, stated by a human or derived from context, and works toward that objective rather than simply responding to a prompt. Second, tool use: the agent can call external tools and services, search the web, query databases, write and execute code, call APIs, and manage files, to accomplish tasks that require interacting with the world beyond pure text generation. Third, multi-step planning: rather than producing a single output, the agent can decompose a complex goal into a sequence of actions, execute them in order, and adjust when intermediate steps produce unexpected results. Fourth, memory and state: the agent can retain information across steps and, in some implementations, across sessions, allowing it to build on prior actions rather than starting from scratch with each exchange.

In practice, most enterprise AI agents today are hybrids they have some but not all these capabilities, and their autonomy is bounded by the tools they have been given access to and the constraints they operate within. A customer service agent might be able to retrieve account information, draft responses, and escalate complex cases, but not process refunds above a set threshold without human review. A procurement agent might be able to request quotes, compare vendors against defined criteria, and generate a ranked recommendation, but require human approval before issuing any purchase order. These bounded forms of agency are already operating inside large organizations. The governance questions they raise are immediate and practical rather than hypothetical.

From AI-as-Assistant to AI-as-Actor

The transition from reactive AI to agentic AI is not an incremental improvement, like faster processors are incremental improvements in computing. It is a change like the relationship between your organization and your AI systems. When AI is an assistant, you prompt it, it responds, and you decide; the human remains the actor. AI is a sophisticated tool in the hands of a person who retains full agency and accountability. When AI is an agent, it receives a goal, plans, acts, observes, and adapts. Humans become a principal: someone who sets objectives, defines constraints, monitors outcomes, and intervenes when needed, but is not present at every decision point.

This principal-agent relationship is not new to management. You experience it every time you delegate a significant initiative to a senior leader or a cross-functional team. You set the objective, provide resources and constraints, monitor progress, and hold the agent accountable for outcomes without personally executing every task. The challenge with AI agents is that the velocity of their action, the scale at which they can operate, and the difficulty of interpreting their decision-making in real time create a governance challenge that traditional delegation frameworks were not designed to handle. An AI agent can make thousands of micro-decisions in the time it takes a leader to read a status report. When they occur, failure modes can propagate at a speed that outpaces organizational response.

The practical implication is that deploying AI agents is a governance design exercise rather than a technology exercise. Before your organization gives an AI system the ability to act to send communications, move data, execute transactions, and manage workflows, you need answers to four questions. What can this agent do without asking? What requires human review? What happens when it encounters a situation outside its training? And who is accountable when it acts in ways that produce harm, even unintentional harm? These questions do not require technical expertise to ask. They require leadership clarity to answer and institutional will to enforce.

Multi-Agent Orchestration

The complexity compounds when multiple AI agents operate simultaneously and interact with one another. Multi-agent orchestration, the coordination of several AI systems working in parallel or in sequence toward a shared goal, is not a distant vision. It is already in production use in organizations that have moved beyond initial experimentation. In these architectures, a primary agent might be tasked with a high-level objective: to analyze this market, generate a regulatory response, optimize this logistics route, and orchestrate a network of specialized sub-agents to handle discrete components: one agent queries external data sources, another analyzes financial models, a third drafts the output, and a fourth checks it against compliance criteria.

The leadership implications of multi-agent systems are significant. When a single agent makes an error, the chain of causality is relatively easy to trace. When multiple agents interact, and a downstream agent acts on flawed output from an upstream agent, error propagation is exponentially harder to diagnose and correct. The concept of trust in these systems extends beyond trusting any individual model; it requires trusting the architecture, handoffs, error-handling protocols, and the monitoring infrastructure that sits above it all. None of this monitoring exists by default. It is designed, built, and maintained by teams that require leadership investment and governance oversight. The organization that deploys multi-agent systems without this infrastructure is not being innovative. It is being exposed.

DIAGRAM 1.3: MULTI-AGENT ORCHESTRATION ARCHITECTURE

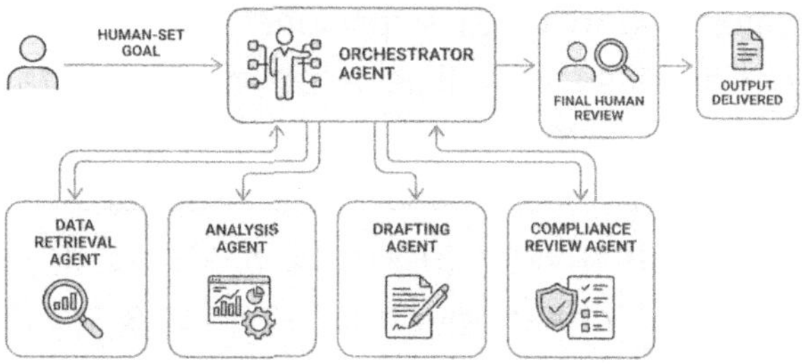

Clean minimrlist infographic diagram for business leadership book, executive/corporate tone, horıntal 16:9 composition

The Learning-Authority Dilemma

One of the most consequential and least discussed challenges of agentic AI in enterprise contexts is what might be called the learning-authority dilemma. As AI agents are given access to more data, more tools, and more operational history, their ability to make effective decisions in their domain can improve to the point where their practical decision-making capability exceeds the formal authority they have been granted. An agent tasked with customer retention might learn, through thousands of interactions, that approving exceptions to standard pricing policies significantly improves customer satisfaction scores, the metric it is optimizing. But those pricing exceptions fall outside the agent's sanctioned authority. The agent is right, in a narrow sense. It is also operating outside its lane.

The dilemma for leaders is that the most capable AI agents, the ones that learn fastest and optimize most effectively, are also the ones most likely to push against the boundaries of their defined authority. Overly tight constraints prevent the system from realizing its potential. Overly loose constraints create organizational and legal exposure. The resolution is not a technical setting; it is a governance structure. Clearly defined authority boundaries, regular audits of agent decision logs, escalation mechanisms with genuine human review (not rubber-stamp approval), and a culture in which boundary violations are flagged and investigated rather than celebrated as innovation are the conditions that allow agentic AI to generate value without generating liability.

The learning-authority dilemma is also a talent challenge. Your organization needs people who can read agent decision logs, identify patterns of boundary encroachment, and translate those findings into governance refinements. These are not purely technical skills. They require domain knowledge, ethical judgment, and organizational authority. The leader who imagines that AI governance can be entirely delegated to the technology team is making the same mistake as the leader who imagines that financial controls can be entirely delegated to the accounting department. Governance is a leadership function. It happens to involve technology.

The Adoption Curve: What the Numbers Reveal

Roughly six in ten large organizations are now experimenting with AI agents in some form, and nearly one in four has begun scaling agent deployments beyond initial pilots. This is not a gradual adoption curve; it compresses the classic technology diffusion timeline into months rather than years, and the organizations scaling agents today were, in most cases, in early experimentation only eighteen to twenty-four months ago.

What this curve reveals for leaders is a window of strategic differentiation that is open but narrowing. Early movers in agentic AI, those who have built governance infrastructure, trained teams to work alongside agents, and established operational patterns for agent deployment and monitoring, are accumulating advantages that will become progressively harder to replicate. These advantages are not primarily technological. They are organizational: the experience of failed deployments, the institutional knowledge of what governance works and what fails in practice, and the teams with firsthand skill in managing AI systems at scale. Technology can be licensed. Experience cannot. The pilot-to-production pathway your organization walks now shapes the capabilities you will have when agentic AI becomes standard infrastructure.

How AI Systems Actually Work at a Conceptual Level

Technical depth is not the goal of this section. What follows is the minimum conceptual grounding needed to enable a leader to ask meaningful questions, evaluate vendor claims, interpret failure reports, and make governance decisions with confidence. You do not need to understand how to train a model. You need to understand what happens during training, what it produces, and what that means for the outputs your organization will rely on.

Diagram 1.4: **The AI System Lifecycle: From Data to Decision**

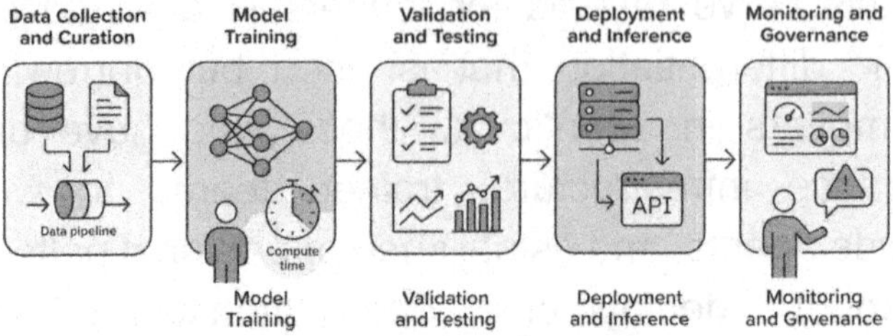

A clean infographic diagram in the business leadership executive and corporate tone.

Training Data, Model Weights, and Why Inputs Determine Outputs

When an AI model is trained, it is exposed to vast quantities of data, text, images, numerical records, or other inputs, depending on its purpose, and it adjusts its internal parameters, called weights, to produce outputs that match the patterns in that data. Training is a computational process that can take weeks and requires enormous infrastructure. Still, conceptually, it is a form of pattern absorption: the model learns which features of the input are associated with which outputs and encodes that learning into billions of numerical weights.

Once training is complete, those weights are fixed, the model is frozen, at least until it is retrained or fine-tuned. This has a critical practical implication: the model's knowledge is limited to what was in its training data, and its biases are those encoded in that data. A model trained on customer service transcripts from five years will have learned communication patterns, resolution strategies, and customer behavior patterns from that period. If the business context has shifted significantly, if customer expectations have changed, or if the data from that period systematically underrepresented certain customer segments, the model will reproduce those limitations in its outputs. "The model was trained on biased data" is not a technical disclaimer to be filed and forgotten; it is a governance finding that demands a human decision about whether and how that model can be responsibly deployed.

The Concept of Inference

Inference is what happens when a trained model is put to work: you provide an input, and the model generates an output based on the patterns encoded in its weights. Unlike training, inference is typically fast, milliseconds to seconds, and does not change the model. Every time a user interacts with a deployed AI system, submits a query, or receives an AI-generated response, they are triggering an inference. At enterprise scale, an AI system may perform millions of inferences per day, each one drawing on the same fixed set of weights derived from training.

The practical leadership implication is that inference at scale is where the consequences of training choices land. A subtle bias in training data, a small systematic error in the model's calibration, or a gap in the training distribution can generate millions of slightly wrong outputs before anyone notices the pattern. This is the mechanism by which AI failures become organizational problems: not through dramatic system crashes, but through the quiet accumulation of small errors that are individually below the threshold of notice but collectively constitute a material problem. The monitoring infrastructure your organization builds around AI deployments- dashboards, sampling protocols, anomaly detection, and human review processes- is what converts this theoretical risk into a manageable operational reality. It requires investment before problems emerge, which is a discipline that separates serious AI governance from reactive management.

Hallucination, Drift, and Confidence Misrepresentation

Three failure modes deserve explicit leadership attention because they are the most consequential and the least intuitively obvious to those with traditional management backgrounds.

Hallucination is the phenomenon in which a generative AI system produces output that is factually incorrect, internally inconsistent, or entirely fabricated, stated with complete linguistic fluency and apparent confidence. A legal research tool that cites non-existent cases, a customer service bot that quotes policy provisions that do not exist. This medical information system describes contraindications that lack evidence of hallucination events. They occur not because the system is malfunctioning in the conventional sense, but because it is doing exactly what it was trained to do: produce plausible, coherent text. Plausible and accurate are not synonyms. For leaders, the governance implication is clear: any AI deployment where factual accuracy is consequential requires a verification layer. Trusting AI output because it sounds authoritative is not a governance strategy. It is an exposure.

Model drift is the gradual degradation of a model's performance over time as the real-world data it encounters diverges from its training distribution. A fraud detection model trained on transaction patterns from two years ago may have been excellent at launch. Still, it is mediocre today because fraud techniques evolve, customer behavior shifts, and the statistical properties of current transactions no longer closely match those used to train the model. Drift is invisible unless you are measuring it. Without regular performance monitoring against ground-truth outcomes, a deployed model can deteriorate significantly before the organization notices that its output is becoming less reliable.

Confidence misrepresentation is, in some ways, the most insidious failure mode. AI systems, particularly language models, can express certainty in their outputs that bear no consistent relationship to actual reliability. A correct answer and a hallucinated answer can emerge with equal fluency and apparent confidence.

Any workflow that relies on humans to flag outputs that seem uncertain will systematically fail because humans accept confident-sounding errors and question correct outputs stated tentatively. The design implication is straightforward: build verification processes that are independent of how confident the AI appears to be, rather than relying on output texture as a signal of reliability.

Diagram 1.5: The Three Critical AI Failure Modes for Leaders

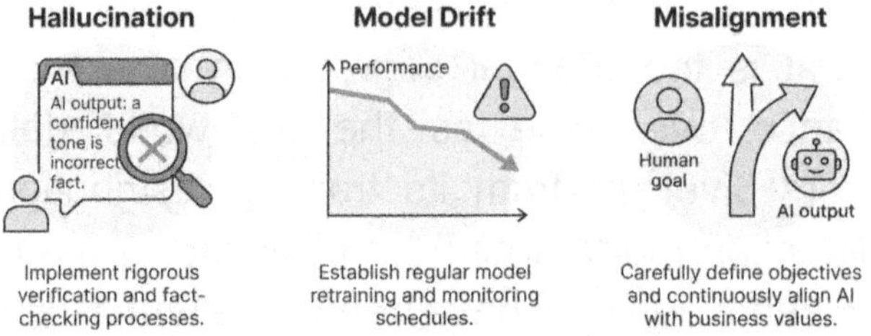

Diagram 1.5: The Three Critical AI Failure Modes for Leaders

Narrow vs. General-Purpose AI

Most AI systems deployed in enterprise contexts today are narrow; they perform a specific task with high competence but cannot generalize outside their trained domain. A document classification model that excels at routing support tickets cannot draft a strategic memo. A demand forecasting model that delivers accurate inventory recommendations cannot answer HR questions about employees. Narrow AI is not a limitation to be embarrassed about; it is a feature of task-specific optimization. Systems that are trained to do one thing well are often more reliable, more explainable, and more governable than systems that attempt general competence.

General-purpose AI systems, primarily large language models and, increasingly, multimodal foundation models, differ in that their training on diverse data gives them capabilities across a wide range of tasks, without being purpose-built for any specific task. The strategic implication is that general-purpose AI and narrow AI are not competitors but complements. A large language model provides breadth; a purpose-built narrow model provides depth and precision within its domain. The organizations that extract the most value from AI are those that design thoughtfully around this distinction, deploying general-purpose AI where breadth is required and narrow AI where precision, reliability, and auditability are required.

Probabilistic Outputs and What That Means for Risk Management

Perhaps the most counterintuitive aspect of AI systems for leaders trained in engineering or operations disciplines is that AI outputs are fundamentally probabilistic rather than deterministic. Run the same input through a large language model twice, and you may receive two different outputs. The same image classification model may categorize the same image differently depending on minor variations in its presentation. This is not a defect; it is a characteristic of systems that generate outputs by sampling from probability distributions rather than executing fixed logical rules.

The risk-management implication is direct: AI systems cannot be governed by the same frameworks you apply to deterministic software. A payroll system that processes the same inputs will produce the same outputs every time you can audit it by replaying transactions. An AI system that generates outputs probabilistically requires a different approach: statistical sampling, performance monitoring across distributions, red teaming with adversarial inputs, and explicit documentation of acceptable output variance. If your organization's risk function has not yet adapted its methodology to account for probabilistic AI behavior, that is a governance gap that warrants urgent attention. The operational clarity required to manage AI risk is achievable. Still, it requires leaders who understand that the tool they are governing is not the same kind of tool as the deterministic software that preceded it.

The Current State of Enterprise AI Adoption

Benchmark data on AI adoption serves a specific leadership purpose: it calibrates your organizational self-assessment against a realistic picture of where your peers and competitors are. Without this calibration, organizations either overestimate their position, believing their early pilots represent a competitive advantage when the rest of their sector has already moved to scale, or underestimate it, feeling behind a curve that their actual data would not support. Both errors lead to misallocated attention and investment.

Diagram 1.6: The AI Adoption Landscape: Three Categories of Adopter

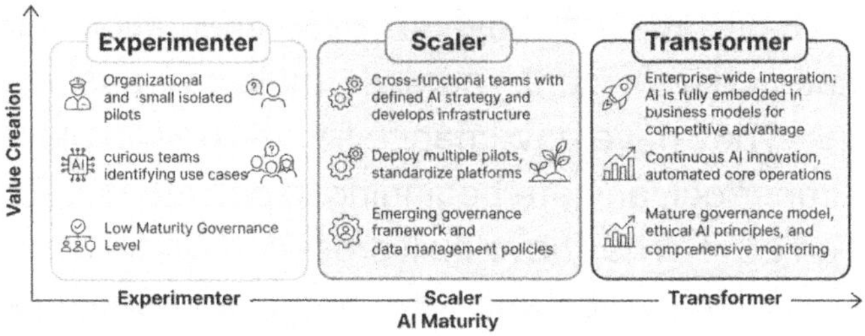

Diagram 1.6: The AI Adoption Landscape: Three Categories of Adopter

What Adoption Actually Means

When the research literature reports that most large organizations use AI in at least one business function, that headline number requires decomposition before it can inform strategy. "Using AI" can mean a marketing team has subscribed to a generative AI writing tool and uses it to draft social media copy. It can also mean a financial institution has deployed machine learning models across credit underwriting, fraud detection, and customer lifetime value functions, with full monitoring infrastructure, governance committees, and model risk management protocols. Both organizations are counted in the adoption statistics. Their strategic positions are not comparable.

The more meaningful cut of the data distinguishes between experimentation, scaling, and transformation. Experimenters are using AI in isolated, non-mission-critical applications. Their deployments produce learning but have a limited financial impact. Their governance infrastructure is nascent, their workforce AI capability is concentrated in small pockets of enthusiasts, and their AI initiatives are often disconnected from their strategic planning process. Scalers have moved beyond experimentation into systematic deployment across multiple business functions. They have governance frameworks in place, even if imperfect, and are beginning to see measurable impact on EBIT. They have built cross-functional teams to support AI initiatives and have begun embedding AI competency into workforce planning. Transformers have integrated AI deeply into their operating model. AI is not a project for them; it is infrastructure. Their competitive advantage increasingly derives from proprietary data, fine-tuned models, and AI-native workflows that take years to build and are difficult to replicate.

Identifying where your organization sits, honestly, not aspirationally, is the starting point for every AI strategy conversation that follows in this book. The leaders who claim Transformer status while operating as Experimenters are not strategic. They are sloppy. And sloppy self-assessment leads to misallocated investment, overpromising to boards and shareholders, and a loss of executive credibility that is hard to recover from.

The Adoption-to-Impact Gap

One of the most consistent findings in enterprise AI research is that high adoption rates coexist with modest EBIT impact. Technology can generate substantial economic returns; well-documented examples across industries clearly establish this. The gap is not a technology problem. It is an execution and leadership problem, and understanding its causes is the precondition for closing it.

Three factors account for most of the adoption-to-impact gap. The first is use-case selection. Organizations experimenting with AI at the periphery-low-stakes, non-core applications that are easy to pilot and easy to shelve- will not generate EBIT impact regardless of how well the technology performs. The path to material returns runs through mission-aligned applications: core business processes where AI can change the economics of operations, not side projects that marginally improve workflows without affecting the bottom line. The second factor is the 10-20-70 principle: roughly 10% of AI investment should go to algorithms and models, 20% to technology and data infrastructure, and 70% to people and process change. Organizations that spend their AI budgets primarily on the ten percent of the models and tools and underinvest in the seventy percent will deploy capable technology into organizational cultures that are not ready to use it, workflows that have not been redesigned to leverage it, and workforces that have not been trained to trust it. The third factor is measurement. Organizations that cannot tell you, with precision, what their AI deployments are producing in quantifiable terms cannot manage those deployments to achieve higher returns. Impact is created by leaders who measure, learn, and adjust, not by those who deploy and hope.

Generative AI Penetration vs. Depth of Use

Generative AI has achieved a penetration rate across large organizations that is remarkable by any historical standard of technology adoption. The majority of large enterprises report using generative AI in some form, primarily in productivity applications, content generation, and code assistance. This is the breadth picture. The depth picture is more nuanced.

Depth of use refers to how far into core business processes generative AI has penetrated, how systematically it is used, and how much of its capability reaches the average knowledge worker versus a small population of power users. On these depth measures, most organizations remain in the early stages, skewed toward individual-level use driven by personal initiative rather than systematic, governed, workflow-integrated use that generates organizational-level returns. Closing this depth gap is a primary leadership responsibility, requiring deliberate choices about workflow redesign, governance infrastructure, and investment in workforce capabilities.

AI in Your Industry: Cross-Sector Patterns and Distinctions

One of the consistent frustrations leaders express in AI strategy conversations is the sensation that the AI examples they encounter in the literature do not map to their specific industry context. The healthcare executive is given examples from the manufacturing sector. The financial services leader is given retail examples. While this frustration is understandable, it can lead to a kind of sector-specific exceptionalism that delays action: "AI works in those industries, but our context is different." It is worth examining which aspects of AI deployment are genuinely sector-specific and which are sector-agnostic.

Common Horizontal Applications

Horizontal AI applications generate value across industries by addressing universal organizational challenges: productivity, communication, data analysis, and content generation. Generative AI tools that assist knowledge workers with writing, summarizing, and synthesizing information are horizontal; a law firm, a pharmaceutical company, and a logistics company all have knowledge workers whose productivity can be enhanced by the same category of tool, even if the specific domain content differs. AI-powered customer service tools that handle routine inquiries, route complex cases, and maintain consistent tone and policy compliance across interactions are horizontal. Code generation assistants that reduce software development cycle times are horizontal in nature. Data analysis tools that accelerate the conversion of raw data into structured insight are horizontal.

For leaders, horizontal applications have a specific strategic implication: they are the fastest path to early organizational AI experience and modest but demonstrable productivity wins. They require less domain-specific model development, they are available from multiple vendors at accessible price points, and they produce benefits that are relatively easy to measure. They are also the applications most vulnerable to commoditization. If every organization in your sector has access to the same productivity tools, those tools become table stakes rather than competitive advantages. The serious leader uses horizontal applications to build organizational AI capability while simultaneously investing in the vertical, domain-specific applications that are harder to replicate and more defensible over time.

Vertical-Specific AI and Competitive Differentiation

Vertical AI applications are domain-specific: diagnostic imaging analysis in healthcare, risk model development in financial services, predictive maintenance in manufacturing, document review and legal research in professional services, demand sensing and route optimization in supply chain. These applications require deep domain knowledge to develop, fine-tune, and govern; they cannot be purchased off the shelf and deployed without an institutional context. A general-purpose model asked to evaluate medical imaging will not perform at the level of a model specifically trained on annotated clinical data from your patient population. The investment required to develop vertical AI capability is substantial. The competitive moat it creates is substantial as well.

The competitive advantage in vertical AI typically lies not in the algorithm but in the data. The organization that has accumulated 10 years of rigorously labeled, proprietary operational data is sitting on the raw material for AI systems that no competitor without equivalent data can replicate. This is why data strategy is inseparable from AI strategy. Organizations that have not yet developed a serious enterprise data capability, governance, lineage, quality standards, and accessibility are not merely behind on a technical dimension. They are depleting a strategic asset through neglect. The leader who understands this will make data infrastructure a priority in board-level strategy discussions, not just in IT budget conversations.

Diagram 1.7: Horizontal vs. Vertical AI Applications by Sector.

Regulated Industries and the Hidden Advantage

Leaders in heavily regulated industries, such as financial services, healthcare, pharmaceuticals, and energy, sometimes face regulatory constraints on AI deployment that can be a competitive disadvantage relative to less-regulated sectors. The opposite is closer to the truth. The governance disciplines that regulators require for AI deployment model risk management, explainability documentation, bias testing, human oversight requirements, and audit trails are the same disciplines that produce reliable, trustworthy, and durable AI systems. An organization that builds AI governance infrastructure because it has no choice is building exactly the infrastructure that responsible-by-design AI deployment requires, regardless of regulatory mandate.

The financial institution that has spent years developing model risk management capabilities is significantly better positioned to govern generative AI responsibly than a technology company that has never needed to justify a model's outputs to a regulator. Regulatory constraint is a forcing function for governance discipline. Organizations that have internalized discipline are better positioned to deploy AI responsibly at scale, avoid governance failures, and earn the institutional trust that becomes a competitive differentiator as AI enters more consequential domains.

The AI Stack: What Leaders Need to Understand About Infrastructure

The AI stack, the layered technology infrastructure that powers enterprise AI, is not a domain where leaders need engineering-level knowledge. It is a domain where leaders need sufficient conceptual clarity to make consequential decisions: about build versus buy, vendor selection, data investment, and security and sovereignty. The following concepts are the minimum infrastructure vocabulary for effective AI leadership.

Diagram 1.8: The Enterprise AI Stack: Layer by Layer

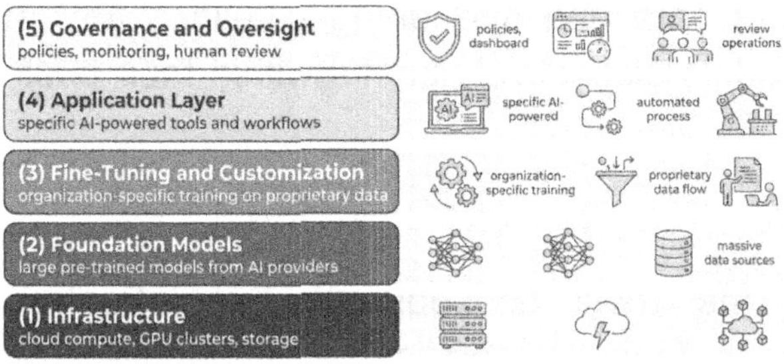

Caption #1c: The Enterprise AI Stack Layer am infographic for a business leadership book

Foundation Models, Fine-Tuning, and Enterprise Customization

Foundation models are large, general-purpose AI models trained by a small number of highly resourced organizations on massive datasets. These models- GPT-4 and its successors, Claude, Gemini, Llama, and their derivatives, and others- form the base layer for most enterprise AI applications. Very few organizations have the resources or the strategic rationale to train their own foundation models from scratch. The competitive question is not whether to train a foundation model, but how to customize and extend it for your specific enterprise needs.

Fine-tuning continues a foundation model's training on a smaller, domain-specific dataset to improve performance on tasks that matter for your organization. A model fine-tuned on your legal documents, compliance policies, and regulatory filings will substantially outperform the base model on those tasks without requiring a build-from-scratch approach. This is where many organizations find their most defensible AI investments: not in the models themselves, but in the proprietary data and fine-tuning pipelines that make those models distinctively useful within their business context.

Build vs. Buy vs. Configure

One of the most consequential AI infrastructure decisions a leader faces is the build-buy-configure decision, and it benefits from clear mental frameworks because it recurs as new AI capabilities become available.

Building training models from scratch and developing proprietary infrastructure is appropriate when your competitive advantage depends on capabilities unavailable commercially, your data gives you a genuine edge, and you have the engineering talent and sustained investment appetite to maintain the system. This is the right path for a small number of organizations where AI capability is truly core to competitive differentiation. It is the wrong path for the vast majority, who are better served by deploying and customizing existing models.

Buying means licensing access to foundation models, AI-powered SaaS applications, or vendor-supplied AI features. This is the right approach for horizontal applications and organizations without specialized AI engineering capability. Risks include vendor dependency, data privacy and sovereignty concerns, and difficulty customizing to organizational context. Configuring a commercial foundation model and customizing it through fine-tuning, retrieval-augmented generation, or prompt engineering is increasingly the right approach for organizations seeking performance benefits without the full build complexity. The pilot-to-production pathway for most enterprise AI looks like configure, start commercial, customize with proprietary data, and reserve build for the narrow set of capabilities where the competitive case is overwhelming.

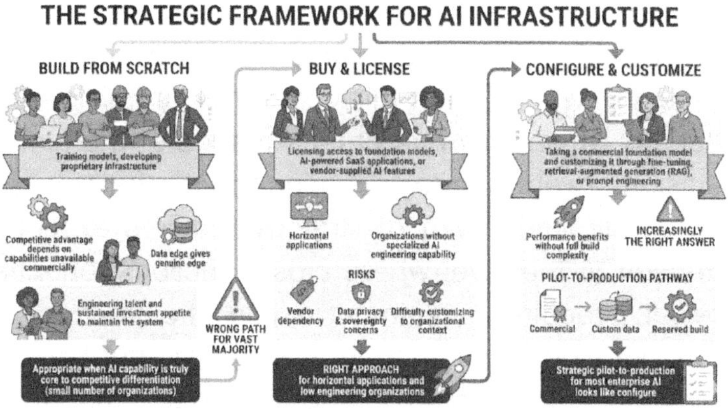

Data Readiness: The Silent Constraint

The single most common cause of AI project failure is not a model problem, a vendor problem, or an infrastructure problem. It is a data problem. Organizations initiate AI projects with significant enthusiasm and investment, only to discover that the data their models need is fragmented across dozens of systems, inconsistently structured, poorly labeled, maintained to varying quality standards by different teams, and encumbered by governance policies that make it difficult to access for AI training. By the time data quality issues surface, typically after significant time and money have been spent, the project's energy and credibility have been substantially depleted.

Data readiness is the silent constraint on AI value creation, and it is a leadership responsibility before it is a technical one. The decisions that determine data readiness, what data is collected, how it is structured and stored, what quality standards are enforced, how data from different systems is integrated, who can access it, and for what purposes are made continuously across an organization, largely invisibly, by people who are not thinking about AI implications because AI was not part of their mandate when those decisions were made. Bringing data strategy into explicit alignment with AI strategy requires executive attention at the level where cross-functional priorities are set. It requires investment in data infrastructure that does not yield immediate, visible returns but lays the foundation for AI returns. The leader who prioritizes data governance as an AI strategy investment, not as an IT housekeeping exercise, is making one of the highest-leverage AI decisions available to them.

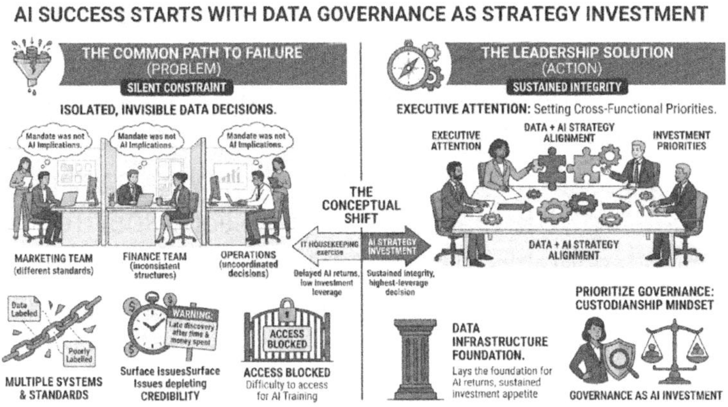

Cloud AI Infrastructure and Sovereignty

Most enterprise AI applications today run on cloud infrastructure provided by a small number of large cloud providers. This concentration creates a dependency that leaders must understand and manage. Cloud AI infrastructure provides access to the computing power needed to run large models, managed services that reduce engineering complexity, and the rapid scalability AI applications often require. It also creates risks that require deliberate governance: data sovereignty concerns when sensitive organizational data is processed by cloud AI services operating under foreign legal jurisdictions, security risks associated with transmitting proprietary data to third-party infrastructure, vendor concentration risk when critical AI capabilities are dependent on a single provider, and cost volatility as AI workloads scale.

Leaders need to ensure their organizations have made deliberate choices about cloud AI strategy rather than defaulting to them. The key questions are: What categories of data should never leave internal infrastructure? What AI workloads belong in public cloud versus private cloud or on premises? What contractual protection is required from cloud AI vendors regarding data use and service continuity? These are risk management questions that require senior leadership judgment. Delegating them entirely to technical teams without executive engagement is a governance gap.

The Serious Manager's AI Primer Checklist

The following checklist translates the concepts from this chapter into concrete leadership behaviors and decisions. Work through it honestly. Items where you cannot confidently say "yes" represent the areas where this chapter's learning has the most immediate application.

Leadership Vocabulary:

- Can you explain the difference between machine learning, deep learning, and generative AI in terms a non-technical board member would understand?
- Can you articulate what makes an AI system "agentic" and why it requires different governance than a reactive AI assistant?
- Can you name and describe the three primary AI failure modes: hallucination, drift, and confidence misrepresentation, and give an example of each in an enterprise context?
- Can you describe the difference between a foundation model and a fine-tuned model, and

explain when each is the right choice for your organization?

Organizational Assessment:

- Have you assessed honestly where your organization sits on the Experimenter-Scaler-Transformer spectrum, not where you would like to be, but where the evidence indicates you are?
- Do you know which of your AI deployments are currently monitored for drift and output quality, and which are operating without active performance oversight?
- Do you have a current understanding of your organization's data readiness, which data assets are accessible, well-governed, and ready to support AI development, and which are fragmented or underqualified?

Governance Readiness:

- Do you have clear authority boundaries defined for any AI agents operating in your organization specifying what decisions they can make independently, what requires human review, and what is outside their scope entirely?
- Is your organization's risk management function equipped to govern probabilistic AI outputs, or does it still operate with frameworks designed for deterministic software?
- Have you reviewed your cloud AI vendor contracts for data sovereignty, data-use-for-training, and service continuity provisions?

- Do you know who in your organization is accountable for AI governance, not project management, but governance: the ongoing oversight of deployed AI systems and their outputs?

Strategic Positioning:

- Do you know whether your organization's current AI investments are weighted toward horizontal applications, vertical differentiation, or a deliberate combination of both?
- Have you mapped the 10-20-70 distribution across your AI investment portfolio, and does the actual allocation align with the principle?

The Leadership Vocabulary of AI

Every concept in this chapter serves a single practical function: equipping you to be a principal in AI conversations, not a passenger. The distinctions between machine learning and deep learning, between reactive and agentic AI, between narrow and general-purpose systems- these are not academic classifications. They are decision tools. The leader who knows them can ask better questions of vendors, hold more precise conversations with technical teams, and make governance decisions that are grounded in an accurate understanding of what technology can and cannot do.

What this chapter has established is a conceptual foundation, not a complete map of the AI landscape. The AI landscape is evolving too rapidly for any complete map to remain current for long. What does not change is the leadership challenge at its center: how to govern systems that are increasingly capable of consequential autonomous action, how to deploy AI in ways that are mission-aligned and responsible by design, and how to build organizational capability that captures AI's value without absorbing its risks. These challenges do not resolve themselves through technology investment alone. They resolve through deliberate, informed, and accountable leadership.

Chapter 2 builds directly on this foundation by examining the mindset shift that separates leaders who treat AI as a tool to be used from those who recognize it as an environment to be led within. The concepts established here, particularly the nature of agentic AI, the probabilistic character of AI outputs, and the learning-authority dilemma, are precisely the concepts that make the mindset shift necessary rather than merely desirable. And Chapter 3 will apply this foundation to the specific challenge of decision-making in an age of algorithmic advice, where understanding what AI systems are and how they fail is the prerequisite for knowing when to trust them and when to override them.

The single most important question to carry from this chapter into every AI vendor conversation, every internal governance review, and every strategic AI discussion is deceptively simple: what does this system do when it is wrong? How it handles its own errors, whether it flags uncertainty, escalates to humans, fails gracefully, or continues generating confident output regardless, tells you more about whether a system is ready for consequential enterprise deployment than any benchmark score or capability demonstration. The answer to that question marks the beginning of serious AI leadership.

Diagram 1.9: The AI Leadership Vocabulary Reference

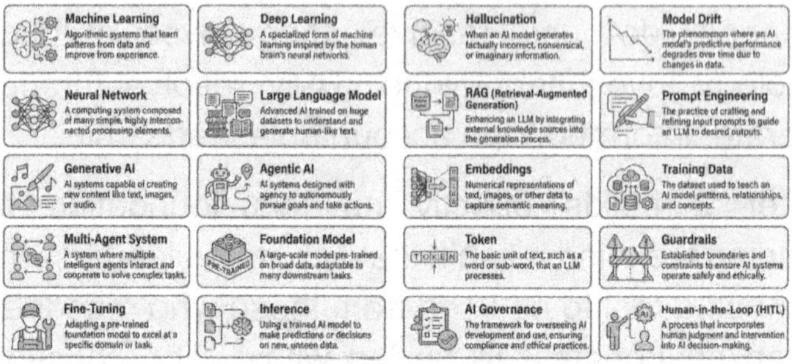

Diagram 1.9: The AI Leadership Vocabulary Referene

3 The Mental Shift That Separates AI Leaders from AI Bystanders

A Monday Morning That Reveals Everything

The investment committee meeting was ninety minutes away. Sandra Okafor, Chief Operating Officer of a mid-size regional insurer, had spent the previous evening reviewing the AI-powered claims forecasting model her data science team had built over six months. The model's precision metrics were strong. The board presentation was polished. The case for an eight-figure automation initiative looked compelling on paper.

But as Sandra reviewed the final deck that morning, something felt wrong. The model had been optimized against three years of historical claims data gathered before a pair of catastrophic weather events had permanently altered regional loss patterns. The numbers were technically correct. They were also strategically misleading. The model was answering the question it had been built to answer, not the question the organization needed answered.

Sandra called the meeting. Not to abandon the initiative, the underlying capability was sound, but to reframe the investment thesis around a forward-looking data strategy rather than a backward-looking efficiency play. Two of her peers were frustrated by the delay. Three were relieved. The board was impressed by the intellectual honesty. Six months later, the recalibrated initiative was producing outcomes the original model could never have sustained.

What Sandra demonstrated that morning was not technical expertise. She had not built the model, did not fully understand its architecture, and could not have explained its training methodology in detail. What she demonstrated was a leadership mindset calibrated for the AI era: she knew enough to ask the right question, was secure enough to act on the answer, and was honest enough to publicly own both the delay and the rationale. That mindset, not the model, was the decisive variable.

Why Mindset Is the Upstream Variable

The single most expensive mistake organizations make with AI is treating it as a technology problem rather than a business problem. They invest in platforms, hire data scientists, stand up governance committees, and measure success in models deployed and automated processes. They are solving the wrong constraint. In many AI initiatives that fall short of expectations, the limiting factor is not algorithmic quality, computational power, or data availability. It is the mental model of the leaders overseeing the work.

Chapter 1 gave you the conceptual grounding of what AI systems are, how they fail, and what the current landscape of enterprise AI actually looks like beneath the marketing layer. That foundation matters because you cannot develop a sound leadership mindset about a technology you do not understand at any level. But conceptual knowledge alone is insufficient. Leaders who understand AI intellectually and still approach it with outdated mental models produce disappointment at scale. The mental shift this chapter describes is not a supplement to technical knowledge; it is the operating system that makes technical knowledge strategically useful.

The stakes are asymmetric. A leader with a strong AI mindset and average technical resources will consistently outperform a leader with a weak AI mindset and superior technical resources. This has been the pattern across every major technological disruption for the past fifty years, from the introduction of enterprise resource planning systems in the 1980s to the mobile revolution in the 2010s. In each case, the organizations that pulled ahead were distinguished not by the sophistication of their technology but by the quality of leadership thinking applied to it. AI is running that pattern faster and has a greater organizational impact than anything that preceded it.

This chapter maps the specific cognitive shifts that distinguish AI leaders from AI bystanders, identifies the mental traps that prevent those shifts from taking hold, and introduces the AI-CLEAR Leadership Model as a diagnostic framework for assessing your own leadership posture. The chapter builds directly on the foundation laid in Chapter 1. It prepares you for the decision-making work of Chapter 3, where the mindsets introduced here become practical frameworks for navigating algorithmic advice without abdicating executive judgment.

Diagram 2.1: The Mindset-to-Outcome Cascade

Caption 2.1: The Mindset-to-Outcome Cascade · Leadership book, executive and corporate tone

The Technology-Adoption Trap

Buying the Tool, Skipping the Transformation

There is a predictable sequence that plays out inside organizations that fail to generate sustained value from AI investments. It begins with a compelling demonstration, a vendor proof of concept, a competitor announcement, or a board mandate to move faster on AI. This triggers procurement activity, which in turn triggers implementation activity, which in turn triggers training activity. Within 12 to 18 months, the organization has deployed AI tools across multiple functions. Usage metrics look acceptable. Then someone asks the hard question: what has changed?

What typically has not changed is how senior leaders make decisions, how middle managers set priorities, how teams evaluate their own work, and how the organization defines success. The tools have been bolted onto existing workflows, processes, and power structures. AI is doing work that was previously done by humans or never done at all, but it is doing that work within a leadership system designed before AI existed. The result is incremental efficiency and marginal workflow improvement, not the strategic transformation that justified the investment.

The trap is seductive because activity appears to be progressing. Procurement is measurable. Deployment is visible. Training sessions can be counted. None of this is a transformation. The organizations that break out of the trap recognize that their goal is a leadership transformation enabled by technology, not a technology transformation supervised by leadership. This distinction drives every consequential decision that follows.

Diagram 2.2: The Technology-Adoption Trap

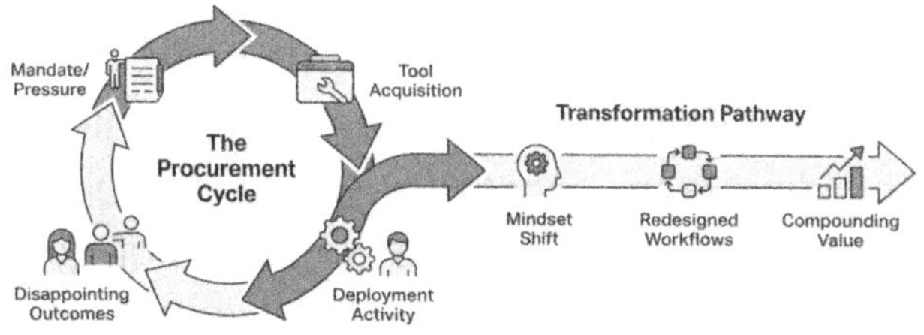

The technology-adoption trap is corrected by transforming mindset and workflows, consistent with each digital deployment.

Why AI Initiatives Fail at the Leadership Layer

Post-implementation analyses of AI initiatives that underperformed almost always surface the same cluster of leadership-layer failure modes. The initiative was scoped by technologists and never translated into the language of business outcomes. Leaders who should have been actively involved in shaping the initiative were passive sponsors who approved budgets but never engaged with the work. Teams were told to use AI tools without being told why, which drove compliance without adoption. And when outputs from the AI system conflicted with existing workflows or established assumptions, the organization defaulted to the familiar rather than examining whether those workflows or assumptions were still fit for purpose.

Each of these failures is a mindset failure before it is a process failure. Leaders who have made the cognitive shift from operational problem-solver to strategic architect do not tolerate vague scoping of initiatives. Leaders who have internalized the human-AI partnership model do not absent themselves from the work. Leaders who understand that AI adoption requires psychological safety do not mandate tools without building team capability. The leadership-layer failures are predictable and preventable, but only by leaders who have already done the internal work of examining and updating their own mental models.

The three CEO archetypes that have emerged from the current AI wave illustrate the spectrum. Followers treat

AI as a compliance activity they invest in when industry norms require it and measure success by not being visibly behind peers. Pragmatists treat AI as a set of efficiency opportunities they invest in where ROI is clearest and manage AI as a portfolio of cost-reduction initiatives. Trailblazers treat AI as a strategic capability; they invest in organizational learning, leadership development, and cultural change alongside technology, and they measure success by competitive differentiation and mission alignment rather than cost reduction alone. The distinction between these archetypes is not primarily budget size. It is the leader's mental model at the top that permeates every decision made below it.

The Core Mindset Shifts Required

From AI as Tool to AI as Organizational Capability

The first and most fundamental shift is categorical. When leaders treat AI as a tool, they ask tool-level questions: What does it do? What does it cost? How quickly can we deploy it? How do we measure whether it is working? These are legitimate operational questions, but they are insufficient as the primary frame for strategic AI leadership. A tool is something you pick up, use for a defined purpose, and put down. A capability is something that fundamentally changes what your organization can do, who can do it, and at what speed and scale.

The shift from tool thinking to capability thinking changes almost every decision. Tool questions produce vendor selection conversations. Capability questions produce architecture conversations. Tool thinking drives procurement. Capability thinking drives workforce development, process redesign, and governance design simultaneously. Tool thinking asks: Did we implement it correctly? Capability thinking asks: Are we building the organizational muscle to use this category of technology across every relevant domain, now and as it evolves?

This shift is particularly difficult for leaders who built their careers on operational excellence. Operational excellence rewards execution discipline: tight processes, clear metrics, fast iteration on defined problems. AI-as-capability requires a different mode, one that tolerates ambiguity during the capability-building phase, invests in learning that may not yield near-term ROI, and rewards experimentation even when it fails. Leaders who have been celebrated for operational rigor frequently experience this shift as disorienting, not because they lack the intellectual capacity to make it, but because it requires them to behave differently from the patterns that earned them their authority.

Diagram 2.3: Tool Thinking vs. Capability Thinking

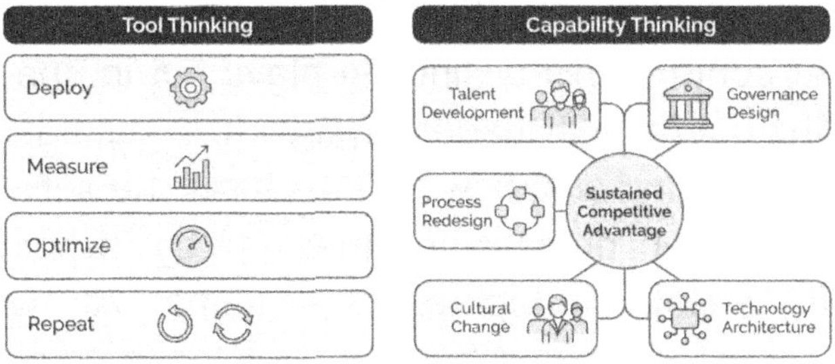

Caption: Executive and corporate-toned clean minimalist infographic diagram for business leadership book

From Operational Problem-Solver to Strategic Architect

The second shift is role-level. Most executives who have succeeded in large organizations have done so by demonstrating the ability to diagnose operational problems, mobilize resources to solve them, and drive measurable improvement in defined metrics. This is a genuinely valuable skill set. It is also a skill set that, when applied as the primary mode of AI leadership, tends to produce locally optimized solutions and globally suboptimal outcomes.

Strategic architecture requires a different cognitive posture. Where the operational problem-solver asks, "What is broken and how do we fix it?", the strategic architect asks, "What capabilities do we need to build, and what decisions today will expand or constrain our options tomorrow?" The architect is comfortable with ambiguity because the full system has not yet been built. The architect tolerates iteration because iteration is the method. The architect values optionality, keeping multiple paths open over premature optimization.

In the AI context, this distinction plays out in specific ways. The operational leader deploys AI to automate a claims-processing workflow and declares the initiative successful when processing times fall by 30%. The strategic architect deploys the same AI while simultaneously asking: What does this teach us about where AI can reduce human cognitive load across our operations? What new questions can our people now address because routine cognition is freed up? What governance structures do we need before applying this capability to higher-stakes workflows? The operational result may be identical in the short term. The strategic trajectory diverges sharply within eighteen months.

Making this shift is uncomfortable because it requires the senior executive to maintain what some researchers have called "productive uncertainty," the ability to act decisively on near-term questions while keeping longer-horizon questions open rather than forcing premature closure. Most high performers have been rewarded for certainty and decisiveness. The strategic architect learns to distinguish between situations that demand closure and situations that reward continued exploration. That distinction is itself a form of leadership judgment that AI cannot supply.

From "AI Does It for Me" to "AI, and I Do It Better Together"

The third shift is relational. Leaders who approach AI with a delegation mindset, treating it as a sophisticated assistant that takes tasks off their plate, tend to get what they ask for, not much more. They are often disappointed, not because the AI performed poorly in absolute terms, but because delegation without genuine engagement produces outputs that fit the average case rather than the specific strategic context that only the leader understands.

The partnership mindset operates differently. In partnership, the leader brings organizational context, ethical judgment, and strategic framing. The AI brings pattern recognition, synthesis speed, and the ability to surface options the leader has not considered. The partnership's output is reliably superior to either party working alone. Still, the quality of the partnership depends on the leader's willingness to engage actively, provide feedback, and accept that their role in the interaction is genuinely different from their traditional role as decision-maker.

This is harder for senior leaders than it sounds. The organizational dynamics around senior executives typically reinforce rather than challenge their existing views. Subordinates filter information before it reaches them. Advisors tell them what they want to hear. Processes are designed around their preferences. AI, when used well, does none of this. It surfaces information that contradicts the leader's assumptions, generates options the leader would not have considered, and produces outputs that do not conform to the organizational narrative. The leaders who genuinely benefit from AI are those with the intellectual security to engage with outputs that challenge rather than confirm their priors.

Diagram 2.4: Partnership vs. Delegation in AI Interaction

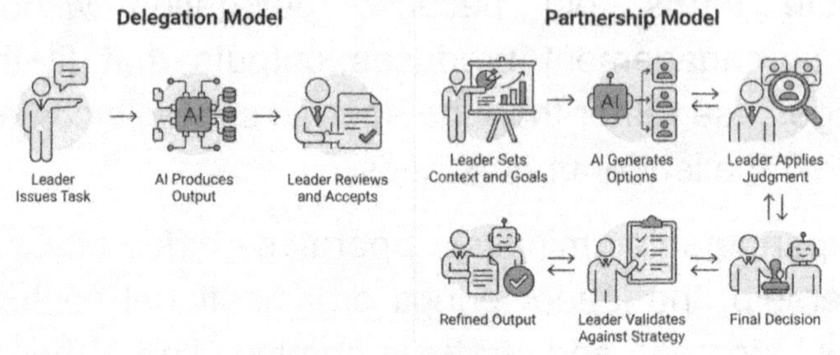

Analyzing two distinct approaches to utilizing AI in strategic leadership: one linear and transactional, the other collaborative and iterative.

Releasing the Perfectionism Trap

AI systems are probabilistic. They produce confident-sounding outputs that are sometimes wrong. They do not consistently or accurately flag their own uncertainty. They can be miscalibrated in ways that are difficult to detect without domain expertise. For leaders who have built their reputation on precision and correctness and are accustomed to signing off on work only when it meets a high standard, this probabilistic nature is genuinely uncomfortable.

The perfectionism trap operates as follows: the leader, aware that AI outputs can be incorrect, responds by demanding extensive human review of every AI-generated output. This review process is slow. It eliminates most of the workflow-level impact that justified AI investment. The team, frustrated by the bottleneck, concludes that AI is not actually useful—the initiative stalls. The leader's unexamined assumption that AI must be right before it is useful has produced exactly the outcome they feared: an expensive tool that added friction rather than removed it.

The resolution is a calibration framework rather than an all-or-nothing quality standard. Serious AI leaders distinguish between categories in which AI errors are low-stakes and easily corrected, where speed matters more than perfection, and categories in which errors are high-stakes and potentially irreversible, requiring heavy human review regardless of cost. This calibration allows the organization to capture genuine AI value where appropriate while maintaining rigorous oversight where it matters most.

Growth Mindset in the AI Context

What Research Actually Predicts About AI Adoption

Carol Dweck's foundational research on fixed versus growth mindsets established a durable insight: individuals who believe their intelligence and abilities can be developed through effort and experience consistently outperform those who treat these qualities as fixed, particularly in novel and challenging domains. The AI environment is, almost by definition, maximally novel and challenging. AI capabilities are changing faster than any individual or organization can keep up with. The field is full of genuine uncertainty, contested claims, and rapidly shifting best practices. A fixed mindset, one that seeks certainty, avoids appearing incompetent, and interprets failure as evidence of inadequacy, is structurally ill-suited to this environment.

A growth mindset predicts specific behaviors that are directly relevant to AI leadership. It predicts willingness to attempt tasks where failure is probable, because failure is understood as a data point rather than a verdict. It predicts genuine curiosity about how AI tools work, rather than performative familiarity designed to maintain status. It predicts comfort in asking questions that might reveal ignorance, because learning is valued more than the appearance of expertise. And it predicts resilience when AI initiatives produce disappointing results, because setbacks are treated as input for iteration rather than evidence that the initiative was a mistake.

Executive vulnerability is real. The higher the organizational position, the greater the social investment in appearing competent and certain. Executives who have built careers as the most informed person in the room face a specific challenge with AI: in this domain, they are frequently not the most informed. The gap between what senior leaders are expected to know and what they understand about AI systems is often substantial. Leaders who manage that gap by projecting false confidence or who surround themselves with advisors who confirm their existing views are making a category error. The executives building genuine AI leadership capability are those willing to publicly occupy beginner status for as long as it takes to develop a real understanding.

DIAGRAM 2.5: FIXED VS. GROWTH MINDSET PATTERNS IN AI LEADERSHIP

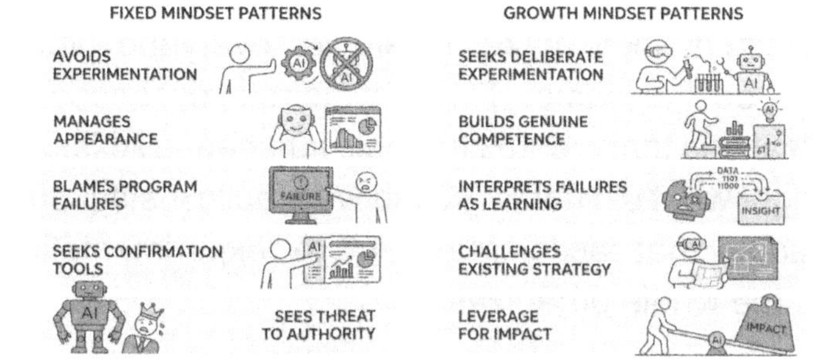

DIAGRAM 2.5: COMPARING FIXED AND GROWTH MINDSET PATTERNS IN AI LEADERSHIP

Building Psychological Safety Around AI Experimentation

The individual mindset shift does not happen in isolation. It happens within organizations whose cultures either enable or suppress experimentation. Leaders who have personally made the growth-mindset shift but lead teams in psychologically unsafe environments will find their teams' AI adoption stunted, regardless of their own posture. Team members who fear that failed AI experiments will be used against them in performance conversations are less likely to experiment. They comply. Compliance looks like adoption from a distance and produces none of its benefits.

Psychological safety in the AI context has three specific components. First, experiment leaders must explicitly communicate that trying AI tools in new contexts is encouraged and that experiments that do not produce value are expected and acceptable. Second, visible leader vulnerability: when senior leaders publicly share AI experiments that did not work as expected, they make it safe for everyone below them to do the same. Third, system-level feedback: organizations that create channels for sharing AI failure learnings- what did not work and why- build institutional knowledge that accelerates future experimentation across the whole organization.

The practical implication for managers is that building psychological safety around AI is not an abstract culture initiative. It is a specific set of behaviors with specific outcomes. A manager who runs a monthly fifteen-minute session where team members share "one AI thing I tried that surprised me," whether the surprise was positive or negative, is doing more to accelerate AI adoption than a manager who mandates AI tool use without creating the conditions for honest learning. Mission-aligned AI adoption is not about compliance rates. It is about building a team that can continuously improve its AI practice.

Introducing the AI AI-CLEAR Leadership Model

Every leader approaches AI with a distinct combination of strengths and gaps. Some leaders are naturally curious about new technology but struggle to translate that curiosity into organizational leverage. Some are excellent at holding their teams accountable for outcomes but have not yet built the readiness infrastructure to keep pace with AI's rapid evolution. Some are skilled at empowering their teams in traditional contexts but have not yet figured out how to extend that empowerment into the unfamiliar territory of human-AI collaboration.

The AI-CLEAR Leadership Model is a five-dimensional assessment framework that provides you with a precise, actionable picture of your current AI leadership posture. Unlike maturity models that measure where an organization is on its journey, AI-CLEAR measures the leader, the human at the center of every AI initiative. The model is diagnostic rather than prescriptive. It does not tell you where you should be on each dimension; it tells you where you are and identifies your highest-leverage development opportunity so you can focus your energy where it matters most.

Diagram 2.6: The CLEAR Leadership Model Overview

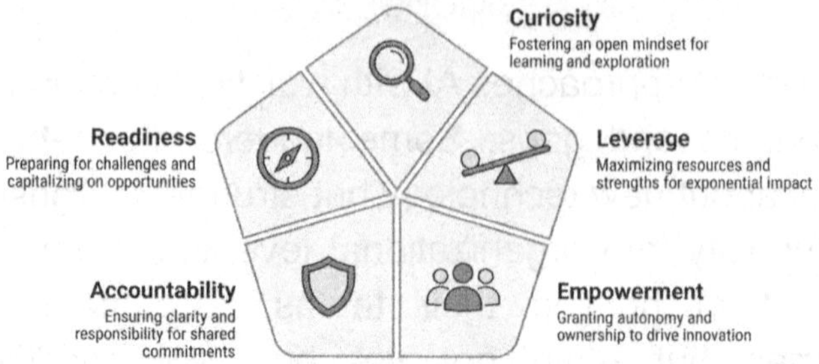

C Curiosity: Disciplined Exploration Without Distraction

In the AI-CLEAR model, curiosity is not the same as enthusiasm. Many leaders are enthusiastic about AI in general, yet intellectually incurious about the specific capabilities and limitations relevant to their domain. Enthusiasm drives investment decisions; curiosity drives learning decisions. The distinction matters because investment without learning produces deployment without adoption, and deployment without adoption is the most expensive outcome in AI leadership.

Disciplined curiosity has a specific texture. It is targeted: the curious leader is not interested in AI in general but in the specific AI capabilities that could reshape their organization's competitive position over the next three to five years. It is skeptical: the curious leader reads vendors' claims with calibrated doubt and insists on seeing evidence rather than accepting demonstrations at face value. It is structured: the curious leader sets aside dedicated time for exploration, not scrolling through technology news, but hands-on engagement with tools, conversations with practitioners, and honest review of both successful and failed implementations.

The failure mode at the low end of the curiosity dimension is not ignorance; it is incuriosity masquerading as pragmatism. The leader who says, "I don't need to understand how the model works; I just need to know if it works," is making a category error. Understanding how AI systems behave, where they are reliable and where they are not, and what organizational conditions are required for them to produce value is not a technical question. It is a leadership question. The leader who cannot answer it is not being pragmatic; they are being uninformed in a domain where informed leadership is the competitive advantage.

Curiosity assessment prompts: In the past ninety days, have you personally experimented with any AI tool in a context that was unfamiliar to you? Have you sought out a case study of an AI initiative that failed and analyzed why it failed? Have you had a genuine conversation with a practitioner who disagreed with the prevailing AI narrative in your industry? Have you asked your team to challenge one of your AI-related assumptions publicly? If the honest answer to most of these is no, the Curiosity dimension is worth attention.

L Leverage: Knowing When AI Adds Value and When It Does Not

Leverage is the discernment dimension of the AI-CLEAR model, and it may be the most consequential. The leader with high Leverage has developed a refined judgment about when AI genuinely improves outcomes and when it introduces more cost, risk, or degraded quality than it delivers in value. This judgment is not algorithmic. It cannot be reduced to a checklist, though a good checklist can help. It develops through deliberate practice, honest review of outcomes, and a willingness to say "AI is not right for this" in the face of organizational pressure to use it everywhere.

The categories of work where AI reliably degrades rather than improves quality deserve particular attention. Ethical judgment deciding how to treat an employee, how to respond to a community concern, and whether a course of action is consistent with the organization's values is fundamentally a human responsibility. Inserting AI into ethical deliberation does not improve ethics; it diffuses accountability and often produces outputs that are technically defensible but morally hollow. Relationship management, the ongoing cultivation of trust with customers, partners, boards, and regulators, depends on signals of genuine presence and authentic engagement that AI-mediated communication systematically undermines. Cultural leadership, the work of shaping organizational identity during periods of uncertainty, requires the leader to be visibly and personally present in ways that no AI tool can replicate.

At the organizational level, Leverage also involves knowing how to size AI initiatives correctly. Over-investment in AI for low-leverage applications (automating tasks that were not bottlenecks) diverts resources from high-leverage applications (reducing cognitive load on decision-makers who are genuinely capacity-constrained). Underinvestment in AI for high-leverage applications (continuing to rely on human judgment for pattern-recognition tasks that AI performs significantly better) is equally costly. The leader with strong Leverage has a clear, regularly updated map of where AI genuinely changes organizational capacity and allocates resources accordingly.

Diagram 2.7: The Leverage Matrix

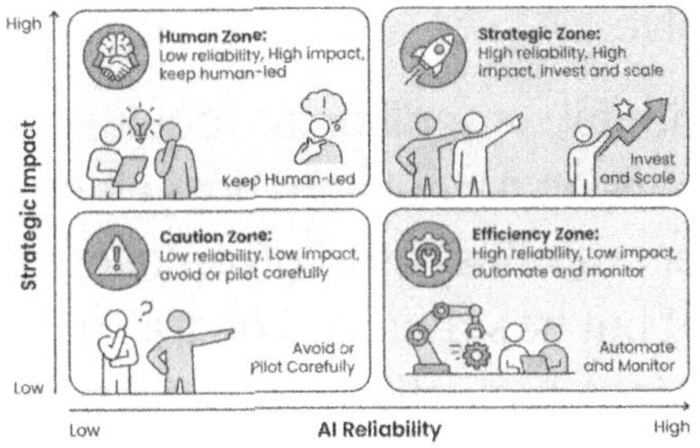

A clean minimalist infographic diagrun designed for executive and corporate tone for a business leadership book.

Empowerment: Creating Conditions for Human-AI Collaboration

Empowerment in the AI-CLEAR model is not about allowing team members to use AI tools. Permission is table stakes. Genuine empowerment is about creating organizational conditions, structural, cultural, and developmental, under which human-AI collaboration becomes productive. These conditions do not emerge spontaneously. They are designed and maintained by leaders who understand what their teams need to work effectively alongside AI.

The structural conditions include clarity about which decisions belong to AI, which to humans, and which are shared responsibilities that require genuine integration of both. Without structural clarity, teams default to either over-delegation (asking AI to make decisions that require human judgment) or under-utilization (avoiding AI for tasks where it would genuinely help due to unclear boundaries). The leader's job is to establish and communicate those boundaries explicitly, and to update them as AI capabilities evolve.

The developmental conditions require the most sustained investment. AI tools are not self-explanatory. A team member who has been given access to an AI writing assistant but has received no training in prompt construction, output evaluation, or workflow integration will use the tool only marginally and eventually stop using it. A team member who has received structured development- not necessarily formal training, but deliberate coaching, peer sharing, and guided experimentation- will progressively build the skill to make AI genuinely amplify their work. The leader who provides access without development is not empowering. They are equipped without enabling.

The cultural condition is psychological safety, discussed earlier in this chapter. It bears repeating in the Empowerment context because the connection is direct: teams that are not psychologically safe to fail in AI experiments cannot develop AI competence. Competence requires iteration, and iteration requires a culture that treats failed experiments as learning rather than evidence of inadequacy. Empowerment and psychological safety are not separate initiatives. They are the same initiative viewed from different angles.

A Accountability: Owning AI Outcomes, Including Failures

Accountability in the AI context has a specific and demanding meaning. It is not accountability for the decision to deploy AI that is ordinary leadership accountability. It is accountability for the outcomes that AI produces, including outcomes that no human explicitly chose or intended. When an AI-powered hiring tool systematically disadvantages qualified candidates from underrepresented groups, the accountable leader does not cite the algorithm as the cause. When an AI-generated financial projection misleads a board decision, the accountable leader does not cite the data scientists who built the model. The leader who chose to deploy the tool, who set the governance conditions, and who acted on the outputs is the accountable party.

This form of accountability requires a specific kind of courage. The organizational instinct when AI produces a problematic outcome is to identify who built the model and hold them responsible. This instinct is wrong and dangerous. It is wrong because the people who built the model typically had less power than those who deployed it and less responsibility for the organizational conditions that shaped its use. It is dangerous because it creates a governance gap: if technical teams are responsible for AI outcomes, then business leaders have a false permission to disclaim outcomes they authorized. That governance gap is where the most serious organizational AI failures originate.

Accountability has a prospective dimension. The accountable leader does not wait for visible failure before taking responsibility for AI behavior. They invest in monitoring and auditability, commission honest post-mortems, and build governance that gives them genuine visibility into how AI systems are behaving, not just the visibility that reporting systems are designed to provide. Accountability is maintenance work, not crisis management.

Diagram 2.8: The Accountability Stack in AI Leadership

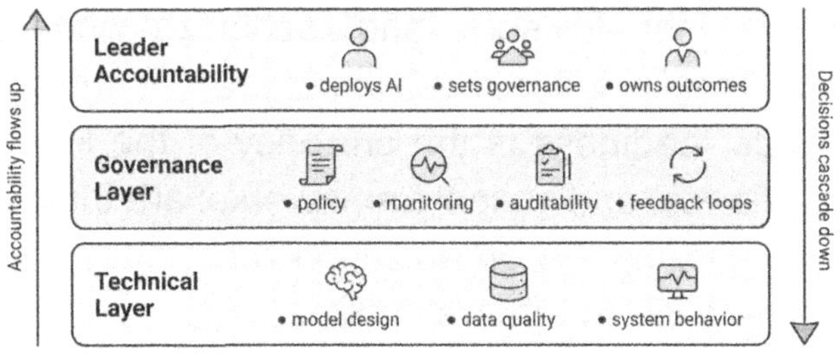

Diagram 2.8: The Accountability Stack in AI Leadership executive designed for business Leadership book

R Readiness: The Continuous Update Posture

Readiness is the temporal dimension of the AI-CLEAR model, the recognition that AI leadership is not a state you achieve but a posture you maintain. The leader who was genuinely ready for AI in 2022 is not automatically ready for AI in 2025, because the technology, the regulatory landscape, the competitive dynamics, and the organizational challenges have all evolved substantially. Readiness requires a continuous practice of updating: deliberate, structured, and regular engagement with how the AI environment is changing and what that change requires of the leader.

The Readiness dimension has three components. Strategic readiness is the leader's current understanding of how AI is reshaping their industry, competitive landscape, and organizational strategic options. Technical readiness is the leader's current ability to evaluate AI-related decisions, not to make those decisions alone, but to ask the right questions, identify the right advisors, and recognize when the answers they are receiving are insufficient. Governance readiness is the currency of the leader's risk, compliance, and ethical frameworks: are they built for the AI systems the organization runs today, or for the systems it ran two years ago?

The failure mode of low Readiness is often invisible until it becomes expensive. The leader who has not updated their AI governance frameworks is not experiencing visible risk until a regulatory inquiry, a high-profile error, or a competitor's move reveals how large the gap has become. The pilot-to-production pathway that worked for an earlier generation of AI tools may be entirely inadequate for generative AI systems capable of producing outputs at scale with minimal human review. Readiness requires leaders to ask regularly: Does our governance infrastructure fit the AI systems we are deploying today?

Building a Readiness practice involves specific habits: quarterly review of AI-related developments in your industry, annual reassessment of governance structures against current AI capabilities, regular conversations with practitioners outside your organization who see patterns you cannot see from inside, and honest self-assessment of where your AI knowledge base has fallen behind your AI deployment footprint. None of these requires technical expertise. They require discipline, intellectual honesty, and organizational authority to act on what you find.

The AI-CLEAR Self-Assessment

Rate yourself on each of the five AI-CLEAR dimensions using the scale below. Be honest, not aspirational: the value of this assessment depends entirely on accurate self-perception, not on producing a flattering profile. Complete the assessment before reading the interpretation guidance; your initial responses are more valuable than responses shaped by knowing what each score implies.

Rating scale: 1 = This dimension is largely absent from my current leadership practice. 2 = I have awareness of this dimension, but limited consistent behavior in it. 3 = I practice this dimension inconsistently, strong in some contexts, absent in others. 4 = This dimension is a consistent part of my leadership practice with identifiable room for improvement. 5 = This dimension is a genuine strength that I actively model for others.

Curiosity: In the past ninety days, I have personally experimented with new AI tools, sought out AI failure cases in my industry, challenged my own AI assumptions through genuine external input, and engaged my team in substantive conversations about AI capabilities and limitations, not just deployment updates.

Leverage: I have a clearly articulated and regularly updated view of where AI adds genuine value in my organization and where it does not. I resist organizational pressure to deploy AI in contexts where human judgment is superior. I can specifically describe the categories of work in my domain where AI should not replace human deliberation.

Empowerment: My team has structural clarity, developmental support, and psychological safety to experiment with AI tools, report failures honestly, and continuously improve their AI practice. I can identify specific actions I took in the past quarter to build this environment, not just the general cultural values I hold.

Accountability: I have personally reviewed the governance conditions under which AI systems in my organization are operating. I can identify the specific mechanisms by which I would know if an AI system under my authority was producing harmful or misleading outputs. I have established clear ownership of AI outcomes at the team and organizational level.

Readiness: My understanding of AI capabilities, risks, and regulatory developments is current relative to the AI systems my organization is deploying. I can identify specific ways my AI knowledge has been updated over the past six months, beyond general awareness of public AI news.

Scoring: Add your five ratings. A total of 20-25 indicates a strong overall posture with targeted development opportunities. A total of 15-19 signals the need for meaningful development across multiple dimensions. A score below 15 indicates that AI leadership development is a strategic priority, not a reflection of general leadership quality, but recognition that this environment requires specific investment.

Interpreting your lowest score: The AI-CLEAR model uses constraint logic. Your lowest-scoring dimension is not the dimension where you are weakest in general terms; it is the dimension where a targeted investment will produce the most significant overall improvement in your AI leadership effectiveness. A chain of five links is only as strong as its weakest link, and a leadership model with four strong dimensions and one underdeveloped dimension will underperform a model with consistent strength across all five. Focus your development energy on the dimension with the lowest score, not the one that is most interesting or most comfortable to work on.

Diagram 2.9: CLEAR Self-Assessment Radar Chart

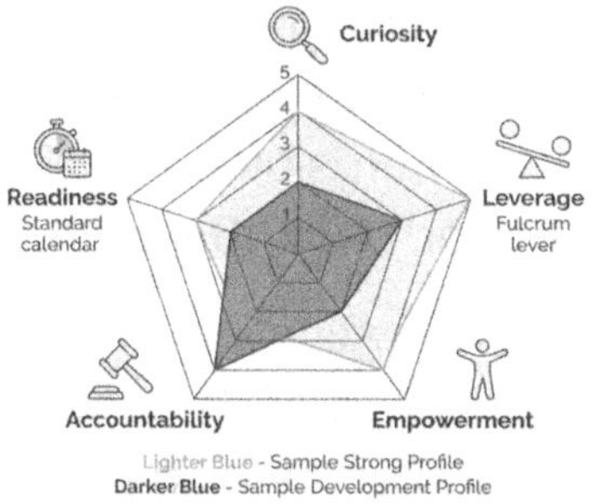

Thisgram ust's CLEAR Self-assessment **radar chart** latemental be executive and corporite corporate.

The Discernment Imperative

"Use AI More" Is Not a Strategy

One of the most dangerous AI leadership positions is also one of the most common: the blanket directive to increase AI adoption across the organization without specification, prioritization, or discernment. This position is dangerous not because AI is harmful; it is not. Applied well, it is not. But it treats every AI application as equally valuable and every human alternative as equally inefficient. Neither assumption is true, nor acting as though they are producing a specific kind of organizational harm: the systematic degradation of the human capabilities that the organization most needs to preserve.

When AI tools are widely available for knowledge work, a significant proportion of users begin to reduce the cognitive effort they invest in tasks that AI can partially handle. This is rational in the short term but has compounding consequences: team members who learn to review AI-generated analysis rather than produce it from first principles gradually lose the analytical capability to recognize when that analysis is subtly wrong. Capability erosion is invisible in the short term but significant over 18 to 36 months.

The discernment imperative is a counsel of AI precision, not AI caution. Use AI where it genuinely amplifies outcomes. Protect human capability where it is irreplaceable. The question "Does using AI here make the outcome better, or just faster?" deserves a specific answer for every significant category of work in your organization.

Where AI Degrades Quality

Ethical judgment is the first category. Decisions that require integrating competing values, weighing harms against benefits in contexts where no algorithm has access to the full range of considerations, and exercising moral courage in the face of institutional pressure are fundamentally human responsibilities. AI can surface relevant precedents, map stakeholder impacts, and generate options for consideration. It cannot make ethical decisions, and leaders who use AI outputs as the primary input for ethical deliberation are not making AI-assisted ethical decisions. They are making algorithmic decisions and calling them ethical.

Relationship management is the second category. The cultivation of trust with customers, employees, partners, board members, and regulators depends on signals that are indistinguishable from genuine human presence: the leader who remembers the specifics of a previous conversation, who follows up without prompting, who shows up differently depending on what a relationship requires in a particular moment. AI-assisted relationship management, drafting communications, summarizing conversation history, and generating follow-up agendas can support the operational infrastructure of the relationship management process. It cannot replace the human signal at its core, and in contexts where stakeholders are sophisticated enough to detect AI mediation, it actively damages trust.

Cultural leadership is the third category. In periods of organizational transformation, which is the permanent condition of any organization navigating an AI-driven environment, employees look to leaders for signals about what is valued, what is expected, and what kind of organization they are being asked to be part of. These signals are transmitted through a leader's visible behavior, the questions they ask in public settings, the discomfort they are willing to absorb publicly, and the consistency between their stated values and their observed decisions. No AI tool produces these signals. The leader who seeks to drive cultural transformation through AI-mediated communications is doing the work without being present for it.

The Both/And Leadership Posture

Rejecting False Binaries

AI leadership discourse is saturated with false binaries. Human OR artificial intelligence. Efficiency OR innovation. Speed OR care. Automation OR employment. These framings are intellectually convenient and strategically misleading. They force leaders into defensive positions, such as "we are pro-human" or "we are pro-AI," that misrepresent the actual leadership challenge. The actual challenge is not choosing between these alternatives. It is developing the organizational capability to hold them in productive tension simultaneously.

The both/and posture requires cognitive maturity developed through practice. It requires disagreeing with framing without replacing it with its opposite, tolerating ambiguity without collapsing into indecision, and communicating complexity to stakeholders who prefer simplicity, saying "it depends" when it does, rather than providing false clarity in the name of decisiveness.

The practical implications are specific. A both/and leader does not respond to team AI concerns by defending the technology; they explore whether the concern points to a genuine limitation, a governance gap, or a capability development need. When facing board pressure to accelerate AI deployment, they provide a specific assessment of where acceleration is safe and where it is not and accept accountability for that judgment. In both cases, the both/and posture consistently outperforms the defensive or the accommodating alternative.

Diagram 2.10: The Both/And Leadership Framework

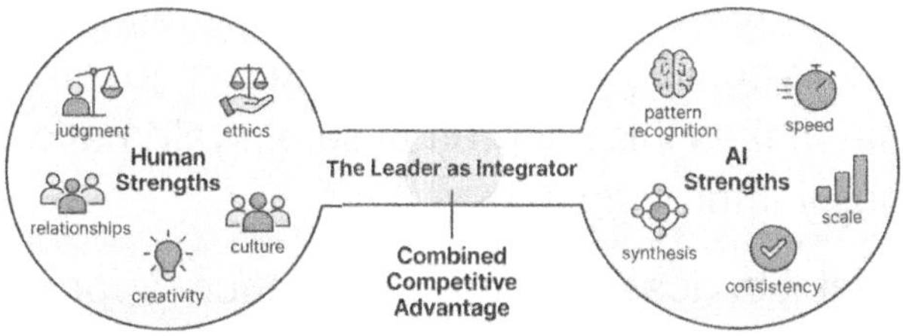

Executive and corporate toned infographic designed for a business leadership book

Hybrid Intelligence in Practice

The concept of hybrid intelligence, the orchestrated combination of human and AI capabilities toward outcomes neither could achieve alone, is more specific than a general endorsement of human-AI collaboration. It implies a particular leadership role: the orchestrator who understands the respective strengths of human and AI contributors well enough to assign each type of capability to the work it is best suited for, and who builds the integration architecture that enables human and AI contributions to complement rather than duplicate one another.

In healthcare, hybrid intelligence appears in clinical decision support systems, where AI flags potential diagnoses or drug interactions for review by clinical staff, whose contextual judgment about the specific patient determines the final recommendation. The AI does not replace clinical judgment; it enriches it by surfacing considerations the clinician might not have generated independently, at a speed that clinical workflow can absorb. The orchestrating leader in this context is not the clinician or the data scientist; it is the healthcare executive who has designed a governance model that makes this integration safe, systematic, and continuously improving.

In financial services, hybrid intelligence appears in compliance monitoring, where AI identifies patterns in transaction data that warrant investigation, and human analysts apply regulatory judgment and relationship context to determine whether investigation is warranted and how it should proceed. The AI's pattern recognition is vastly superior to human scale. Human judgment regarding organizational context, regulatory intent, and proportional response is vastly superior to that of AI. The integration produces a compliance capability that neither party could replicate on its own.

In professional services, hybrid intelligence appears in due diligence processes, contract analysis, competitive research, and client communication preparation, all domains where AI can compress hours of synthesis into minutes. At the same time, experienced practitioners apply judgment about what the synthesis means for the specific client situation. The workflow-level impact is real, but it requires the professional services leader to have designed the workflow, to determine which AI syntheses receive human review, what constitutes sufficient review, and how the organization learns when the integration produces errors.

In manufacturing, hybrid intelligence shows up in quality control, predictive maintenance, and supply chain optimization, all domains where AI processes sensor and operational data at volumes beyond human capacity. But decisions about how to respond to AI-generated alerts require operational judgment that must remain in human hands. The leader who abdicates those judgment calls to the algorithm has not accelerated decision-making; they have eliminated accountability.

Mindset for Mid-Level Managers and Product Owners

The Unique Position of Operational Managers

Mid-level managers and product owners occupy the most demanding position in the AI-transforming organization. They are simultaneously subject to AI-skeptical team members worried about job security and workflow disruption, and to AI-overenthusiastic executives who underestimate the complexity of implementation and overestimate near-term organizational readiness. They are expected to execute AI initiatives designed by technical teams that do not fully understand operational constraints, and to manage human performance in contexts where AI capabilities are redefining good work in real time.

This position requires a specific adaptation of the mindsets described earlier in this chapter. For the mid-level manager, the growth mindset is not primarily about developing personal AI capabilities, though that matters. It is about maintaining intellectual openness in the face of genuinely difficult daily implementation pressures. The AI tool that was supposed to reduce the team's workload is creating unanticipated review categories. The AI-generated outputs that looked excellent in the proof of concept are producing workflow friction in production. The team member who was most enthusiastic about AI in the initial training is now the most frustrated by it. None of these developments should be treated as evidence that the initiative was a mistake. They are the normal texture of transformation that is working.

For the mid-level manager, the posture is most evident in how they translate between the executive and team layers. When an executive issues a directive that is AI-maximalist and insufficiently nuanced to guide practical implementation, the operational manager's job is not to execute it literally. It is to translate it into implementation guidance that preserves the strategic intent while building in the operational clarity that makes execution safe. When a team member raises a legitimate concern about an AI application, the operational manager's job is not to defend the executive position. It is to take the concern seriously, escalate it if it indicates a genuine risk, and provide the team member with honest feedback on what can and cannot be changed.

Product Owner Mindset: Three Simultaneous Lenses

Product owners in AI-transforming organizations have a particularly complex responsibility: they must treat AI simultaneously as a feature, a platform, and an ethical responsibility. As a feature, AI is a capability that needs to be designed for the user, rigorously tested before deployment, iterated based on real usage data, and retired or redesigned when it fails to deliver the experience it was built to provide. Product discipline applies to AI features just as it applies to any other product capability, and product owners who relax that discipline because AI seems inherently innovative are setting themselves up for failure.

As a platform, AI is the architectural layer on which future product capabilities will be built. Product owners who treat each AI feature in isolation fail to build the institutional knowledge, governance infrastructure, and feedback architecture that allow AI platforms to compound value. Platform thinking requires asking for every AI feature decision: Does this build or erode the organization's ability to use AI more effectively in the future?

As an ethical responsibility, AI imposes obligations on product owners that do not arise with most other product capabilities. AI systems can produce outputs at scale that affect users in ways no individual team member intended or would have authorized. AI systems can encode biases present in training data, leading to disparate outcomes across user populations. AI systems can fail in subtle, difficult-to-detect ways without active monitoring. The product owner who treats ethical responsibility as someone else's domain- the legal team's, the governance committees', and the data scientists'- is not distributing responsibility appropriately. They are creating an accountability gap that will eventually produce a visible failure.

Diagram 2.11: The Product Owner Three AI Lenses

Caption: The rat of AI product owner a as ethical responsibility content firrs as compouiding value, business leadership.

Building Your Personal AI Literacy Practice

AI literacy for senior managers and product owners is not a credential program, a certification course, or a training module completed once and checked off. It is a practice, an ongoing, structured set of activities that progressively builds and maintains the specific knowledge and judgment that serious AI leadership requires. The managers who build genuine AI literacy consistently do several specific things, not occasionally.

They engage with primary sources rather than relying solely on synthesis. Reading technology journalism and consulting research gives you the curated narrative about AI. Reading actual post-implementation case studies, regulatory guidance documents, and technical overviews of specific AI capabilities gives you the texture you need to evaluate the narrative critically. Serious managers who have developed genuine AI literacy can typically point to specific sources they have engaged with, specific tools they have tested, and specific assumptions they have revised based on their findings.

They build a network of genuine practitioners rather than relying solely on internal expertise. The AI landscape is evolving faster than any single organization can keep up with from the inside. Practitioners working with AI systems across adjacent domains, industries, or scales see patterns and failure modes that are not visible within a single organization. This network does not require extensive formal cultivation. It requires the willingness to be genuinely curious in conversations, to ask substantive questions rather than networking questions, and to engage with perspectives that challenge rather than confirm internal assumptions.

They maintain a personal AI experiment log, a simple record of what they have tried, what happened, and what they concluded. This makes learning cumulative rather than episodic and provides honest evidence of where AI literacy is genuinely strong versus where it is thinner than preferred. Evidence-based self-assessment produces the calibrated accuracy that the AI-CLEAR model requires.

They explicitly tie AI literacy to organizational decisions, including evaluating vendor proposals, designing governance structures, coaching teams through adoption, and communicating AI risks to the board. Learning anchored to a specific decision application is retained more reliably than learning acquired for its own sake.

Manager's Checklist: Applying the Mindsets

The following checklist translates the chapter's mindset framework into specific, observable leadership behaviors. Use it as a quarterly self-audit. A behavior you cannot point to with a specific recent example is aspirational rather than operational.

Mindset Shifts

- You can articulate the difference between treating AI as a tool and treating it as an organizational capability. You can describe at least one recent decision you made differently because of this distinction.
- You have had at least one conversation in the past quarter in which you publicly occupied beginner status on an AI-related topic rather than managing the appearance of expertise.
- You can identify at least one AI application in your domain where you said, "not here," where you explicitly chose human judgment over AI assistance, and can explain why.
- You have shared at least one AI experiment failure with your team and used it as a learning conversation rather than a performance conversation.

AI-CLEAR Leadership

- You have completed the AI-CLEAR self-assessment in this chapter and identified your lowest-scoring dimension.
- You have developed at least one specific development action for your highest-leverage AI-CLEAR dimension, with a timeline and a measurable indicator.
- You have reviewed your AI-CLEAR scores with at least one trusted colleague or advisor who can provide honest calibration.
- You have scheduled an AI-CLEAR reassessment for approximately ninety days from today.

Team Empowerment

- Your team can describe the boundaries between AI responsibility and human responsibility in the workflows that affect their work.
- You have created at least one structured opportunity in the past quarter for team members to share AI experiments, successful or not, in a context that does not feel evaluative.
- You can identify at least one team member whose AI capability you have actively developed through coaching, not just tool access.
- You have not forced any AI tool adoption without also investing in the development support required to use it effectively.

Accountability and Readiness

- You can describe the specific mechanisms by which you would currently know if an AI system under your authority was producing misleading or harmful outputs.
- You have reviewed your AI governance frameworks in the past six months against the specific AI capabilities your organization is currently deploying.
- You have updated your AI knowledge base not through general news consumption but through engagement with substantive primary sources or practitioner conversations in the past ninety days.
- You can describe one specific AI development in the past twelve months that changed how you think about a decision in your domain.

Where These Mindsets Lead

The mindsets introduced in this chapter are not self-contained leadership virtues. They are the cognitive infrastructure for every practical framework in the chapters that follow. Chapter 3 will introduce the Serious Decision Spectrum, a tool for classifying decisions by data density and human stakes, and the leaders who will use it most effectively are those who have already made the shift from operational problem-solver to strategic architect. The decision-making discipline the Serious Decision Spectrum demands requires exact discernment, the tolerance for ambiguity, and the accountability posture developed by the AI-CLEAR model.

Chapter 9 will synthesize the AI-CLEAR model, the Serious Decision Spectrum, and the Trust Architecture into an integrative framework for the AI leader operating at full organizational scale. The synthesis will make clear that these frameworks are not separate tools but interlocking components of a coherent leadership system. Your AI-CLEAR assessment today is the baseline from which synthesis will be most useful. Revisit it before reading Chapter 9.

The mindset work in this chapter is not a prerequisite to be completed and then moved past. It is an ongoing practice you return to as your AI environment evolves. The leader who completed the AI-CLEAR assessment honestly, identified a specific development target, and made one concrete behavior change is already operating differently from the majority of senior managers navigating the AI era. That operational difference compounds. It produces better decisions, more effective team development, more credible AI governance, and a more robust organizational AI capability, all of which are examined in detail in the chapters ahead.

The mental shift described in this chapter is, ultimately, a leadership shift. It is the difference between leading an organization through an AI transformation and watching an organization attempt one. Sandra Okafor pulled that Monday morning meeting because her mindset gave her the right question at the right moment. The technical competence to deliver the right answer lay with her team. But the leadership clarity to know that the question needed asking- that is the AI-CLEAR model in practice- before any of its dimensions had a name.

Diagram 2.12: Chapter Connections: Mindsets as Cognitive Infrastructure

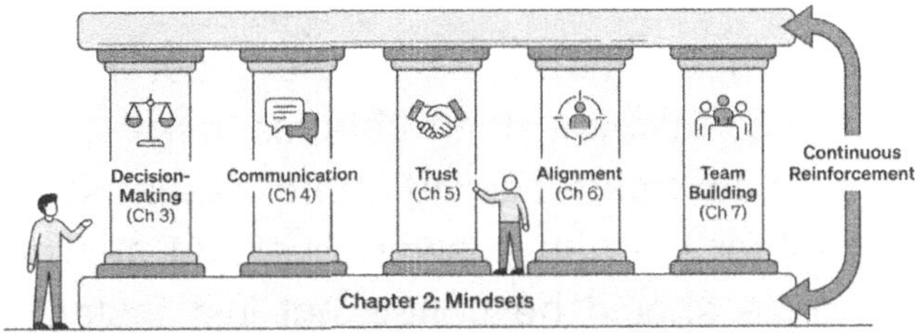

Caption 2.12: Continuous connection around key capabilities built upon Mindsets as Cognitive Infrastructure

The Essential Point

The organizations pulling ahead in the AI era are not primarily the ones with the largest AI budgets, the most sophisticated models, or the most aggressive deployment timelines. They are the organizations whose senior leaders have made a genuine cognitive shift: from tool thinking to capability thinking, from operational problem-solving to strategic architecture, from AI delegation to human-AI partnership, and from the certainty-seeking mindset that previous environments rewarded to the productive-uncertainty mindset that the AI era requires.

The AI-CLEAR Leadership Model gives that shift a diagnostic structure. Curiosity, Leverage, Empowerment, Accountability, and Readiness are not abstract virtues. They are specific, measurable dimensions of leadership behavior that can be developed and continuously improved. Your lowest-scoring dimension is not a weakness; it is a direction. The leader who knows their direction is already ahead of the one who does not.

The discernment imperative is the most important individual commitment this chapter asks for: the commitment to treat "use AI more" as a strategic question rather than an answer. Every AI application you authorize should be better, not just faster, than what it replaces. That standard, applied consistently, is the difference between an AI-active organization and an AI-effective one. It is the difference that this guide is designed to help you build.

4 Making Better Decisions in an Age of Algorithmic Advice

A Decision That Could Not Wait

The CFO of a mid-sized logistics company received an alert on Tuesday morning: the AI-powered demand forecasting system recommended an immediate 22 percent reduction in contract staffing across three regional distribution hubs. The model's confidence score was high. Its reasoning, laid out in a neatly formatted dashboard, cited a projected 14-week softening in freight volumes, seasonal compression, and a competitor's reported capacity expansion. The numbers were coherent. The presentation was clean. The recommendation was unambiguous.

She had forty-eight hours before the board's operating committee convened. Her operations VP was already citing the AI recommendation in pre-meeting emails as "what the data says." Her HR director was asking which vendor to notify first. The machine had spoken, and the organization was already moving toward execution.

She paused. Not because the analysis was wrong; it may well have been right. She paused because she recognized that the decision before her was not actually a forecasting problem. It was a people problem. It was a community-relations problem. It was a signal-to-the-market problem. It was a values problem. And not a single one of those dimensions appeared in the model's output.

She convened a two-hour working session that afternoon not to second-guess the forecast, but to interrogate the decision. The AI analysis remained on the table as one voice, not the final word. By the end of the session, the team had agreed on a different path: a voluntary hour-reduction program at one hub, a hiring freeze at the other two hubs, and a 60-day review gate. The cost savings were comparable. The human cost was materially lower. The reputational exposure was minimal.

That CFO did not ignore the algorithm. She used it exactly as it should be, as a rigorous, data-rich input to a decision that ultimately required human judgment, organizational context, and moral clarity. What she demonstrated deliberately and under pressure is the skill this chapter is designed to build.

Why This Matters Now

Decision-making is not one of a leader's responsibilities; it is the responsibility from which all others flow. Every strategy, every resource allocation, every team structure, every response to a crisis begins with a decision. And artificial intelligence has permanently altered the environment in which those decisions are made.

The change is not simply that AI provides more data or faster analysis, though it does both. The bigger change is that AI has introduced a new participant into the decision process, one that speaks with numerical authority, produces confident-sounding outputs, and does not announce its limitations unless specifically asked to. In organizations without deliberate decision governance, this participant can quietly shift from advisor to authority without anyone explicitly choosing to do so. The workflow-level impact is significant: when an AI system's recommendation becomes the de facto starting point and ending point of a decision, the organization has ceded judgment without realizing it.

Most organizational decision-making frameworks were designed before this participant existed. They account for cognitive bias, stakeholder input, escalation protocols, and scenario planning, but they were built for environments where all the voices in the room were human. Leaders who have not updated their frameworks are operating with a map that pre-dates the territory. They are either trusting AI outputs more than they have earned, or dismissing data-rich analysis because it conflicts with intuition. Neither posture serves the organization well. This chapter gives you a structured, practical framework, the Serious Decision Spectrum, for calibrating the right level of AI authority for the right types of decisions, every time.

Diagram 3.1: The Three New Decision Realities

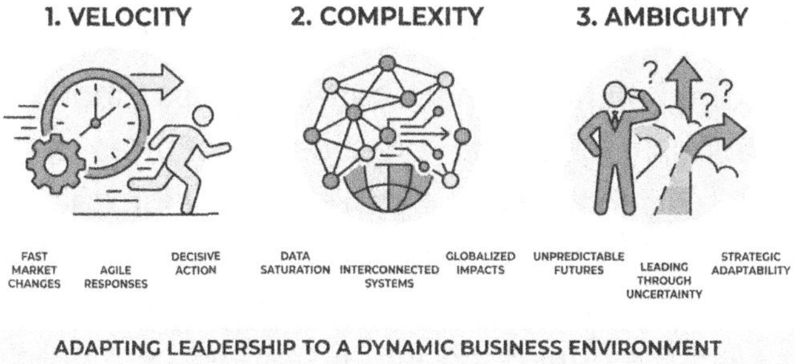

How AI Has Changed the Decision Landscape

The Three New Decision Realities

The decision environment that most senior leaders learned to navigate no longer fully describes the one they operate in. Three developments have made the gap significant enough to warrant a deliberate response.

Speed pressure has intensified in ways that go beyond competitive dynamics. AI-powered tools can generate market analysis, financial projections, and operational recommendations in minutes that would previously have taken analytical teams days. This is a genuine capability advantage when used well. It is a liability when it creates organizational pressure to consume and act on that output with the same speed at which it was generated. The half-life of organizational decisions is shrinking, but the irreversibility of many of them has not. A workforce restructuring decision does not become less consequential simply because a model produced the analysis in four minutes rather than four days.

Data abundance is the second reality. Leaders at every level now have access to more relevant data than at any point in their careers. This should be unambiguously good. In practice, it creates a new challenge: distinguishing between plentiful data and reliable, representative, and correctly interpreted data. Volume can masquerade as rigor. An AI system that ingests vast amounts of data and produces a precise-looking recommendation may be masking significant assumptions about data quality, recency, and applicability. Serious leaders ask not only what the data says, but also what data is and is not in the model, and what the model cannot see.

Algorithmic influence is the third, and least-examined, reality. AI outputs carry a form of authority that human recommendations often do not. A percentage, a confidence score, a ranked list: these communicate quantitative certainty that can overwhelm qualitative judgment in a group setting. When a system presents a recommendation with a 91 percent confidence score, it takes a confident and informed leader to say, "I know what that number means and what it cannot mean." Most organizational cultures have not yet developed the norms and language to push back productively on algorithmic outputs. The result is a subtle but significant shift in how decisions are made, not by policy, but by default.

The False Efficiency Trap

There is a persuasive logic to the idea that AI-enabled decisions are inherently more efficient. The analysis arrives faster, the data coverage is broader, and the bias of any single human analyst is partially mitigated. All of this is true, and it creates genuine value in the right context.

What this logic misses is the difference between decision speed and decision quality. Moving faster toward the wrong answer is not an improvement. It is an acceleration of organizational error. The false efficiency trap occurs when leaders treat the speed of AI-generated analysis as a signal that the decision itself should be made quickly. A two-minute AI brief does not imply a two-minute decision. The synthesis of analysis into action still requires judgment, stakeholder consideration, ethical review, and contextual intelligence that no system can fully supply.

The leaders who avoid this trap ask a simple clarifying question before acting on any AI-generated recommendation: *What would change if I had an additional forty-eight hours?* If the honest answer is "very little," then speed may be appropriate. If the answer is "I'd have time to consult the operations team, review the assumptions, and consider the downstream effects," then the efficiency gain of the AI analysis is being sacrificed to a different kind of inefficiency: the cost of a poorly executed or subsequently reversed decision.

The Emerging Decision Audit Imperative

As AI becomes a more regular participant in organizational decisions, a new governance expectation is taking shape: the decision audit. This is the organizational practice of tracking not only what was decided but also how and why, which inputs were used, which AI systems contributed, which assumptions were made explicit, and who exercised final judgment.

Decision audits are not bureaucratic overhead. They are operational clarity in documented form. They protect the organization in regulatory environments that are increasingly interested in how AI-influenced decisions are made. They create an institutional learning record that allows leaders to identify patterns: which decision types consistently perform better with more AI input, which consistently require human override, and where the gap between AI recommendations and final human decisions has been most costly or most valuable.

Building a decision audit practice does not require sophisticated technology. It requires discipline. A consistently maintained shared log that records the decision, the AI systems consulted, the recommendation they offered, the human judgment applied, and the outcome reviewed quarterly is sufficient to begin building the organizational intelligence that makes future decisions better.

Diagram 3.2: The Decision Audit Framework

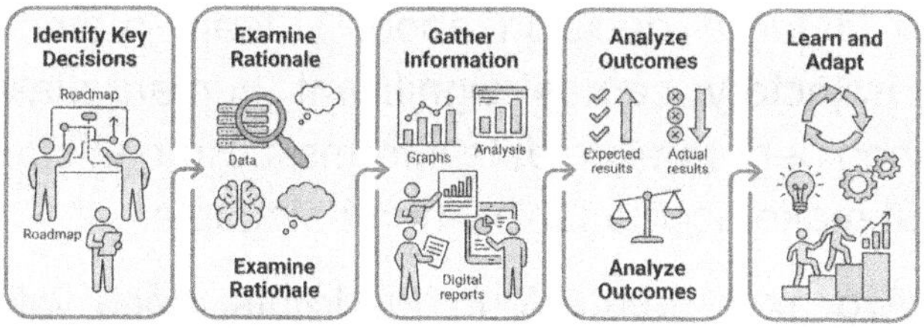

A comprehensive review process to evaluate decision-making effectiveness and outcomes for continuous improvement.

Introducing the Serious Decision Spectrum

Most decision frameworks ask leaders to think about decisions in terms of urgency and importance. This is useful but incomplete for an AI-augmented environment. The Serious Decision Spectrum adds two axes that are specifically calibrated to the AI leadership context: **data density** and **human stakes**.

Data density refers to how much relevant, reliable, and accessible data exists to inform the decision. This is not just about volume. A decision can be surrounded by vast amounts of low-quality or poorly applicable data, and that does not make it high in data density. Equally, a decision can be genuinely data-rich: historical patterns are strong, comparable situations are numerous, and the data is clean and up to date. High data density makes AI assistance more powerful. Low data density limits what AI can reliably contribute.

Human stakes refers to the extent to which a decision directly affects people, ethics, culture, or organizational identity, including those both inside and outside the organization. A decision about server capacity allocation has low human stakes even if it involves complex data. A decision about a team member's career trajectory carries significant human stakes, even when performance data informs it. Human stakes are what make accountability non-delegable.

These two axes create four quadrants, each with a distinct prescription for how much authority AI should hold in the decision.

DIAGRAM 3.3: THE SERIOUS DECISION SPECTRUM: FOUR QUADRANTS

ADAPTING THE DECISION-MAKING APPROACH BASED ON STAKES AND COMPLEXITY DRIVES ORGANIZATIONAL EFFECTIVENESS.

Quadrant 1 Automate: Let the System Lead

Decisions that fall into the Automate quadrant share two characteristics: the relevant data is rich and well-structured, and the consequences of a wrong decision are low in human terms. These decisions are well-suited to AI execution with minimal real-time human oversight, though not without governance.

Examples include dynamic pricing adjustments within pre-authorized bands, inventory reordering triggered by stock-level algorithms, IT ticket routing and categorization, and fraud detection flagging in payment systems. These decisions happen at a volume and velocity that no human team could match, and the cost of individual errors is typically low and recoverable.

The leadership responsibility in the Automate quadrant is not moment-to-moment oversight but **guardrail design**. You are accountable for setting the parameters within which the system operates: the floors and ceilings for automated actions, the exceptions that trigger human review, and the audit mechanisms that detect when the system behaves outside expected patterns. Automation without guardrails is not efficiency; it is exposure.

One critical discipline: review your Automate quadrant decisions periodically and ask whether the conditions that put them there still apply. A pricing algorithm that was appropriate when margins were stable may behave destructively in a margin-compressed environment. Automated systems do not know when their context has changed. Their human overseers must.

Quadrant 2 Augment: AI Informs, Humans Decide

The Augment quadrant is where AI provides its most significant organizational value and where the greatest risk of misuse exists. These decisions are both data-rich and high-stakes. AI can process the data with a depth and speed no human team can match. But the stakes mean that getting the decision wrong has real consequences for real people, and those consequences require human accountability.

Performance evaluations, strategic vendor selection, workforce restructuring analysis, significant capital allocation decisions, and product discontinuation decisions all fall within this quadrant. The AI contribution is genuine and important: it surfaces patterns in the data, identifies comparisons across time periods or peer organizations, flags outliers, and generates scenario projections. None of that work should be bypassed or duplicated manually when a capable system exists.

What AI cannot contribute to in this quadrant is the synthesis layer. That is where context, experience, ethical judgment, organizational knowledge, and leadership wisdom work that data cannot. The leader who uses AI output as the starting point of a decision, not the ending point, is using the Augment quadrant correctly. The leader who signs off on whatever the model recommends because "the data says so" has abdicated the judgment this quadrant explicitly requires.

The AI-CLEAR model's Leverage dimension, introduced in Chapter 2, is most directly activated in the Augment quadrant. Leverage is the discernment to know when AI is adding genuine value to your analysis and when it is substituting for judgment you need to provide yourself. In Augment decisions, both are true simultaneously: the AI analysis is valuable, and the human synthesis is non-negotiable.

DIAGRAM 3.4: THE AUGMENT QUADRANT IN PRACTICE

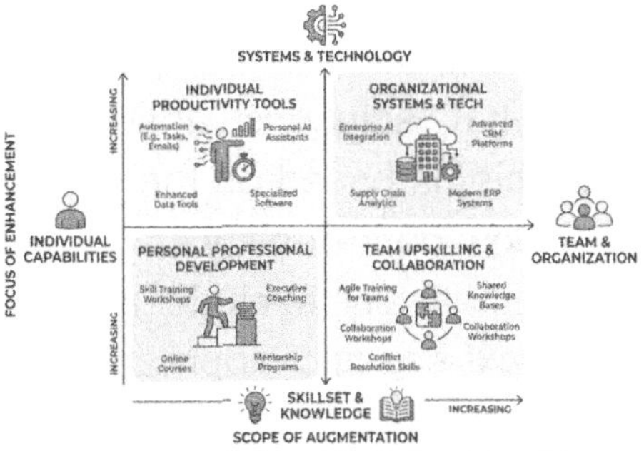

A strategic framework for increasing organizational performance through deliberate enhancement of human and technological resources.

Quadrant 3 Advice: AI as One Voice Among Several

The Advice quadrant covers decisions in which the data is sparse, incomplete, or of uncertain quality, but the human stakes are relatively low. These are often exploratory decisions: early-stage market research, initial product feature brainstorming, preliminary vendor shortlisting, or operational experiments where the cost of being wrong is contained.

In this quadrant, AI can be genuinely useful as a pattern-matcher and options generator. A generative AI system that is asked to brainstorm use cases for new technology or to identify analogous cases in adjacent industries is doing work that would otherwise take a research team weeks. That contribution has real value. But it should be treated with proportionate skepticism, not because the AI is performing poorly, but because the underlying data environment does not support high-confidence outputs.

The discipline in the Advise quadrant is resisting the tendency to treat AI-generated options as a definitive list or to accept AI framing as the only frame available. Experienced leaders know that the way a problem is defined shapes what solutions appear visible. AI systems frame problems based on the data they have been trained on. In low-data-density environments, that framing may systematically exclude unconventional, emerging, or context-specific approaches. Treat AI outputs in this quadrant as a useful first draft, not a final inventory of possibilities.

Quadrant 4 Assert: The Decisions That Belong to Leaders

The Assert quadrant is the most important and the most uncomfortable. These decisions combine low data density; there is not enough reliable information for an AI system to produce a high-confidence recommendation with the highest human stakes. They involve ethics, culture, identity, values, crisis response, and the moments that define what an organization is and is not willing to do.

Examples include: deciding how to respond when an AI system produces a discriminatory output and a regulatory inquiry follows; determining whether to proceed with an acquisition that would displace a significant portion of the acquired workforce; navigating a crisis of organizational trust after a product failure; making the call to pause an AI deployment because the team is not ready, even when the technology is. None of these decisions can be meaningfully delegated to a model. They require the full integration of experience, values, organizational judgment, and moral clarity that defines leadership at its highest level.

The Assert quadrant is where self-trust, the fourth layer of the Trust Architecture that Chapter 5 will develop, is most directly tested. Self-trust is not arrogance or the rejection of evidence. It is the disciplined confidence that your judgment, organizational knowledge, and human values matter, especially in circumstances where the data cannot tell you what to do. A leader who defers to algorithmic authority on assertive decisions is not being humble. They are absent.

Establishing your personal policy on Assert decisions before a crisis occurs is one of the highest-leverage preparations you can make. Know in advance: Which decisions will I always claim as human responsibility, regardless of what any system recommends? What are my non-negotiables? The answer to that question is not a limitation on your use of AI. It is a definition of your leadership.

Diagram 3.5: Assert Quadrant Decision Protocol

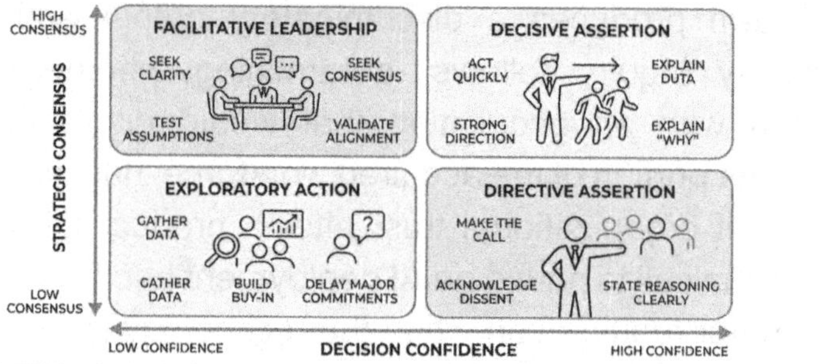

THIS PROTOCOL GUIDES LEADERS ON WHEN TO ASSERT DECISIONS BASED ON ALIGNMENT AND CERTAINTY.

Applying the Spectrum: Three Worked Examples

A finance decision. A financial services organization is reviewing its credit risk scoring model after a regulatory inquiry raised questions about disparate impact across demographic groups. The model uses extensive historical data (high data density). Still, the decision about how to respond- whether to revise the model, pause its use, issue a public statement, or restructure the review process- directly affects customers, staff, and the organization's regulatory standing (high human stakes). This is an Augment decision at minimum, and in its ethical and reputational dimensions, it crosses into Assert territory. The AI analysis of the model's performance remains essential input. But the decision about what to do belongs to the organization's leaders, and the accountability for the choice cannot be attributed to the system.

An HR decision. A technology company is conducting its annual talent review. An AI-powered performance analytics system has generated ranked scores for all employees, flagging candidates for promotion, development, and managed exit conversations at the lower end of the distribution. The data is extensive (high density). The impact on individuals is direct and significant (high stakes). This belongs squarely in Augment. The AI-generated analysis provides a starting framework that would take weeks to produce manually. But every individual decision, promotion, development investment, and conversation about performance must go through human review, human conversation, and human accountability. A leader who approves the bottom-quartile list without reviewing individual cases has allowed an Augment decision to function as an Automate decision. That is not efficiency. It is abdication.

A product development decision. An early-stage product team is deciding which features to prioritize for the next development cycle. They have customer feedback data, usage analytics, and NPS scores, a useful but incomplete dataset, and the competitive landscape is shifting faster than the data can capture. The stakes for individual customers are low, and the cost of building the wrong feature, although not trivial, is recoverable. This is Advice territory. The AI-generated prioritization model is a useful input, but the team should treat it as one voice alongside customer interviews, competitive intelligence, and their own product intuition. The features that appear highest-ranked in an algorithmic model may not be the features that define market differentiation.

The Most Common Mistake: Moving Assert Decisions into Augment Under Time Pressure

If there is one pattern in AI-augmented decision-making that experienced leaders encounter most reliably, and most harmfully, it is this. When time pressure intensifies, decisions tend to gravitate toward the quadrant that feels faster to resolve.

Assert decisions are ethically complex, value-laden, high-stakes, and low-data; they are inherently slow. They require deliberation, consultation, and the kind of careful synthesis that cannot be rushed without increasing the risk of error. Under time pressure, these same decisions get reclassified not officially, but practically. The team anchors on whatever data is available, treats partial analysis as sufficient, and moves to a recommendation that the AI system's output has made it easier to reach a quick decision. An Assert decision has been converted to Augment, not because the conditions changed, but because the clock said so.

This migration is one of the most consequential leadership failures in the AI era, and it is entirely preventable. The countermeasure is establishing your decision classification practice before the pressure arrives, building the habit of asking "where on the Spectrum does this decision belong?" as a routine step before analysis begins, not after the calendar has compressed your options. When a crisis arrives, and someone says, "the AI recommends X," the leader who already knows this is an assertive decision is not slowed by that recommendation. They are liberated by knowing exactly how to weigh it.

Cognitive Biases in the AI Decision Environment

AI does not eliminate cognitive bias from organizational decision-making. It rearranges it. Some previously significant biases have become less so. AI systems, for example, are often more consistent than individual human analysts in applying a set of criteria across a large data set. But other biases are intensified or take new forms in an AI-augmented environment. Leaders who understand which biases are most active in this environment can design structural countermeasures before those biases cost the organization.

Automation Bias

Automation bias is the tendency to over-trust algorithmic recommendations, specifically, to accept AI output without appropriate scrutiny because the system appears authoritative. It operates below the level of conscious choice. Most leaders affected by it would sincerely say they critically review AI outputs. But the research evidence is consistent: when a confident algorithmic recommendation is available, humans routinely give it more weight than they would a similar recommendation from a human colleague who stated it without supporting data.

In the Serious Decision Spectrum context, automation bias causes the most harm when it operates in the Augment quadrant, convincing a leader that AI analysis is sufficient without the synthesis layer, or in the Assert quadrant, convincing a leader that a recommendation with a high confidence score settles a question that is fundamentally about values, not probabilities.

The structural countermeasure for automation bias is pre-commitment: before consulting the AI system, articulate what you believe the decision should look like and why. This is not about ignoring the analysis; it is about establishing an independent baseline that gives you something concrete to compare the AI output against. A leader who already has a hypothesis is far more likely to notice when the AI's recommendation diverges from it and to ask why, rather than simply adopting the machine's view.

Algorithm Aversion

Algorithm aversion is the mirror image of automation bias: the reflexive rejection of AI outputs when they conflict with existing intuition or established practice.

While automation bias under-scrutinizes AI recommendations, algorithm aversion over-scrutinizes them, particularly when the system produces a result the human decision-maker does not want to hear.

Algorithm aversion is more common in organizations where AI is new or where leaders have not developed a working understanding of how the systems they use produce their outputs. When a model is a black box, it is psychologically easier to dismiss results that feel wrong than to interrogate the reasoning behind them. The problem is that "feeling wrong" is not always a reliable signal. Sometimes AI outputs conflict with intuition precisely because they have identified a pattern the human analyst missed, and that is exactly when the output is most valuable.

The antidote is not uncritical acceptance but structured engagement. When an AI recommendation conflicts with your intuition, commit to a two-step process: first, articulate specifically what the recommendation is claiming; second, identify precisely which element of your intuition it conflicts with and why you believe your intuition reflects information the system may not have. If you can articulate that gap clearly, you can make a reasonable judgment about who has the better view of the relevant facts.

Confirmation Bias Amplified

Confirmation bias, the tendency to seek, interpret, and remember information that confirms existing beliefs, is not new. But AI-powered information environments can significantly amplify it. When recommendation systems learn from past behavior, they tend to surface information that resembles information the user has engaged with before. Over time, an executive who consumes AI-curated briefings, analyses, and news feeds may develop a view of their competitive landscape, talent market, or strategic environment that is systematically shaped by what they already thought.

This is a workflow-level impact that operates slowly and invisibly. No individual AI output is distorting the picture, but the cumulative effect of thousands of AI-curated interactions can narrow the intellectual aperture through which a leader sees their environment. The countermeasure is deliberate: schedule regular exposure to information sources and perspectives that are not AI-curated, and specifically seek out analysts, colleagues, and advisors who are likely to offer views that diverge from your current strategic assumptions.

Anchoring on AI Outputs

Anchoring is a well-documented cognitive bias in which the first number or estimate encountered in a decision process exerts disproportionate influence on the outcome, even when subsequent information suggests it should be revised. In an AI decision-making environment, the model's output often becomes the anchor, even in group settings where no one explicitly intends it to be.

When a meeting opens with "the AI forecasts a 7 percent revenue decline," the specific magnitude and direction of that number shape every subsequent discussion. Even teams that believe they are critically evaluating the forecast will typically produce final estimates that cluster around it more than around any independent calculation. The anchor has done his work.

The practical countermeasure is sequencing: in high-stakes decisions, do not share AI outputs with the full team before independent human estimates have been made. Ask your team to develop their own projections, range estimates, or scenarios first. Then introduce the AI analysis as a third perspective to compare against, not as a framing device to react to. This single procedural change has a measurable effect on the quality and independence of group judgment.

Countermeasures: Building Anti-Bias Infrastructure

Addressing cognitive bias in AI-augmented decisions requires structural countermeasures, not willpower. Individual commitment to "thinking more critically" is valuable but insufficient. Three practices have proven consistently effective.

Structured devil's advocacy assigns a designated team member, rotating across decision events, the specific responsibility of challenging the AI recommendation. The devil's advocate is not simply tasked with skepticism; they are tasked with identifying the most plausible scenario in which the AI recommendation is materially wrong and presenting it as if they genuinely believed it. This forces the group to engage with counter-evidence actively rather than passively.

Second-opinion protocols require that any decision above a defined threshold of consequence be analyzed by a second source, either a different AI system configured with different parameters, a human analyst working independently, or both. The purpose is not redundancy for its own sake. It is to expose the extent to which the primary analysis reflects genuine insight rather than an artifact of the model's training or configuration.

Pre-mortem analysis asks the decision team to assume, before the decision is finalized, that the outcome has been a significant failure and to identify the most likely reasons why. Pre-mortems are most valuable in the Augment and Assert quadrants, where the consequences of error are significant. They surface assumptions that feel settled yet are uncertain, and they give organizational permission for team members with doubts to articulate them constructively.

DIAGRAM 3.6: ANTI-BIAS INFRASTRUCTURE: THREE COUNTERMEASURES

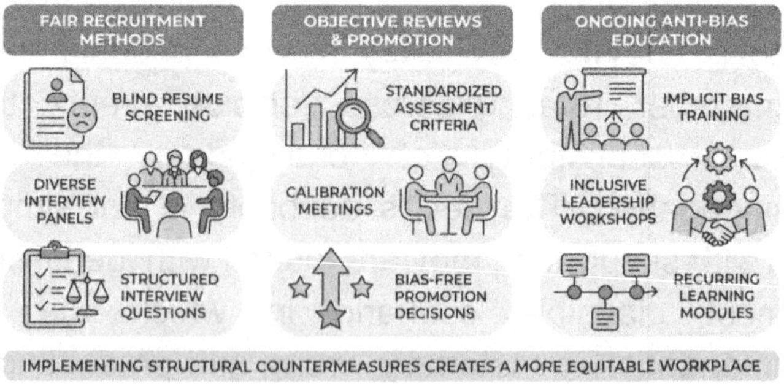

Data-Driven Decision Culture: What It Actually Requires

Data-Informed vs. Data-Dependent

One of the most consequential distinctions in AI leadership is the difference between a data-informed organization and a data-dependent one. The distinction is not about the amount of data used or the sophistication of the analytical tools deployed. It is about where the decision ultimately lives.

A **data-informed** organization uses data to reduce uncertainty, identify patterns, surface options, and test assumptions, while recognizing that data has limits, that context matters, and that judgment is a leadership responsibility, not an analytic output. Data is a powerful input. The decision is a human output.

A **data-dependent** organization has quietly transferred decision-making authority to the data itself, or, more precisely, to the systems that generate it. Leaders in these organizations are reluctant to act without algorithmic confirmation. They experience organizational paralysis when data is unavailable or conflicting. They confuse the confidence of a model's output with the quality of the underlying decision. Over time, this culture erodes exactly the leadership judgment that the organization most needs when the data environment shifts, which it inevitably does.

Building a data-informed culture requires actively modeling the distinction. When leaders narrate their own decision process, "the AI analysis showed X, and here is how I weighed that against Y and Z," they demonstrate what healthy data engagement looks like. When leaders sign off on AI recommendations without narrating any judgment, they model something else.

Data Quality as a Leadership Responsibility

Data quality is almost universally treated as a technical problem. In the AI leadership context, it is a leadership problem because the quality of the data that feeds your decision systems determines the quality of every AI-assisted decision your organization makes. Leaders are the ones who authorize the data environment, data governance practices, and data investment priorities that shape the quality.

Poor data quality in AI systems often goes unnoticed until a significant decision goes wrong. Training data that reflects historical biases produces recommendations that perpetuate those biases, flagging talent acquisition candidates, prioritizing credit applications, or allocating service resources in ways that systematically disadvantage groups the organization intends to serve equitably. Data that is technically accurate but outdated produces confident-seeming analysis that describes a reality that no longer exists.

The leadership practice is not to become a data engineer. It is to ask the right questions. Before deploying or relying on an AI system for significant decisions: How old is the training data? Does it represent the population this decision will affect? What events or dynamics in the past eighteen months might have made historical patterns less predictive? Who is accountable for maintaining data quality? These questions do not require technical expertise. They require the leadership habit of treating data as infrastructure, something that requires ongoing investment and oversight to remain mission-aligned.

Governance of AI-Generated Data in Decision Pipelines

As AI systems become more integrated into decision workflows, a new governance challenge emerges: the data that feeds decisions is itself increasingly AI-generated. Forecasts, summaries, risk assessments, scenario projections, and many of the inputs to human decision-making are now outputs of prior AI processes. This creates a circularity risk that is difficult to detect and important to manage.

When an AI system generates a forecast, which is then used as input to another AI system that generates a recommendation, which is then presented to a human decision-maker, the provenance of that recommendation is complex. If the first model contained an error or reflected a flawed assumption, that error may propagate through the pipeline in ways that are not visible at the point of final decision.

Source transparency, knowing which systems generated which inputs, is a governance prerequisite, not a nice-to-have. Version control for analytical models matters for the same reason that version control matters in software development: when an output changes unexpectedly, you need to be able to trace whether the cause was new data, a model update, a parameter change, or a configuration error. Organizations that cannot answer that question are operating with accountability gaps that create both reputational and regulatory exposure. The audit trail is not bureaucracy. It is the operational infrastructure of responsible decision-making.

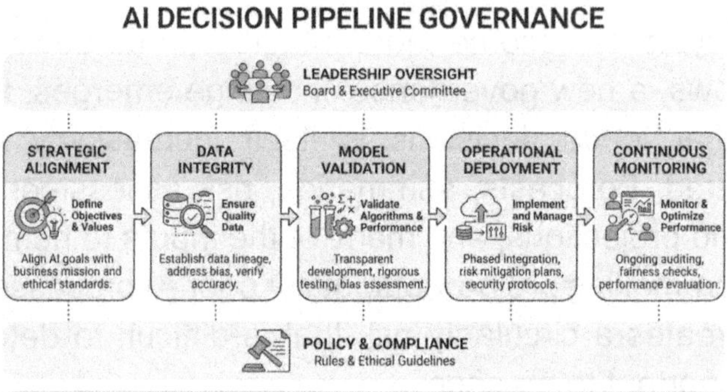

Diagram 3.7: AI Decision Pipeline Governance

Speed vs. Accuracy: The AI-Era Tradeoff

Why AI-Enabled Speed Is a Double-Edged Capability

AI-enabled decision speed is one of the most frequently cited arguments for AI adoption in enterprise environments. And it is a real benefit. The ability to compress analysis timelines from weeks to hours, generate scenario projections in real time, and surface anomalies in data sets that would take human analysts months to review creates a genuine organizational advantage.

But speed is only valuable when applied to the right things. The same capability that allows an organization to make good decisions faster also allows it to make bad decisions faster, and the scale at which AI operates means that a systematically wrong decision can propagate through an organization's processes and customer relationships before any human has noticed the error. The cost of a fast wrong decision is not just the cost of the error itself. It is the cost of the error multiplied by the speed at which it was implemented.

This is why the question every serious leader should ask before accelerating any AI-enabled decision process is: Have we invested as much in quality controls as in speed? A two-hour turnaround on a credit risk assessment is an asset when the model is well-governed, and the outputs are reviewed. It is a liability when the model operates outside its validated parameters and no human is in the review loop.

The Deceleration Paradox

One of the less intuitive insights in AI-era decision management is what might be called the deceleration paradox: slowing down the decision-making process at the right junctures can produce faster organizational results. This is counterintuitive in cultures that have built their identity around decisiveness and speed. But the evidence from organizational decision research is consistent: decisions that skip the review, deliberation, and stakeholder alignment stages move faster to implementation and then back far more often than decisions that incorporate those stages at the appropriate time cost.

The deceleration paradox is particularly relevant to Augment and Assert decisions, where the complexity of human stakes means that implementation without adequate preparation generates resistance, revision, and remediation that cost far more time than the deliberation stage would have taken. A workforce restructuring decision that moves from AI analysis to announcement in five days may require six months of employee relations repair. A strategic partnership decision that was rushed to capture a perceived window may require a year of integration work to correct a misalignment that forty-eight hours of deliberation would have revealed.

The practical implication is to design decision processes calibrated to the quadrant, not to the executive's schedule. Automated decisions can be fast by design. Augmented decisions should include built-in deliberation gates. Assert decisions should have explicit time minimums that cannot be compressed without leadership escalation. This is decision architecture, the intentional structuring of how decisions flow through an organization, and it is one of the most important and underinvested leadership competencies in AI-adopting organizations.

Decision Checkpoints That Preserve Speed While Maintaining Quality

The goal is not to slow every decision down; it is to slow the right decisions down at the right points and accelerate everything else. Decision checkpoints accomplish this by creating explicit pause-and-verify moments in the decision workflow without adding bureaucratic drag to decisions that do not need it.

An effective checkpoint is narrow, fast, and mission-aligned. It asks a small number of specific questions. Is the AI output within the expected parameter range? Has a human reviewed the output against real-world context? Does this decision trigger any escalation criteria? and moves quickly when those questions are answered satisfactorily. The overhead is measured in minutes for routine decisions. For significant decisions, the checkpoint expands into the deliberation stage required by Augment and Assert decisions.

Checkpoint design is a leadership task, not a systems design task. Leaders who build checkpoints into their team's decision processes and model the discipline of using them, including when time pressure argues against it, create the organizational norm that makes AI-enabled speed both safe and credible.

DIAGRAM 3.8: DECISION SPEED VS. QUALITY CHECKPOINT DESIGN

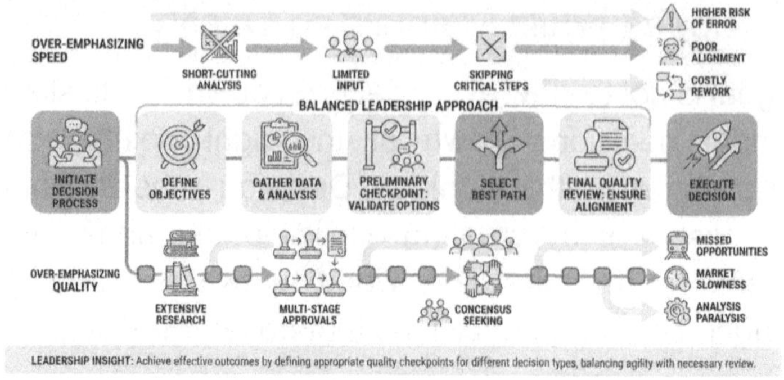

Strategic Decision-Making at the C-Suite Level

How Agentic AI Is Entering Strategic Analysis

Until recently, AI's contribution to strategic decision-making was primarily analytical: processing competitive data, financial projections, and market signals to inform human deliberation. This is still the dominant mode. But a newer generation of agentic AI systems is beginning to participate more actively, not only surfacing information but also synthesizing scenarios, identifying strategic options, and, in some early deployments, proposing and evaluating strategic alternatives in real time.

This is a meaningful shift. When AI moves from supplying data to framing strategic options, it is doing work that was previously the exclusive domain of senior leadership teams and strategy functions. The framing of strategic options is not neutral; the options you see shape the options you choose. An AI system that consistently frames choices in terms of near-term financial impact may systematically underweight strategic options with longer payoff horizons, options that are difficult to quantify, or options that require organizational change rather than market moves. Leaders who are not alert to this framing influence may find that their strategies are more AI-shaped than they realize.

The Risks of Strategy-by-Algorithm

Competitive advantage in most industries depends on decisions that, by definition, are not obvious from historical data patterns. The moves that create durable market positions tend to be contrarian, creative, and informed by a synthesis of context, timing, and organizational capability that no system can currently replicate. AI systems are, by design, pattern-recognition engines. They are excellent at identifying what has worked in similar situations. They are limited in their ability to identify what will work in situations that do not closely resemble past cases, which is often precisely when strategic decision-making matters most.

Strategy-by-algorithm, the practice of delegating strategic choices to AI-generated recommendations without robust human synthesis, produces strategies that are incrementally optimized versions of the past rather than genuine bets on the future. This is a rational-seeming but strategically dangerous posture. It is comfortable because the analysis is rigorous, and accountability appears to be distributed. But the organization that makes only AI-validated strategic moves will find itself arriving slightly late to places where the competitive landscape is already forming.

The antidote is not to remove AI from strategy; it is to be deliberate about what role AI plays and where human creativity, contrarian thinking, and organizational judgment must reassert themselves. The question "what does the data recommend?" should be followed immediately by "and what does the data miss?" That second question is where the strategic advantage lives.

The CEO as Chief Discernment Officer

The most important AI leadership function at the top of the organization is not technology selection, AI investment strategy, or governance policy, though all those matters are important. It is the personal practice of discernment: the ongoing, demonstrated commitment to distinguishing between decisions that AI should inform and decisions that humans must claim.

When a CEO is visibly thoughtful about this distinction in their reasoning, asks hard questions about AI recommendations in executive settings, and holds themselves and their leadership team accountable to the decision-making process rather than just the decision outcome, they are setting the organizational standard. The culture of discernment flows from the top, or it does not flow at all. Executives further down the hierarchy take their cues from what they observe in the C-suite. If the CEO treats every AI recommendation as authoritative, that posture propagates when the CEO demonstrates disciplined engagement, honoring AI analysis and asserting human synthesis, and that, too.

Chapter 5: Trust Architecture builds directly on this foundation. The organizational trust environment that makes AI adoption both sustainable and safe is not the product of policy documents and governance frameworks alone. It is the product of leadership behavior that is consistently visible, consistently mission-aligned, and consistently anchored in the principle that accountability belongs to people, not to systems.

DIAGRAM 3.9: THE CEO AS CHIEF DISCERNMENT OFFICER

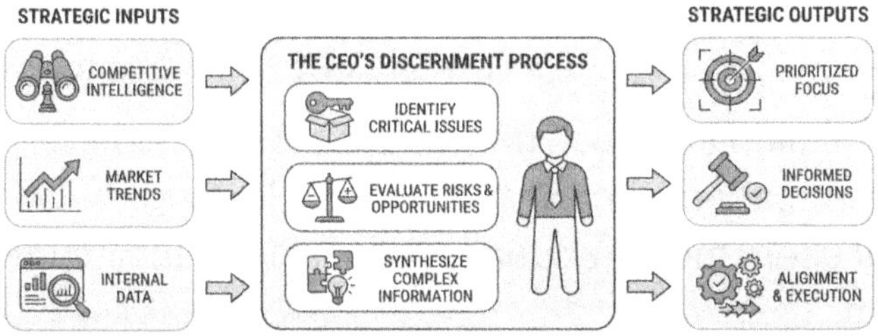

A focus on discernment enables CEOs to filter complexity, identify critical factors, and make informed decisions that drive effective execution.

Practical Decision Frameworks for Product Owners and Operational Managers

The AI-Assisted Product Roadmap Decision

Product roadmap decisions are among the most consequential recurring decisions in technology organizations. They allocate scarce development capacity, signal strategic priorities to customers and investors, and shape the organization's ability to compete over the next planning horizon. They also attract AI assistance from multiple directions: usage analytics, customer feedback synthesis, competitive intelligence tools, and market sizing models all have a claim on the conversation.

The risk in product roadmap decisions is not too little AI input; most product organizations now have more data than they can process. The risk is insufficient synthesis. When a product team builds its roadmap primarily by ranking AI-generated feature scores, it produces a roadmap that reflects current usage patterns and stated customer preferences. That is useful input. It is not a strategy. Strategy requires asking which features will create the competitive differentiation that does not yet exist in the market. That question cannot be answered by looking at what current users most frequently request from their current product.

The mission-aligned product roadmap decision uses AI analysis to map the current landscape clearly and quickly what customers want, what competitors offer, what usage data reveals and then explicitly reserves a portion of the planning conversation for human synthesis: where do we believe the market is going, what do we uniquely know that the data does not capture, and which bets require us to build ahead of demand rather than in response to it? Those questions are not AI-resistant. They are AI-required in one direction and human-requiring in another.

Prioritization with AI: Starting Point, Not Endpoint

Algorithmic prioritization tools have become standard equipment in product and project management environments. They generate ranked lists, weighted scores, and effort-impact matrices at the click of a button. The efficiency gain is real; what used to require a half-day planning workshop can now be pre-populated in minutes.

The discipline is treating the AI-generated ranking as a starting point for the conversation, not the conversation itself. A ranked list is a hypothesis. It reflects the weights assigned to the scoring criteria, the quality of the underlying data, and the model's assumptions about what constitutes value. Every one of those elements is contestable. The team's job is to bring their collective judgment to the ranked list: to identify the items that are ranked higher than they deserve because the data flatters them, the items ranked lower than they deserve because the relevant data does not exist yet, and the items that do not appear on the list at all because no data supports them, but which experienced judgment says should be explored.

The pilot-to-production pathway for any AI-assisted prioritization process should include an explicit human-review stage in which the team interrogates the ranking rather than simply endorsing it. This stage does not have to be long; a focused thirty-minute team review of the top and bottom quartiles of any AI-generated list will surface the most important mismatches between algorithmic scoring and human judgment. Over time, those mismatches become the learning data that improves both the model and the team's judgment about how to weigh it.

When AI Recommendations and Stakeholder Preferences Conflict

One of the most practically challenging situations for managers deploying AI in decision workflows is when an AI recommendation and a significant stakeholder preference point are in opposite directions. This happens more often than organizations typically acknowledge because it is uncomfortable and because there is no clear protocol for navigating it.

The scenario is familiar: the AI analysis recommends a course of action A. A senior stakeholder, based on experience and judgment, prefers course of action B. The manager in the middle must navigate between them without either dismissing the analysis or overriding the stakeholder.

The productive resolution begins with precision: What specifically does the AI recommendation claim? What specific evidence or assumption drives the preference for B? Frequently, conflict dissolves when the two positions are stated precisely, because they are not actually contradicting each other; they are answering different questions. The AI system may be optimizing for near-term cost efficiency while the stakeholder is optimizing for long-term relationship quality. Those are not incompatible answers to the same question; they are answers to different questions, both of which deserve to be on the table.

When the conflict is genuine, when both positions address the same question and arrive at opposite conclusions, the decision process should return to the Serious Decision Spectrum. Where does this decision sit? If it is in the Augment quadrant, AI analysis deserves significant weight, but the stakeholder's contextual judgment is also a legitimate input. If it is in the Assert quadrant, the stakeholder's judgment is primary, and the AI recommendation is advisory. Making this explicit removes the political charge from the conversation and replaces it with a structural logic that both parties can engage with professionally.

Building Your Personal Decision Log

The most enduring individual practice this chapter recommends is simple: keep a personal decision log for AI-influenced decisions. This does not require a sophisticated system. A structured record of the decision, where it sat on the Spectrum, what the AI recommended, what you decided and why, and what happened, reviewed monthly, will generate more decision-making insight than any course or framework you will encounter.

The decision log serves multiple purposes. It builds your personal database of AI decision patterns: which systems have been most useful, which have been most frequently overridden, which override decisions turned out well, and which did not. It creates a running narrative of your AI leadership practice that is available for mentoring conversations, performance reviews, and the kind of honest self-assessment that the AI-CLEAR model's Accountability dimension requires. And it builds the institutional memory that makes your successor's leadership better, which is the definition of a serious leader's impact.

The AI-CLEAR model's Readiness dimension, the commitment to continuously updating your mental models and governance structures, is operationalized in the decision log more directly than in any other single practice. You cannot read your way into AI leadership readiness. You build it one decision at a time, and only the leaders who are paying close enough attention to learn from those decisions systematically will compound that readiness over time.

DIAGRAM 3.10: THE PERSONAL DECISION LOG TEMPLATE

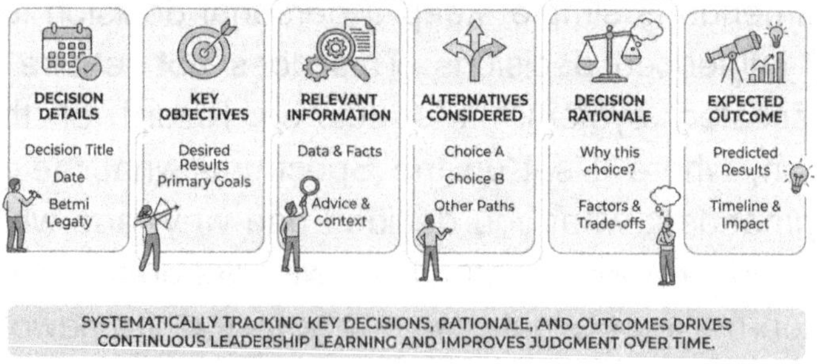

Manager's Checklist: Making Better AI-Augmented Decisions

Before acting on any significant AI-augmented recommendation, work through the following disciplines.

Classify the decision first.

- Plot the decision on the Serious Decision Spectrum before the analysis begins, not after.
    - Ask: Is the data density genuinely high, or does it just feel high because a lot of numbers are present?
    - Ask: What are the human stakes? Who is affected, and how directly?
    - If you are unsure of the quadrant, treat the decision as belonging to the higher-stakes quadrant.

Interrogate the AI output.

- What data was this output based on? How recent is it? Does it represent the population affected by this decision?
- What are the top three assumptions embedded in this recommendation?
- What scenario would cause this recommendation to be materially wrong?
- Is the confidence score a reflection of data quality or just model self-consistency?

Manage your own cognitive response.

- Have you formed an independent view before looking at the AI recommendation?
- If the recommendation conflicts with your intuition, can you articulate specifically why your intuition may hold information the system does not?
- Is the team anchoring on the AI output, or are independent perspectives present in the discussion?

Apply the appropriate decision governance.

- For Augment decisions: has a human synthesis layer been applied to the AI analysis?
- For Assert decisions: have you convened the appropriate human council, regardless of what any system recommends?
- Has a devil's advocate reviewed the recommendation from the perspective of how it could fail?
- For decisions above your defined consequence threshold, has a second opinion been obtained?

Document and learn.

- Record the decision, the Spectrum classification, the AI recommendation, and your final judgment in your decision log.
- Note the assumptions you accepted and the ones you overrode.
- Schedule a review checkpoint thirty, sixty, or ninety days after the decision to evaluate how the decision is performing against your reasoning at the time.

DIAGRAM 3.11: THE DECISION GOVERNANCE CHECKLIST IN PRACTICE

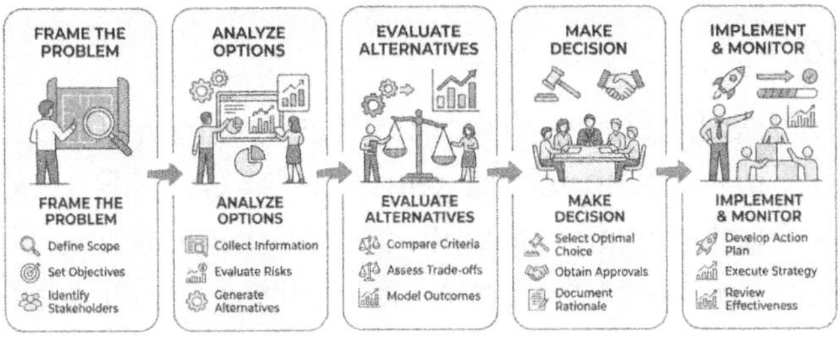

A STRUCTURED PROCESS FOR ROBUST AND ACCOUNTABLE STRATEGIC DECISION MAKING.

Looking Forward: Where This Chapter Connects

The decision classification practice introduced in this chapter builds directly on the AI-CLEAR model's Leverage dimension from Chapter 2, the discernment capacity that distinguishes leaders who deploy AI with precision from those who deploy it reflexively. Every placement on the Serious Decision Spectrum is an act of leverage: identifying exactly how much AI authority is appropriate and claiming exactly as much human judgment as the situation demands.

The decision governance disciplines outlined here- the audit trail, the source transparency requirements, and the escalation criteria are foundational to the Trust Architecture that Chapter 5 will develop in full. Trust between leaders, their teams, and the AI systems they deploy is not built through declarations of confidence. It is built through the consistent practice of decision integrity: making the reasoning visible, owning the outcomes, and maintaining the distinction between what the system recommended and what the leader decided.

The Serious Decision Spectrum will return in Chapter 9, where it is synthesized with the AI-CLEAR model and the Trust Architecture into an integrated leadership compass. Leaders who have internalized the Spectrum by that point will recognize it as the practical instrument it is designed to be: not a theoretical framework for categorizing decisions in the abstract, but a real-time tool for navigating the constant, consequential question that defines AI leadership at every level of the organization: when to trust the machine, and when to trust yourself.

What Serious Leaders Take Away

The fundamental shift this chapter asks you to make is from an intuitive, context-dependent relationship with AI recommendations to a structured, principled one. Most leaders who have been in their roles for a decade or more have developed sophisticated judgment about when to trust their analysts, when to push back, and when to override. That same sophistication needs to be deliberately developed with respect to AI systems.

DIAGRAM 3.12: THE SERIOUS DECISION SPECTRUM: COMPLETE REFERENCE

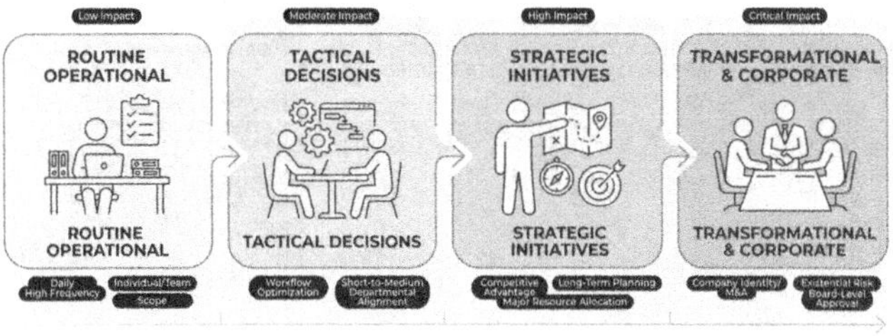

This reference guides leadership teams in categorizing decisions by their impact, complexity, and scope to determine the appropriate level of analysis and authority.

The Serious Decision Spectrum is the tool that makes that sophistication transferable across decision types, leadership contexts, and AI capabilities that did not exist when your judgment was formed. It gives you a shared language for decision governance conversations with your team. It gives you a personal standard against which to evaluate whether AI is genuinely augmenting your leadership or quietly replacing it.

The leaders who will navigate the AI era most effectively are not the ones who use AI the most or the least. They are the ones who use it with the most precision who know, for each decision in their domain, exactly where on the Spectrum it lives, exactly what AI can contribute, and exactly where human judgment must assert itself without apology. That precision is not instinctive. It is built. This chapter gives you the foundation. The practice is yours to develop.

DIAGRAM 3.13: CHAPTER 3 TO CHAPTER 5: DECISION GOVERNANCE BUILDS TRUST

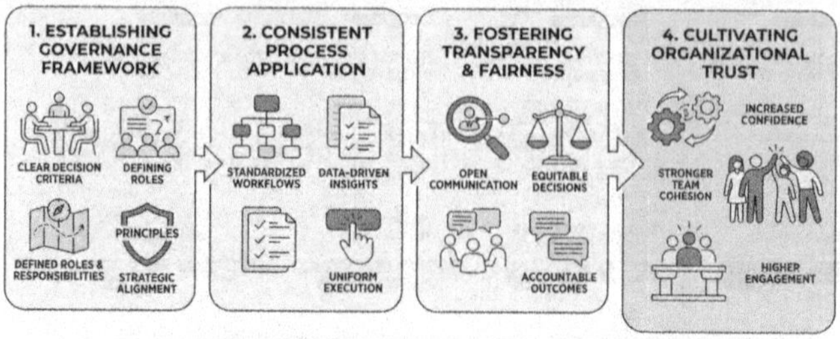

CONSISTENT, TRANSPARENT DECISION-MAKING PROCESSES STRENGTHEN CONFIDENCE AND BUILD LASTING TRUST BETWEEN LEADERS AND TEAMS

5 The Language of AI Leadership: Translating Technology into Trust

When the Words Get in the Way

The board meeting had gone well by most measures. The Chief Digital Officer had walked the directors through eighteen months of AI investment: three production deployments, measurable cycle-time reductions in two operating divisions, and a roadmap that positioned the company ahead of its nearest competitor in process automation. The slides were polished. The data was solid. The presenter was confident. And yet, as the meeting broke, the board chair pulled the CDO aside with a single quiet question: "Are we being told what we need to hear, or what you want us to believe?"

It was not a hostile question. It was an honest one, and it revealed something important. The board had received a great deal of information about AI. They had received almost no help understanding it. The distinction matters enormously. Information without interpretation creates a gap, and in that gap, skepticism forms. The CDO had communicated efficiently. She had not communicated effectively. The board left the room informed about metrics and uncertain about leadership.

This chapter is about closing that gap. Not by simplifying AI until it is unrecognizable, and not by overwhelming stakeholders with technical precision that obscures rather than illuminates, but by developing what might be called communicative leadership: the capacity to translate technical reality into language that builds genuine understanding, calibrated trust, and confident action. Every concept introduced in Chapter 2 about the AI mindset, every framework from Chapter 3 for decision-making under uncertainty, all of it depends on a leader who can articulate those ideas clearly to the right audience at the right moment. Communication is not the soft side of AI leadership. It is the load-bearing wall.

Section 1: The Multi-Directional Communication Challenge

Most organizational communication flows in one direction at a time. Annual reports go to investors. Memos come down to teams. Announcements go out to customers. AI leadership does not work that way. The AI leader must communicate simultaneously upward to boards and C-suite colleagues who control resources and set risk tolerance, downward to teams who carry out the work and absorb the disruption, outward to customers, partners, and regulators who need assurance that the organization is operating responsibly, and inward in honest conversation with themselves about what they actually know, what they are uncertain about, and where they are operating on intuition rather than evidence. Failure in any one direction creates problems that compound across the others.

What makes this four-directional challenge difficult is not the volume, but the audience mismatch. The most common AI communication failure is failing to deliver a consistent message. It is a message calculated by one audience delivered to another. Technical precision designed for the engineering team, presented unchanged to the board, produces confusion and a subtle erosion of confidence. The enthusiasm calibrated for an investor roadshow, repeated verbatim to the employees who will be displaced by the systems being celebrated, produces fear and resentment. Audience mismatch is the root cause of most communication failures in AI leadership, and the remedy is not to speak less; it is to listen more carefully before you speak.

The Four Communication Directions

Upward communication with boards, C-suite peers, and external investors operates in the language of strategy, risk, and financial return. This audience does not want technical details. They want clarity on three things: what the investment is expected to produce, what it will cost in monetary and organizational capacity, and what can go wrong. Leaders who answer these questions directly, honestly, and with appropriate acknowledgment of uncertainty consistently earn more credibility than those who lead with technical sophistication or project unbounded optimism.

Downward communication with the teams doing the work operates in the language of meaning, security, and practical implication. Employees confronting AI in their workplace are not primarily thinking about organizational strategy. They are thinking about their own roles, their value to the organization, and whether the people leading them have considered their interests. The phrase "AI won't take your job" is almost always perceived as either dismissive or untrue. Better communication is honest and specific: this is what AI will change in your work, this is what it will not change, and this is what I am committed to doing to help you navigate this transition. That is the conversation teams need.

Outward communication to customers, regulators, and external partners operates in the language of transparency, accountability, and demonstrated reliability. These audiences do not trust assertions about AI responsibility. They trust evidence: clear disclosures of how AI is used, visible mechanisms for human oversight, accessible processes for raising concerns, and honest responses when things go wrong. The Chapter 5 Trust Architecture, which rests on stakeholder trust as one of its four load-bearing layers, depends directly on the quality of outward communication.

Inward communication, the honest internal dialogue a leader maintains with themselves, is perhaps the most overlooked dimension. Leaders who communicate beyond their actual confidence, who express certainty about AI outcomes they privately doubt, who fail to acknowledge gaps in their own understanding, are building on sand. The AI-CLEAR model from Chapter 2 is useful here: the Readiness dimension demands that leaders continuously update their own understanding, and that process is impossible without honest inward communication about what you actually know versus what you are performing knowing.

DIAGRAM 4.1: THE FOUR COMMUNICATION DIRECTIONS

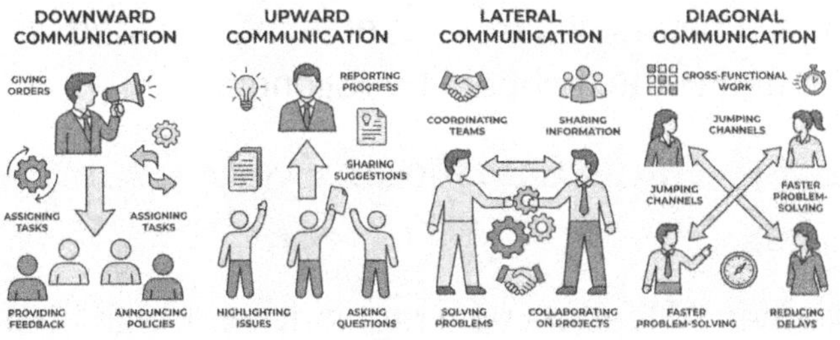

A balanced flow of information in all directions ensures organizational alignment and efficient collaboration.

Section 2: Communicating AI Value to Senior Executives & Boards

The boardroom is a specific communication environment with specific rules. Time is compressed. Attention is selective. Stakes are high. Decisions made in this room have organizational consequences that can take years to correct. Leaders who understand these conditions communicate differently from those who treat board presentations as extended technical reviews, or worse, as performance opportunities designed to demonstrate sophistication rather than to produce alignment.

The foundational principle of boardroom AI communication is this: translate capabilities into outcomes and translate outcomes into the language of risk and return. A board does not need to understand how a transformer model works. A board needs to understand that a specific AI deployment is expected to reduce a particular process cost by a quantifiable amount, carries identifiable risks with named mitigating controls, and positions the organization in a strategic direction consistent with its stated priorities. That is a complete communication. Everything beyond it is context, and context should be rationed.

The Three Questions Every Board Will Ask

Experienced AI leaders who regularly work with boards report that substantive questions consistently converge on three core concerns, regardless of industry, organization size, or AI maturity. Preparing for these three questions before any board presentation is not merely good practice; it is the minimum standard for responsible upward communication.

The first question is: what will this cost? The honest answer always includes more than the technology license or cloud compute invoice. It includes the organizational change management effort, the workforce development investment, the governance infrastructure, the ongoing monitoring and maintenance burden, and the opportunity cost of leadership attention. Leaders who present only the technological cost and later discover additional expenses erode trust in ways that are difficult to recover from. Present the full cost picture with appropriate confidence intervals, and the board will trust your subsequent projections.

The second question is: what will this produce? Here, the discipline is precision. Leaders frequently characterize AI initiatives in terms of theoretical maximum impact, what technology could produce under ideal conditions. Boards deserve realistic projections based on your organization's specific context, your data quality, your implementation capacity, and the competitive dynamics of your market. Honest optimism, the communication style that acknowledges uncertainty while maintaining conviction about strategic direction, is more credible and ultimately more effective than either unbounded enthusiasm or defensive conservatism.

The third question is: what can go wrong? This question is the most important and the most frequently avoided. Leaders who preemptively identify AI risks, name their likelihood and potential impact, and describe the specific controls they have established to manage them consistently outperform those who present risk as an afterthought or deflect it entirely. The board is not looking for a risk-free AI program; such a thing does not exist. They are looking for evidence that the leader has carefully considered what could go wrong and taken responsible steps to prepare. Chapter 5's trust architecture is built, in part, on exactly this kind of visible risk stewardship.

DIAGRAM 4.2: THE THREE BOARD QUESTIONS FRAMEWORK

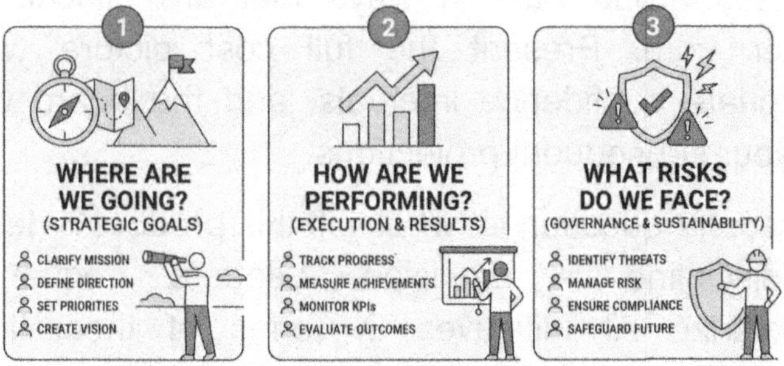

ESSENTIAL INQUIRY FOR STRATEGIC LEADERSHIP AND GOVERNANCE

Framing AI as Strategic Positioning

One of the most consequential communication choices an AI leader makes is how to frame AI investment. Organizations that frame AI primarily as a cost-reduction tool invite boards to evaluate it exclusively on efficiency metrics, a framework that tends to lead to underinvestment, unrealistic timelines, and disappointment when the first deployment does not deliver a dramatic cost headline. Organizations that frame AI as strategic positioning invite boards to evaluate it on competitive terms: where does this capability place us relative to our competitors in three years, and what would it cost us not to develop it?

This reframing is not spin. It is accurate. The organizations that are building serious AI capabilities today are not doing so primarily to reduce headcount. They are doing so because the competitive landscape will look materially different in thirty-six months, and the organizations that have invested in AI infrastructure, talent, and governance during this period will have structural advantages that are expensive to replicate later. The pilot-to-production pathway that delivers operational clarity today is also the capability-building engine that creates strategic flexibility tomorrow. Making this argument clearly and credible, with evidence from your own initiative, progress, and honest acknowledgment of what remains uncertain, is one of the highest-value communications an AI leader can deliver.

Managing Executive Expectations: The Art of Honest Optimism

The phrase "honest optimism" deserves careful attention because it names a specific communication posture distinct from both pessimism and marketing. Honest optimism means expressing genuine confidence in AI's strategic direction and realistic potential while maintaining complete transparency about uncertainty, risk, and the limits of current knowledge. It is the posture of a serious professional who has done the work, understands the landscape, and is willing to be accountable for their assessments, not that of a promoter whose confidence is inversely proportional to complexity.

In practice, honest optimism sounds like this: "We expect this deployment to reduce processing time by between thirty and forty-five percent, based on our pilot results and comparable deployments in the industry. We have identified three risk factors that could affect that range, and we have specific mitigations in place for each. I will report back in ninety days with actual performance data." That is a sentence a board can trust. It contains a projection, an evidence base, an uncertainty acknowledgment, specific risk awareness, and a commitment to accountability. Compare it to "this AI system will transform our operations," a sentence that sounds confident and communicates nothing.

Section 3: Communicating About AI to Your Teams

The communication challenge with teams is almost the mirror image of the board challenge. With boards, the risk is too much technical detail and too little strategic framing. With teams, the risk is too strategic framing and too little honest engagement with the questions people are carrying. Those questions, in most organizations, center on a single anxiety that expresses itself in many forms: Will I still have a meaningful role in this organization when AI is more fully deployed?

That question deserves a direct, honest, and specific answer, not reassurance. Reassurance without substance ("AI won't take your job") is experienced as either dismissive or as something to be said when the real answer is something the speaker cannot yet bring themselves to deliver. Employees in serious organizations are sophisticated enough to recognize when they are being managed rather than spoken to. The leaders who build the most durable team trust around AI are those who communicate as though their teams are full adults capable of handling honest information, because they are.

The Employee Fear Equation

Understanding what employees are worried about is the first step in communicating effectively with them. The fear is rarely monolithic, and it is rarely simply about job loss. It typically has several distinct components that require different responses. First is role uncertainty: employees do not know which parts of their job will be affected, enhanced, or may disappear, and ambiguity is more distressing than even difficult clarity. Second is capability anxiety: employees worry that they lack the skills to work effectively alongside AI, and that this gap will be visible and costly. Third is trust in leadership intent: employees want to know whether the people making AI decisions genuinely have their interests in mind, or whether AI is being deployed in ways that will benefit the organization at the employees' expense.

Each of these fears calls for a specific type of communication. Role uncertainty is addressed through specific, task-level transparency: how this AI system will interact with your workflow, what it will handle, what it will not, and how your role will evolve. Capability anxiety is addressed through investment commitments: here is what we are doing to help you develop the skills required for this transition, and here is the timeline. Trust in leadership intent is addressed through visible accountability: here is how AI will not be used against you, and here is how decisions about workforce implications will be made and communicated. None of this is easy. All of it is necessary.

DIAGRAM 4.3: THE EMPLOYEE FEAR EQUATION

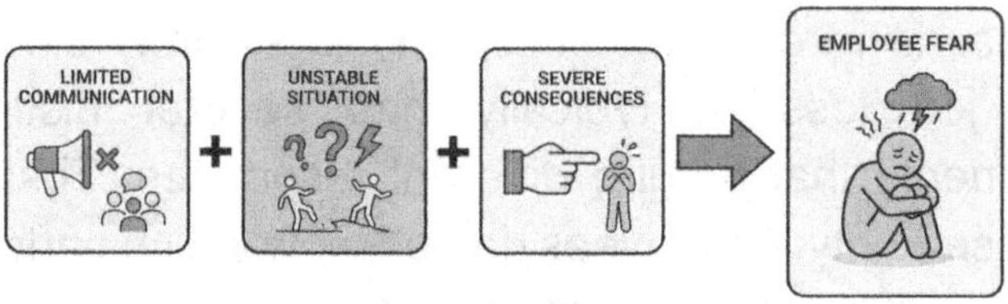

VISUALIZING KEY DRIVERS THAT INCREASE WORKPLACE ANXIETY AND HINDER PERFORMANCE.

What to Say Instead of "AI Won't Take Your Job"

The phrase "AI won't take your job" has become so reflexive in organizational AI communication that it has lost whatever reassurance it once carried. Employees hear it as a non-answer, and they are right; it is a non-answer. It does not engage with the specific changes they can observe in their work environment. It does not acknowledge the legitimate disruption that AI adoption creates. And in many cases, it is simply not accurate: some roles will change so significantly that their current form will effectively cease to exist, even if the people filling them are retained and retrained.

The more effective communication is specific, honest, and forward-looking. It might sound like this: "Here is what we know about how AI will affect this team's work over the next twelve months. Here are the tasks that will change, and here are those that will remain human-led. Here is what we are investing in to prepare everyone for those changes. And here is the specific commitment I am making to you: if your role changes significantly as a result of AI deployment, you will know that before it happens, not after, and you will have support in navigating the transition." That is not a promise that nothing will change. It is a promise to lead honestly through change, and one that serious leaders can make and keep.

The leaders who communicate at this level of specificity, describing workflow-level impact rather than organizational abstractions, build the kind of team trust that sustains AI adoption through difficult periods. When employees can see that their leader understands not just what AI means strategically but what it means for the specific tasks they perform each day, the conversation shifts from anxiety to partnership.

Building Psychological Safety for AI Questions

The Empowerment dimension of the AI-CLEAR model, introduced in Chapter 2, defines one of its core behaviors as creating psychological safety for experimentation and honest dialogue about AI. In the communication context, psychological safety means that employees can ask questions about AI without fear of appearing uninformed, can raise concerns without fear of appearing obstructive, and can report problems with AI tools without fear of being blamed for surfacing them. In organizations that lack this safety, employees manage the appearance of AI competence rather than developing actual competence, and problems accumulate invisibly until they become visible crises.

Building this safety is primarily a behavioral discipline rather than a policy intervention. Leaders who ask their own honest questions in public and model intellectual humility about AI by saying openly, "I'm still developing my understanding of this," permit others to do the same. Leaders who visibly reward employees who surface an AI tool's failure mode, rather than treating the report as a nuisance, send a clear signal about what the organization values. The culture of a team is set more precisely by what leaders do when information is uncomfortable than by what they say when it is easy.

Transparent Communication About AI in Performance Contexts

One of the most trust-sensitive communication challenges in AI leadership is how to handle the use of AI in contexts that directly affect employees' professional standing, performance evaluation, workload allocation, monitoring, and developmental assessment. These uses are legitimate, often valuable, and potentially problematic if implemented without clear communication. The absence of transparency in this area does not create ignorance; it creates suspicion. Employees who know or suspect that AI is informing decisions about them but cannot see how or to what degree will fill the information gap with the worst available interpretation.

The communication standard in this domain should be proactive disclosure. If AI tools are used to support performance data analysis, employees should know that before the analysis happens, not after they encounter its conclusions. They should know what data is used, what questions the AI is helping to answer, how human judgment is applied to AI-generated insights, and what recourse exists if they believe an AI-assisted evaluation is inaccurate. This level of transparency is not only ethically appropriate but also strategically sound. Organizations that operate AI systems affecting employees without clear communication create the conditions for the kind of trust breakdown that Chapter 5 will address in detail.

Section 4: Narrative Architecture for AI Initiatives

Individual conversations are necessary but insufficient for AI leadership communication. What sustains an AI initiative through the inevitable setbacks, budget cycles, personnel changes, and competitive pressures of organizational life is a coherent narrative, a consistent story that explains why this organization is investing in AI, what it is trying to accomplish, and what values are guiding the decisions. Without that narrative, each communication event stands alone, and the accumulation of events does not build toward understanding. With it, each conversation reinforces a shared framework that helps stakeholders make sense of what they see and hear.

A narrative is not a marketing message. It is not a tagline or a vision statement. It is the genuine, substantive account of the organization's AI journey, told with enough honesty about challenges and uncertainties to be credible, and with enough clarity about direction and values to be orienting. Building this narrative is one of the most important yet underinvested-in activities in AI leadership. Most organizations have an AI strategy. Far fewer have an AI story.

The Five Elements of a Compelling AI Narrative

Effective AI narratives, in organizations where leaders have genuinely invested in building them, consistently contain five elements. The first is a grounded account of why AI is not "because AI is transforming every industry," which is true but uninspiring, but rather a specific account of the competitive, operational, or mission-based pressures that make AI investment necessary for this organization at this moment. The second is a clear statement of what this organization is trying to accomplish with AI: not a list of technology capabilities, but a description of the specific outcomes that will constitute success.

The third element is an honest account of how AI decisions are made, including who holds authority, which values guide decisions, and how the organization will handle situations where AI recommendations conflict with human judgment. This element is the one most frequently omitted, and its absence is precisely what leaves stakeholders feeling that AI is being deployed to them rather than with them. The fourth element is a commitment to transparency about progress, setbacks, and learning, a signal that the narrative will be updated when reality diverges from projection. The fifth is an account of the human dimension: what this AI journey means for the people doing the work, and what the organization is prepared to invest in their development.

DIAGRAM 4.4: THE FIVE ELEMENTS OF AN AI NARRATIVE

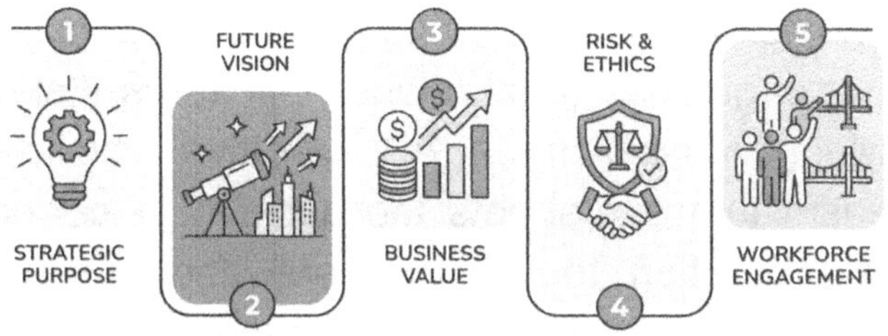

A FRAMEWORK FOR LEADERS TO EFFECTIVELY COMMUNICATE AI STRATEGIES, ALIGN STAKEHOLDERS, AND DRIVE ORGANIZATIONAL INTEGRATION.

The Problem with AI Enthusiasm Without Context

One of the most reliably damaging communication patterns in AI leadership is what might be called contextless enthusiasm, an effusive commitment to AI's transformative potential, delivered without specific grounding in this organization's actual situation, capabilities, or constraints. Contextless enthusiasm creates several problems simultaneously. It sets expectations that operational reality cannot meet, producing the inevitable disappointment that turns initial excitement into cynicism. It signals to employees and middle managers that leadership is operating from aspiration rather than analysis. And it frequently produces exactly the narrative vacuum it is designed to avoid. Because enthusiasm cannot be sustained as implementation complexity becomes apparent, communication becomes more cautious over time, and the gap between the early narrative and the current reality becomes a source of organizational anxiety.

The test of a sound AI narrative is whether it can survive contact with reality. A narrative that acknowledges uncertainty, sets realistic expectations, and commits to honest reporting survives setbacks and even strengthens trust when leaders clearly acknowledge problems. A narrative built on enthusiasm that overshoots the achievable corrodes trust in proportion to the gap between what was promised and what was delivered. The most sophisticated AI communicators in serious organizations are not those who inspire the most excitement, but those whose stakeholders feel most accurately prepared for what happens.

Consistency as a Communication Discipline

Inconsistent leadership messaging is one of the most common and costly AI communication failures. When the CEO frames AI as a workforce augmentation strategy in an all-hands address, a business unit leader frames it as a cost-reduction program in a team meeting, and an HR communication emphasizes monitoring capabilities without mentioning investment in development, each message may be technically accurate in isolation. Collectively, they produce organizational confusion, and, in the context of AI and employment, confusion tends to resolve fear.

Consistency is discipline, not an accident. It requires that leaders who communicate about AI within an organization align on the key messages, commitments, and boundaries before speaking publicly. It requires a shared understanding of the AI narrative that is substantial enough to withstand translation across different organizational contexts. And it requires a feedback mechanism that identifies inconsistencies quickly before they harden into conflicting organizational beliefs that become expensive to reconcile. The executive alignment work addressed in Chapter 6 directly depends on establishing this communication discipline at the leadership level.

Section 5: Communicating Risk, Uncertainty, and Failure

Every AI initiative will encounter moments of visible difficulty. Systems will produce outputs that are wrong, biased, or harmful. Deployments will fall short of projections. Third-party AI providers will have incidents that affect your organization. Regulatory inquiries will arrive. These moments are not exceptional; they are predictable features of operating at the frontier of organizational technology. The leaders who navigate them most effectively are those who have prepared their communication approach in advance, not those who improvise under pressure.

The foundational principle of communicating risk and failure is the transparency imperative: proactively and honestly disclosing AI limitations, setbacks, and failures creates less organizational damage than concealing them and having them discovered. This is true for multiple reasons. Concealment requires the ongoing effort to manage information that tends to surface anyway, usually at the worst possible time. Discovery of concealed problems generates not only the original problem but also a secondary trust crisis centered on the concealment itself. And transparency, handled well, is an opportunity: the leader who names a problem clearly and describes how they are addressing it signals exactly the kind of accountability and operational discipline that builds durable credibility.

Language for Communicating Uncertainty

There is a specific skill in communicating uncertainty, the state of not knowing precisely, without undermining confidence in the overall initiative or in the leader's competence. Leaders who conflate uncertainty with weakness either refuse to acknowledge it (which destroys credibility when reality diverges from projection) or acknowledge it in ways that trigger disproportionate alarm. The goal is calibrated disclosure: communicating what you know, what you do not know, and how you are managing the gap, with language precise enough to be informative and composed enough to be steady.

Specific linguistic patterns are more effective in this context than others. "Our current data suggests" is more credible than "we believe." "We expect a range of outcomes between X and Y, with the most likely outcome near the middle of that range" is more useful than "results will vary." "We have identified the following factors that could affect performance, and we are monitoring each of them" is more confidence-inspiring than either "this will definitely work" or "there are many things that could go wrong." Precision in uncertainty language is a communication skill that can be developed deliberately, and it pays substantial dividends in both boardroom credibility and team trust.

Diagram 4.5: Language for Communicating Uncertainty

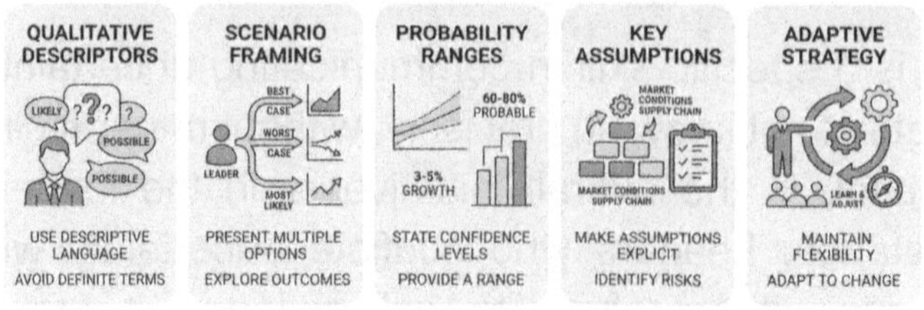

STRATEGIES FOR COMMUNICATING AMBIGUITY, BUILDING TRUST, AND MANAGING RISK IN BUSINESS LEADERSHIP

Crisis Communication When an AI System Fails

When an AI system produces a harmful, biased, or significantly wrong output at an organizational scale, the communication response in the first forty-eight hours will determine whether the incident becomes a contained setback or an enduring trust crisis. The leaders who navigate these moments most effectively follow a consistent four-step response pattern.

The first step is to acknowledge early. Do not wait for complete information before communicating. The worst outcomes in AI crisis communication occur when leaders delay acknowledgment while they gather facts, and stakeholders fill the silence with speculation, which becomes the dominant narrative. I know that an incident has occurred, that you are taking it seriously, and that you will provide more information as it becomes available. This step can and should be taken within hours, not days.

The second step is to maintain honesty. Describe the scope of the incident with precision, who was affected, in what way, and what immediate actions have been taken to stop or mitigate ongoing harm. Do not minimize scope in ways that subsequent information will contradict. Honest containment communication is the difference between a crisis that erodes trust and one that demonstrates operational discipline.

The third step is to explain without deflecting. Stakeholders need to understand what went wrong. This does not require an exhaustive technical post-mortem in public communication; it requires a substantive and honest account of the failure mode that avoids the two most common deflection strategies: blaming the AI ("the algorithm made an error we couldn't predict") and blaming the data ("the training data had inherent biases"). Both deflections are experienced as accountability avoidance, and they are. Leaders who accept organizational responsibility for AI failures and explain what they are doing to understand the root cause build more credibility than those who locate the cause entirely outside their authority.

The fourth step is to commit to systemic change. The final element of effective crisis communication is a specific, credible commitment to the changes that will prevent recurrence. Not "we will review our processes" but "we have identified the specific control gap that allowed this outcome, we are implementing these three changes to address it, and we will report back on their effectiveness in this timeframe." Specificity is what separates a commitment from a reassurance.

DIAGRAM 4.6: THE FOUR-STEP AI CRISIS COMMUNICATION FRAMEWORK

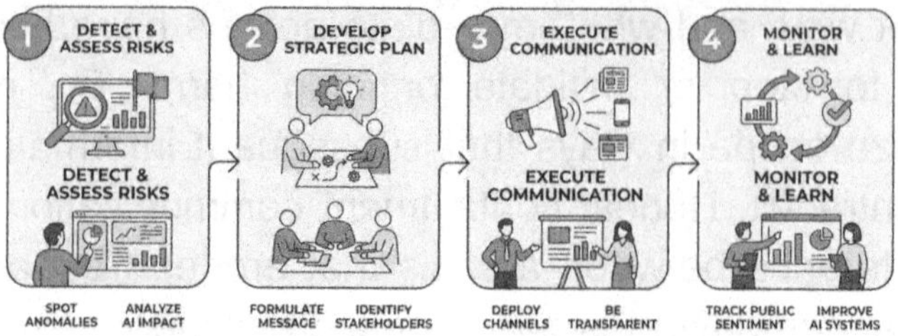

THE DIAGRAM 4.6: THE FOUR-STEP AI CRISIS COMMUNICATION KIT A BUSINESS LEADERSHIP BOOK SUMMARY CLINTIFY AIS INVUVATORST AND CMK, IMPROVE, AID EXECUTIIVE SYSTEMSE.

Post-Failure Narrative Reconstruction

The most experienced AI leaders understand that a well-handled failure is, paradoxically, one of the strongest trust-building events available to them. This is not a rationalization; it is an observation about how trust works. Stakeholders who see a leader acknowledge a serious problem promptly, contain it responsibly, explain it honestly, and implement genuine systemic changes gain something they could not have gained from a flawless deployment: direct evidence of how this leader behaves when things go wrong. That evidence is irreplaceable.

Post-failure narrative reconstruction is the deliberate work of reintegrating a setback into the organization's AI story in a way that is honest about what happened and maintains genuine conviction about the direction. It is not spin. It requires that the leader has learned something from the incident, has made meaningful changes, and can communicate both the lesson and the change with specificity. Organizations that have done this work well consistently report that their stakeholders' confidence in AI leadership increased after a significant incident, not because the incident was good news, but because the response demonstrated the accountability that makes further investment feel safe.

Communicating with Regulators

Regulatory communication about AI operates under a specific set of constraints and expectations that differ meaningfully from internal or investor communication. Regulators are not looking for strategic vision or inspiring narratives. They are looking for evidence that the organization knows what its AI systems are doing, has implemented appropriate governance controls, can demonstrate compliance with applicable standards, and will respond honestly to inquiry. The worst regulatory communication approaches are those that try to apply marketing logic to a compliance context, emphasizing benefits while minimizing concerns, using language that is technically accurate but constructed to foreclose uncomfortable follow-up questions.

The standards that consistently serve organizations best in regulatory communication are clarity and completeness. Answer what is asked, completely and without evasion. Do not volunteer information beyond the scope of inquiry in ways that create new compliance surface, but do not construct answers designed to obscure. If any aspects of the organization's AI operations are not yet fully compliant, acknowledge them and describe the specific remediation plan with a timeline. Regulators consistently report distinguishing between organizations that have problems and those that hide them, and the regulatory consequences for the latter are substantially more severe. Operational clarity in the regulatory context means being able to answer any reasonable question about your AI systems with confidence, specificity, and honesty.

Section 6: Being the Bridge Between Technical Teams and the Boardroom

The organizational AI communication landscape has a structural fault line that runs between the technical teams that build and operate AI systems and the business leaders who allocate resources, set strategy, and manage stakeholders. On the technical side, there is often deep expertise, but limited fluency in business communication and an inability to translate what the system does into what it means for the organization. On the business side, there is often strategic acumen accompanied by a reluctance to develop substantive AI understanding, a tendency to delegate technical questions entirely, and a surprise at the technical consequences.

The leader who can bridge this gap, who is genuinely bilingual in both technical reality and business consequence, holds one of the most valuable positions in the AI-era organization. This is not about becoming a data scientist. It is about developing enough technical literacy to ask good questions, understand the answers, and translate the relevant implications into language that different audiences can act on. The AI-CLEAR model's Curiosity dimension is the engine of this development: leaders who maintain active intellectual engagement with how their AI systems work are consistently better communicators about those systems than those who engage with AI only at the level of outputs and cost centers.

Common Translation Errors

Two translation errors appear with enough regularity to warrant naming. The first is over-technicizing: the executive who has developed genuine AI literacy and deploys it inappropriately by introducing technical specificity into conversations that require business clarity. This pattern often emerges from the understandable desire to demonstrate competence. Still, it consistently produces the wrong effect; audiences disengage from the technical detail and lose confidence in the leader's ability to communicate at their level. Technical understanding should inform executive communication, not constitute it.

The second error is oversimplifying: reducing AI capabilities and limitations to language that is so vague it misleads rather than informs. "Our AI system analyzes data to help us make better decisions" contains no information that any stakeholder could use. It does not describe what data, what analysis, what decisions, or what "better" means in this context. Over-simplification is often well-intentioned, a desire not to overwhelm, but its effect is the opposite of the trust-building transparency that effective AI communication requires. The standard to aim for is the level of specificity that allows the audience to ask the next intelligent question. If they cannot formulate a meaningful follow-up question, you have not communicated.

Diagram 4.7: The Translation Gap: Technical Reality to Business Consequence

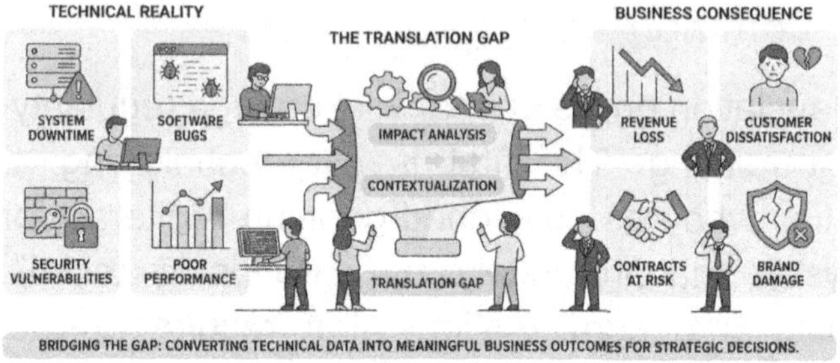

Building a Shared Vocabulary

One of the most high-leverage and underused communication tools available to AI leaders is the organizational AI glossary. This shared vocabulary defines key terms consistently across technical and business functions. This is not a jargon document. It is a precision tool. When "model accuracy" means different things to the data science team and the business unit that relies on the model, the result is not just miscommunication; it is misaligned expectations that lead to genuine operational problems when the model meets the technical definition of accuracy but not the business unit's implicit expectations.

An effective organizational AI vocabulary document defines the terms that matter most for governance and communication: what the organization means by AI, what it means by automated decision-making, what it considers high-risk versus low-risk AI applications, how it defines bias and what standards it applies, and what escalation and review processes are triggered by what types of AI decisions. This document should be written in plain language, reviewed by both technical and business stakeholders, and updated as the organization's AI environment evolves. It is not a compliance artifact; it is a mission-aligned communication infrastructure investment that pays dividends in every governance conversation, every board briefing, and every team discussion about AI implications.

Running a Governance Briefing That Produces Alignment

Governance briefings are a specific form of organizational AI communication that deserves dedicated attention because they are frequently delivered poorly, creating the appearance of alignment without its substance. The typical governance briefing presents AI initiative status, reports metrics, identifies risks, and ends with a question period that produces few genuine questions because attendees are not sufficiently oriented to ask them. Leaders leave believing alignment has been achieved. Subsequent decisions contradict the understanding of governance, revealing that the alignment was superficial.

A governance briefing that produces alignment has a different structure. It begins not with status updates but with a brief orientation: what questions is this briefing trying to answer, and what does this governance body need to understand or decide by the end of the session? It surfaces genuine disagreements rather than managing around them. If there is a substantive dispute about risk tolerance or investment priority, the governance briefing is the right place to resolve it, not to defer it. It ends with explicit decisions and names accountabilities, not with a general sense that the matter was discussed. And it includes a visible feedback loop: how will this governance body know whether the decisions made today produced the intended outcomes?

Diagram 4.8: The Governance Briefing Structure

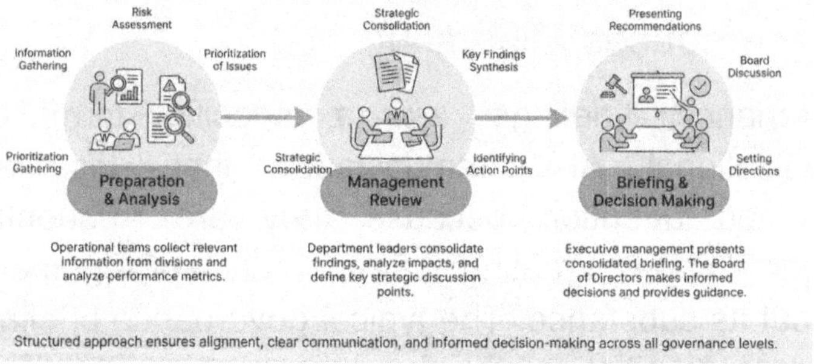

Section 7: AI Communication for Product Owners

Product owners occupy a distinctive position in the AI communication landscape. They are responsible for communicating AI capabilities both inward to the engineering and data teams building the systems and outward to the customers and users who interact with AI features in products and services. They often serve as the primary translation layer between technical possibility and user experience, and the quality of that translation has direct consequences for both product adoption and organizational trust.

The external communication challenge for product owners is managing expectations about AI capabilities without either underselling features that could provide genuine value or overselling capabilities that the system cannot reliably deliver. AI-powered product features are particularly prone to mismanaged expectations because the technology is genuinely impressive in controlled conditions but genuinely variable in production. A customer who encounters an AI recommendation feature that works brilliantly three times and then produces a clearly wrong output on the fourth interaction does not simply discount the fourth interaction; they retrospectively reinterpret the first three. Building trust in AI-powered products requires proactively communicating the system's limitations before users encounter them in disappointing ways.

Communicating AI Capabilities to Customers

The standard for customer-facing AI communication is accuracy and proportionality. Accuracy means describing what the AI system does, not what it theoretically could do, not what it does in ideal conditions, but what users can reliably expect in the range of situations they will encounter. Proportionality means calibrating the confidence of the communication to the reliability of the underlying system. A recommendation engine that performs consistently within a narrow, well-defined domain should be communicated with greater confidence than one deployed across a broad, variable set of inputs.

The product owner who communicates accurately about AI capabilities, including their limits, builds the kind of customer trust that survives the inevitable moments when the system underperforms. The product owner who oversells AI capabilities, whether implicitly or explicitly, creates initial excitement that quickly turns into distrust when reality diverges from expectations. In AI-powered products, as in organizational AI leadership more broadly, the long-term competitive advantage belongs to those who have earned calibrated trust rather than those who have generated maximum initial enthusiasm. Products built responsibly by design, where transparency and disclosure of limitations are treated as features rather than liabilities, consistently outperform those where honesty is treated as a communication risk.

Diagram 4.9: The Customer AI Communication Spectrum

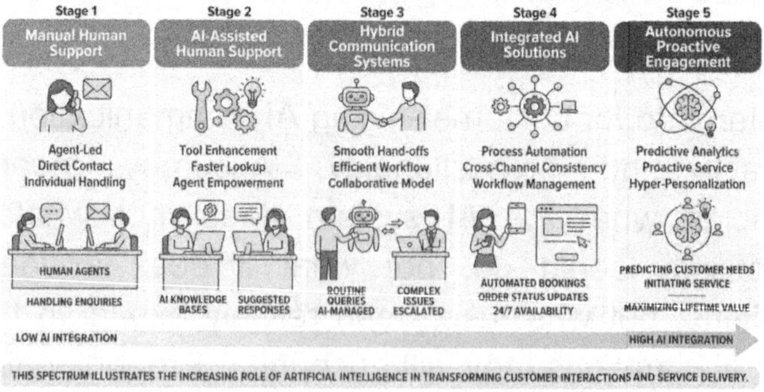

Handling User Feedback About AI

User complaints and concerns about AI outputs are among the most valuable signals available to product owners and organizational AI leaders, and they are among the most frequently mishandled. The typical organizational response to negative user feedback about AI is defensive: the feedback is classified as a misunderstanding of how the system works, or an edge case outside the intended use profile, or simply a reflection of user error. Each of these dismissals may occasionally be accurate. They are never an adequate response.

What user feedback about AI reveals, when treated as a diagnostic signal rather than a complaint to be managed, is where the gap between system design intent and user experience is largest. Users who report that an AI recommendation is wrong are often right. Still, even when they are not, their feedback reveals something important about expectation calibration, interface design, or the range of inputs the system encounters in production that were not represented in testing. Product owners who build systematic feedback channels for AI-related user concerns and who report those concerns transparently to technical teams create a learning loop that improves AI system performance over time. Those who treat complaints as reputational threats to be deflected accumulate technical debt in the form of unaddressed edge cases that will ultimately lead to larger failures.

Internal Communication of AI Product Decisions

Product owners also face a significant internal communication challenge: explaining AI-related product decisions, including the trade-offs, risk assessments, and value choices embedded in those decisions, to engineering, design, and business stakeholders, each with different contexts and priorities. An AI feature that the product owner has decided not to ship due to fairness concerns requires a different kind of explanation than a feature deprioritized for technical reasons. A decision to apply the Serious Decision Spectrum's Augment quadrant, keeping a human in the loop for AI-assisted decisions about individual users, requires communication that both technical and business stakeholders can understand and support.

The product owner as an AI translator occupies a uniquely important position in organizations building AI-powered products. They are often the first person in the organization who must articulate, in real terms, what responsible AI development requires at the product level, which data practices are acceptable, which use cases are in and out of bounds, how user consent should be handled, and when a technically possible feature should not be built. These are not purely technical decisions, nor are they purely business decisions. They are leadership decisions, and communicating those decisions to engineers, executives, and customers is one of the most consequential forms of AI leadership available to anyone in the organization willing to exercise it.

Diagram 4.10: The Product Owner as AI Translator

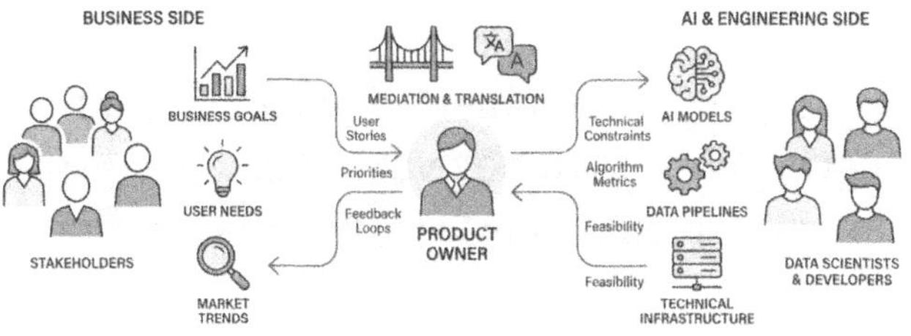

The Product Owner translates complex business requirements into actionable AI specifications and communicates data insights back to stakeholders to ensure alignment and value delivery.

The Serious AI Leader's Communication Checklist

Use this checklist to assess your AI communication practice. It is not an aspirational list; it is a behavioral inventory of what serious AI leaders do.

Upward Communication:

- Have you articulated your AI investment case in terms of strategy, risk, and return without leading with technical detail?
- Can you answer the three board questions: cost, outcome, and risk, with specific, evidence-based, honest responses?
- Are your executive expectations calibrated to realistic projections rather than theoretical maximums?
- Do you distinguish between what you know, what you project, and what you are uncertain about in board communication?

Downward Communication:

- Have you given your teams specific, task-level clarity about how AI will affect their work, not generic reassurance?
- Have you made explicit commitments about workforce development investment that are specific enough to be evaluated?
- Do your teams have a genuine, friction-free channel to raise concerns and questions about AI without fear of judgment?
- Have you proactively communicated about any AI use in performance or evaluation contexts before employees discover it independently?

Narrative and Consistency:

- Does your organization have a coherent AI narrative that contains all five elements: why now, what we're building toward, how decisions are made, how we stay accountable, and what this means for our people?

- Have you aligned key leaders across the organization on the core AI messages, so that team-level communications reinforce rather than contradict the organizational narrative?
- Is there a mechanism for identifying and correcting messaging inconsistencies before they harden into conflicting organizational beliefs?

Risk and Crisis Preparedness:

- Have you established a crisis communication protocol for AI failures before any failure occurs, including designated spokespersons, escalation paths, and approval processes?
- Do you use precise uncertainty language rather than either false confidence or vague hedging?
- Have you communicated proactively with regulators about your AI governance approach, rather than waiting for an inquiry?

Bridge and Translation:

- Do you have a shared AI vocabulary document that defines key terms consistently across technical and business functions?
- Is your governance briefing structure designed to produce actual decisions and accountabilities, rather than the appearance of review?
- Can you identify the specific ways your technical teams' communication is not landing with business stakeholders, and are you actively helping close that gap?

DIAGRAM 4.11: THE AI LEADER COMMUNICATION CHECKLIST OVERVIEW

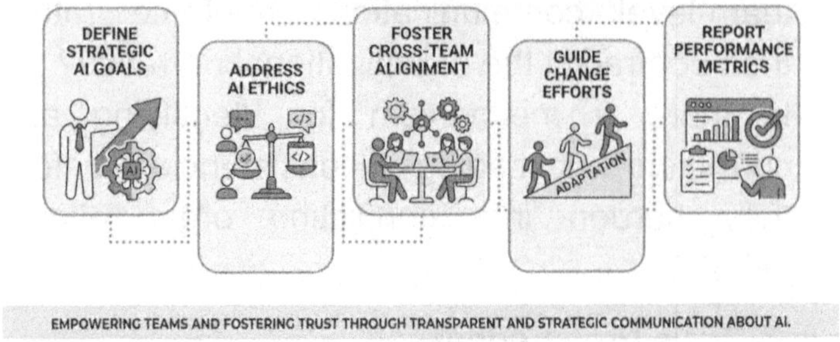

What Communication Makes Possible

The work of this chapter has been to establish communication not as a soft skill adjacent to AI leadership but as the mechanism through which AI leadership becomes real. Every insight from Chapter 2 about the mindsets that distinguish AI leaders, every framework from Chapter 3 for making better decisions alongside algorithmic advice, these are only as valuable as the leader's ability to translate them into language that different audiences can understand, trust, and act on. The trust architecture introduced in Chapter 5 is not a structure that exists in governance documents. It is built or eroded in the conversations, briefings, team meetings, and crisis responses that AI leaders deliver every day. Communication is where architecture becomes either solid or fragile.

The AI leaders who consistently build durable organizational trust are not those who project the greatest confidence or demonstrate the deepest technical knowledge. They are those who have developed the discipline to speak accurately about what they know, specifically about what they are uncertain of, and honestly about what can go wrong. They are those who have invested in understanding their audiences well enough to meet each one where they are, rather than where it would be convenient for them. And they are those who regard every communication event, the board briefing, the team announcement, the regulatory inquiry, the crisis response, as an opportunity to demonstrate exactly the kind of accountability and integrity that makes the next communication easier to receive.

The most effective AI communicators are not simplifiers. They are sense-makers. Their gift to their organizations is not the reduction of complex reality to comfortable abstractions, but the creation of a shared framework for engaging with it together. In an era when AI will continue to evolve faster than most organizations can fully absorb, that is not just a matter of communication. It is the foundation of organizational resilience.

Diagram 4.12: Communication as the Foundation of AI Trust

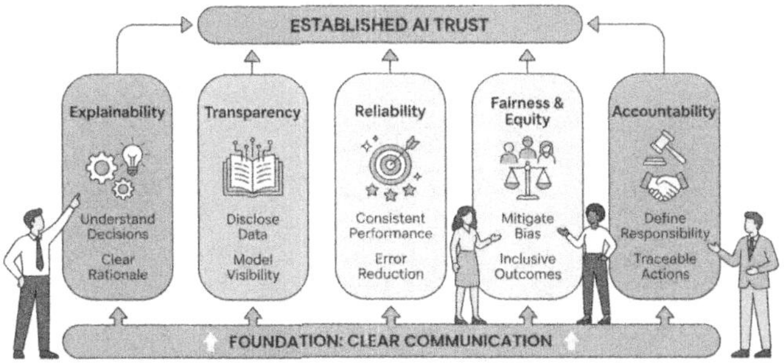

CONSISTENT, TRANSPARENT COMMUNICATION IS ESSENTIAL FOR BUILDING CONFIDENCE AND ENSURING ETHICAL AI DEPLOYMENT.

6 Trust Is the Infrastructure: How Serious AI Leaders Build and Protect It

A Crisis That Did Not Have to Happen

The operations review was supposed to take forty-five minutes. Instead, it consumed three days.

The SVP of Operations at a large financial services firm had championed a new AI-assisted contract analysis platform for over a year. The system had been piloted carefully, rolled out across three regional offices, and was generating measurable efficiency gains. Analysts were processing the contract volume three times per week. Leadership was impressive. Then a client discovered that an addendum to their master services agreement, one that capped the firm's liability exposure in a specific scenario, had been flagged by the AI as low priority and routed to a secondary review queue. No human had read it before the contract was passed. The clause was activated six weeks later.

The legal exposure was manageable. The reputational damage was harder to contain. But what unsettled the SVP most was not the error itself; every system fails somewhere; it was what she discovered in the aftermath. When she began asking questions, she found that her analysts had long suspected AI's priority-flagging logic was inconsistent, but had not raised concerns because the previous performance culture had penalized slowdowns, and slowing down to escalate AI anomalies felt risky. Her clients had not been told that AI was reviewing their contracts. Her board had received upbeat AI deployment metrics but had never seen a risk assessment. And she herself had approved the system's expansion based on throughput data, without ever asking what went wrong.

Four trust relationships had quietly eroded: with the AI system itself, with her team, with her clients, and with her own judgment. Not suddenly, and not through anyone's malice. Simply through the absence of intention. Trust does not maintain itself. In AI-powered organizations, architecture is required.

Why Trust Is the Infrastructure, Not the Outcome

Leaders who treat trust as a byproduct of good results are making the most expensive mistake in AI governance. They are not wrong that results build trust, but they are wrong about the sequence. In AI-driven organizations, trust must be built in advance of the results, because results that cannot be explained, governed, or accounted for do not generate durable trust. They generate fragile adoption that collapses under the first significant failure.

The trust deficit most organizations face with AI is paradoxical. Research consistently shows that most of the workforce wants the benefits of AI: faster workflows, reduced administrative burden, and better analytical support. Yet a substantial portion of those same workers report being unwilling to trust AI outputs without verification, uncertain whether their organization's AI governance protects them, and reluctant to flag AI-related concerns to leadership. This is not a skepticism problem. It is a structural problem. Workers want AI to succeed, but the systems, the policies, and the leaders around them have not yet earned the trust needed for that success to be sustainable.

Chapter 4 established that the language of AI leadership must translate complexity into clarity, and that the way leaders communicate about AI determines whether their teams can work effectively with it. That capacity for communication depends entirely on a prior condition: the communicator must be trusted. The AI-CLEAR model's Empowerment dimension, which creates the conditions for teams to work confidently alongside AI, only functions when Team Trust has been built. You can say all the right things about AI's role in your organization, but if your team does not trust that you are telling the truth about how AI outputs will be used in workforce decisions, the communication fails at the receiver. Trust is the infrastructure on which every other AI leadership capability runs.

Chapter 9 will synthesize the Trust Architecture, the AI-CLEAR model, and the Serious Decision Spectrum into a complete leadership operating system. But trust is introduced here, at the center of this book, for a reason. Everything before Chapter 5 was about what the leader knows and how the leader thinks. Everything after it is about what the leader builds and sustains in the organization around them. Without trust as the connecting tissue, those two halves never become a whole.

DIAGRAM 5.1: TRUST AS ORGANIZATIONAL INFRASTRUCTURE

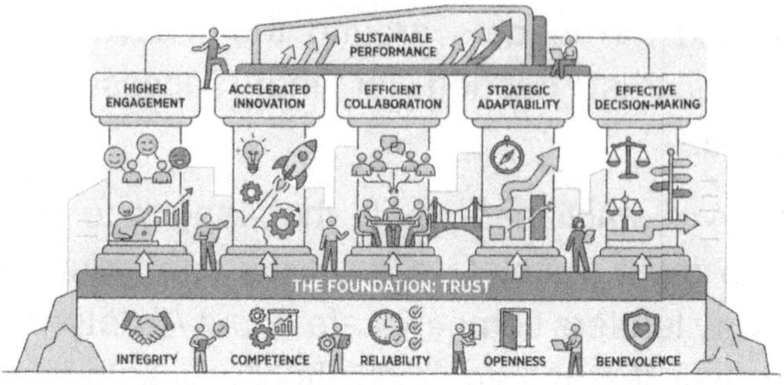

A STRONG FOUNDATION OF TRUST UNDERPINS AND ENHANCES KEY ORGANIZATIONAL CAPABILITIES AND RESILIENCE.

Introducing the Trust Architecture

Trust Architecture is the third branded framework introduced in this book. Where the AI-CLEAR model measures the leader's internal readiness and the Serious Decision Spectrum guides the appropriate allocation of AI authority, the Trust Architecture maps the four distinct trust relationships that a serious AI leader must simultaneously build and maintain. These relationships are not hierarchical; none is more important than the others. They are interdependent. Neglecting any one layer creates structural weakness throughout the whole.

Leaders who treat trust as a single, undifferentiated concept run into a predictable problem: they make general statements about its importance without diagnosing which specific trust relationship is most at risk. The SVP in the opening scenario did not have a generic trust problem. She had four specific trust deficits, each with its own cause, evidence, and repair strategy. The Trust Architecture gives leaders diagnostic precision to act on the right problem.

The Four Layers

Layer 1: System Trust is the leader's calibrated confidence in the AI tools and platforms they deploy. Calibrated is the operative word. System Trust is neither optimism about AI capabilities nor reflexive skepticism that undermines AI's genuine value. It is earned confidence, built through transparency about how models work, systematic validation of outputs, and honest governance of failure modes. A leader with well-calibrated System Trust can articulate what their AI systems do well, what they do poorly, where human review is essential, and what governance mechanisms are in place when outputs are wrong. A leader without it is either overconfident in AI outputs or paralyzed by uncertainty about them, and neither posture serves the organization.

Layer 2: Team Trust is employees' belief that AI will be used for them, not against them. This is not simply about whether teams like the AI tools they use. It is about whether they believe their leadership is honest about AI's role in decisions that affect them, such as performance evaluations, workload assignments, career development, and workforce planning. When Team Trust is low, employees do not raise AI concerns, do not admit AI-related mistakes, and do not engage in the honest feedback loops that enable organizations to govern AI well. The cost of low Team Trust is not moral; it is a matter of governance blindness. Leaders stop seeing the problems that matter most because the people closest to those problems have learned that raising them is not safe.

Layer 3 Stakeholder Trust is the confidence that customers, partners, boards, and regulators place in the organization's AI governance. It encompasses how clients are informed about AI's role in the services they receive, how boards are briefed on AI risk, how regulators are engaged on compliance matters, and how partner organizations are held accountable within the AI supply chain. Stakeholder Trust is the most publicly visible layer of the Trust Architecture; it is the one that makes headlines when it breaks down. But it is also the most difficult to rebuild, because external parties have less visibility into your remediation efforts and more exposure to the consequences of your failures.

Layer 4: Self-Trust is the leader's confidence in their own judgment when it diverges from AI recommendations. This is among the most underappreciated leadership skills in AI-powered organizations. The pressure to defer to algorithmic recommendations is real. Algorithms don't have career ambitions, don't suffer from fatigue, and carry a veneer of objectivity that makes disagreement feel presumptuous. But the leader who cannot assert human judgment when it matters, who defaults to the AI recommendation because overruling it feels like a risk, has effectively abdicated leadership over some of the most consequential decisions the organization makes. Self-Trust is not arrogance. It is the disciplined belief that leadership wisdom, organizational context, and human values are legitimate inputs that algorithms cannot fully encode.

Diagram 5.2: The Trust Architecture: Four Layers

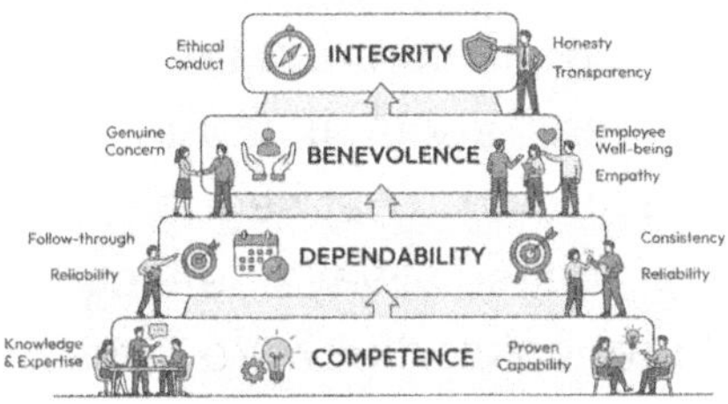

A robust framework for building and maintaining strong organizational trust.

The Cascade Principle

The Trust Architecture functions as a system, not a checklist. This means that failures in any one layer create pressure across all four, and, specifically, predictable patterns. Understanding these cascade dynamics is what separates leaders who maintain trust architecture proactively from those who spend their careers in reactive trust repair.

System Trust failures cascade into Team Trust when employees observe that leadership is deploying AI tools that produce unreliable outputs without adequate governance and expects them to continue using them regardless. The implicit message is that speed matters more than accuracy. If speed matters more than accuracy in AI outputs, it may also matter more than accuracy in how AI outputs are used to evaluate the team's own performance. That inference, fair or not, is the one your team draws. It is rational.

Team Trust failures cascade into Stakeholder Trust when low psychological safety within the organization prevents honest internal escalation, so problems go unaddressed until they become external events. The client who discovered the contract error in the opening scenario did not hear about it from the firm. They discovered it on their own. That sequence of events is rarely random. It almost always reflects an internal environment where concerns were present but not raised.

Self-Trust deficits cascade to all other layers simultaneously. A leader who cannot assert confident human judgment when AI systems produce counterintuitive outputs cannot build a governance environment that takes human judgment seriously. Their team will observe the leader deferring to algorithms in high-stakes situations and draw the appropriate conclusion: that their own judgment is not particularly valued either. The downstream consequences for Team Trust, System Trust governance, and stakeholder communication are substantial.

The audit tool introduced later in this chapter operates on the principle of cascading. The goal of the quarterly audit is not simply to inventory trust levels across the four layers, but to identify which layer is most at risk of triggering a cascade, and to act before the cascade begins.

Building System Trust

Calibrated Confidence Is the Goal

System Trust is not a binary condition. Leaders do not simply trust or distrust the AI tools; they calibrate their confidence in those tools for specific tasks, in specific contexts, with specific data. The leader who says "I trust our demand-forecasting AI" is making a statement that is too broad to be useful. The leader who says, "I trust our demand-forecasting AI for short-range inventory planning in our established markets, but I hold its outputs loosely for new market entries where our historical data is thin," has the kind of calibrated System Trust that translates into sound operational decisions. Calibration requires knowing both what AI does well and where its confidence should not be shared.

This calibration is the direct operational expression of the Serious Decision Spectrum introduced in Chapter 3. Recall that the Spectrum's two axes are data density and human stakes. A demand forecast for established markets with high historical data and moderate stakes belongs in the Augment or even Automate quadrant, where AI authority is appropriate. A market-entry recommendation for a new geography, with sparse data and high strategic stakes, sits squarely in the

Assert quadrant, where human judgment must dominate, with AI providing supporting analysis at best. System Trust calibrated to the Serious Decision Spectrum is the System Trust that informs sound governance. Uncalibrated System Trust overconfidence or underconfidence applied uniformly across all use cases is a governance failure mode.

Explainability as a Leadership Requirement

Serious managers do not approve of AI systems that they cannot explain at an appropriate level of abstraction. This does not mean technical mastery; it means the ability to answer the questions that matter for governance. How does this system make its recommendations? What data does it use, and what are the known gaps or biases in that data? What does the system do when it encounters conditions outside its training range? Who in this organization can explain why a specific output was generated? If these questions do not have clear answers available to the leader approving the system, the system is not ready for deployment at scale.

The explainability requirement is not bureaucratic caution. It is the foundation of accountability. When an AI-assisted decision produces a poor outcome, and it will, because no system is error-free, the serious manager needs to be able to answer two questions from the board, from the client, and from the regulator: What went wrong, and what have you changed? Neither question can be answered if the leader does not understand how the system works. "The AI decided" is not an answer. It is an abdication. And no board, no regulator, and no serious client will accept it.

DIAGRAM 5.3: THE EXPLAINABILITY HIERARCHY

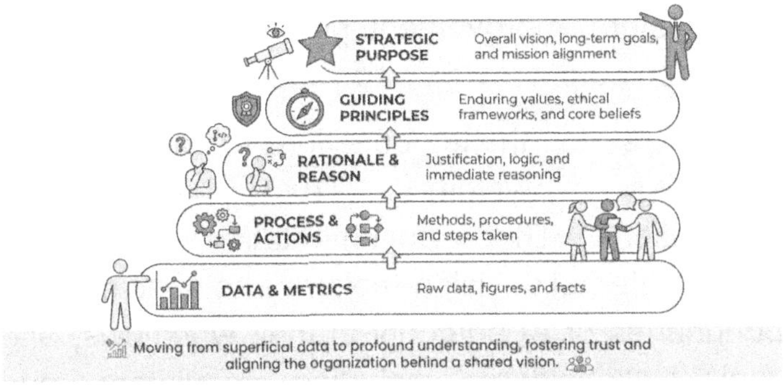

Output Validation Protocols

System Trust is built not through assumption but through verification. Serious managers establish validation protocols that define, before deployment, how AI outputs will be checked, by whom, at what frequency, and with what escalation procedure when outputs fall outside expected ranges. These protocols are not expressions of distrust in the AI system; they are the governance infrastructure that makes trust rational.

A rigorous output validation framework addresses four questions. First, what is the expected accuracy range for this system's output in production, and how does that range vary with input conditions? Second, what is the sampling protocol for human review of outputs:

random sampling, threshold-triggered review, or mandatory review for specific decision categories? Third, who holds the authority to pause or override AI outputs when anomalies are detected, and what is the communication protocol when that authority is exercised? Fourth, how are validation findings fed back into the system improvement process? What is the loop between output review and vendor accountability?

The answers to these questions constitute the organization's System Trust governance documentation. That documentation has two audiences: internal decision-makers who need to know the boundaries of AI authority in their workflows, and external stakeholders, including regulators and auditors, who may ask how AI governance is implemented rather than what it promises. Governance that exists only in policy documents rather than in operational protocols will not withstand scrutiny.

Confronting AI Failure Modes Honestly

AI systems fail in ways that differ from conventional software. They fail at the boundary of their training data. They fail on edge cases not represented in the datasets used to train their models. They fail when real-world conditions shift in ways that violate the assumptions embedded in their design. And critically, they sometimes fail with high confidence, producing wrong outputs without any signal that the output is unreliable. This last failure mode is the most dangerous for leaders who have not anticipated it.

Building genuine System Trust requires honest governance that assumes error as a design condition, not an edge case. The leader who builds governance on the assumption that AI will be accurate, with error handling as an afterthought, has created a fragile system. The leader who builds governance on the assumption that errors will occur, that the question is not whether but when and at what rate, has built a resilient one. Resilient governance includes monitoring for performance degradation over time, clear escalation paths for anomalous outputs, and a documented response protocol that does not begin with "determine whether the AI was responsible."

Evaluating the Vendor, Not Just the Product

System Trust extends to the organizations that build and maintain the AI tools an enterprise deploys. Vendor evaluation is a governance imperative, not simply a procurement exercise. The serious manager's framework for vendor trust assessment covers four dimensions: transparency about model training data and known limitations; responsiveness to reported errors and update cadence; contractual accountability for output quality and data handling; and evidence of the vendor's internal governance structures. A vendor that cannot answer questions about their model's known failure modes, does not commit to error-remediation timelines, or resists audit provisions in their contract is not a trustworthy AI partner, regardless of the product's benchmark performance. Choosing an

AI vendor means extending your governance perimeter to include their practices. Make that extension deliberately.

Diagram 5.4: System Trust Building Blocks

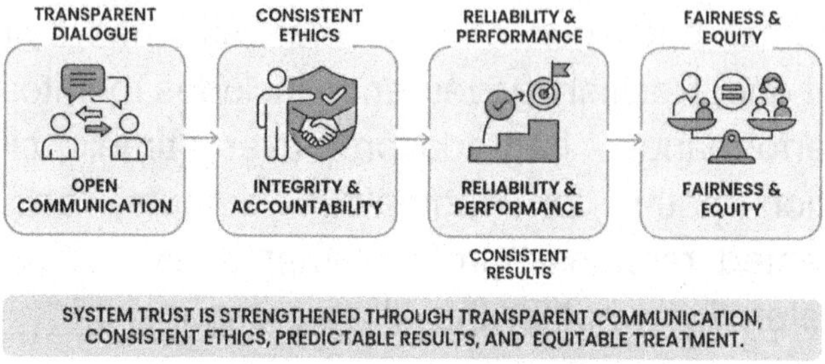

Building Team Trust

The Employee Trust Equation

Team Trust is built on a specific belief: that AI is being deployed to improve employees' working lives, not to make their positions more precarious. This belief is not created by communication alone; it is created by the cumulative experience of seeing how AI is used in decisions that directly affect employees. When employees observe that AI outputs are used to set productivity benchmarks that become impossible to contest, or to generate performance assessments without meaningful human context, or to identify "redundant" roles without transparent criteria, they draw the rational conclusion that AI is a tool directed at them rather than for them. No communications campaign overcomes that experience. Only changed behavior does.

The AI-CLEAR model's Empowerment dimension addresses this directly. Empowerment means creating the conditions for teams to work confidently alongside AI, and psychological safety is required for that confidence. Psychological safety around AI means employees can raise concerns about AI outputs without fear of being dismissed as technologically resistant. It means they can admit AI-assisted mistakes without fear of disproportionate consequences. It means they can suggest improvements to AI workflows without fear of being blamed for problems. Leaders who score low on the Empowerment dimension of their AI-CLEAR assessment typically find exactly this: their teams are using AI tools but not honestly, and the feedback loops that governance depends on are compromised.

Transparency About AI's Role in Workforce Decisions

The most corrosive form of Team Trust erosion is the use of AI in workforce decisions without disclosure. When employees later learn that AI output influenced how their performance was assessed, how their workload was structured, or how their roles were classified, the violation of trust is compounded by the absence of transparency. The damage is not simply "the AI made a bad call." The damage is "leadership used AI to make decisions about me and did not tell me."

Transparent communication of AI's role in workforce decisions is not a legal requirement in most jurisdictions; it is a leadership choice. The serious AI leader makes that choice proactively for reasons unrelated to regulatory compliance. Transparency creates the conditions for legitimate feedback. When employees know that AI is involved in their performance evaluation, they can identify and raise concerns about inputs the AI may have missed, contextual factors the model may not capture, or outputs that conflict with their direct manager's assessment. That feedback is invaluable governance data. Organizations that suppress it by hiding AI's role in workforce decisions are governing blindly.

DIAGRAM 5.5: THE TEAM TRUST FRAMEWORK

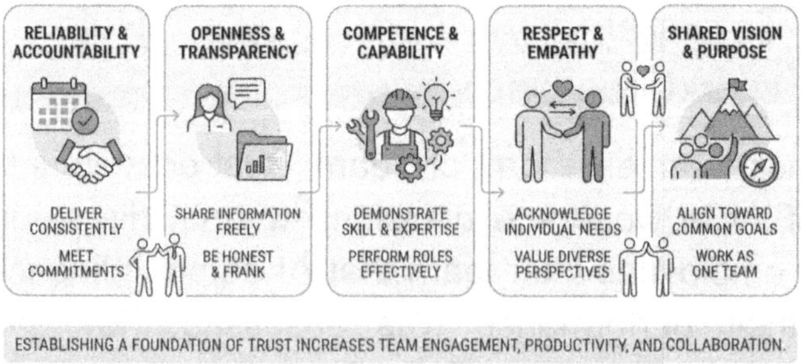

The Reskilling Covenant

The most powerful demonstration that AI is intended to augment rather than replace is investment. Words about AI augmentation cost nothing. A serious reskilling commitment in budget, in time, and in career pathway design is a tangible signal that leadership means what it says. The reskilling covenant is not a one-time training event. It is a sustained organizational commitment that has three visible components: dedicated learning resources that are actually accessible during working hours (not relegated to after-hours self-directed learning expectations), clearly articulated career development pathways that incorporate new AI-adjacent skills as advancement criteria rather than replacement conditions, and leadership visibility in the reskilling investment senior leaders who publicly acknowledge their own AI learning journeys rather than presenting themselves as fully formed AI experts.

The reskilling covenant is also the most direct expression of the AI-CLEAR model's Empowerment dimension in practice. It is the organizational infrastructure that transforms empowerment from a value statement into a verifiable commitment. Teams assess sincerity not by what leaders say about AI augmentation, but by whether the organization invests in their capability to navigate an AI-augmented future.

Psychological Safety and AI Failure

How a leader responds when a team member makes an AI-assisted mistake is one of the most consequential moments of trust in AI governance. The response does not just affect the individual involved; it broadcasts a policy to every observer. If the response is punitive, observers learn that AI errors are personal failures rather than system events, leading to future AI errors being hidden rather than escalated. If the response is curious and constructive, what happens? Where did the AI output diverge from what you expected? What governance improvement would prevent this? Observers learn that the organization treats AI errors as information. That organizational learning posture is the prerequisite for continuous improvement in AI governance.

The leader who maintains psychological safety around AI failure is not lowering accountability standards. They are applying accountability correctly: at the system and governance level, where it can drive actual improvement, rather than at the individual level, where it drives error concealment. There is a meaningful distinction between an employee who disregards known AI limitations recklessly and an employee who acts in good faith on AI outputs that the organization's own validation protocols failed to catch. Governance that cannot make this distinction trains people to hide problems.

Co-Designing AI Policies with Teams

Participatory governance, involving team members in the design of AI policies that affect their work, is both a trust-building and a governance-improvement strategy. Employees who work with AI tools daily have insights into failure modes, workflow gaps, and edge cases that leaders and technology teams lack. Excluding that knowledge from policy design is a governance error. Including it is a competitive advantage.

Participatory governance does not mean that every policy decision is subject to consensus. It means that, before deploying significant AI policies, acceptable use standards, output review protocols, and AI-assisted performance frameworks, leadership creates genuine input mechanisms, listens to what emerges, demonstrates that input has been incorporated, and explains where input was not incorporated and why. This cycle of genuine consultation and honest feedback builds the specific kind of Team Trust that makes governance durable: trust that the organization is not doing AI governance to the team, but with them.

Building Stakeholder Trust

Customer Trust: Transparency Before Obligation

Customers who learn that AI was involved in decisions affecting them, from service recommendations to pricing to risk assessments, after the fact, and without their knowledge or consent, do not simply lose trust in the AI. They lose trust in the organization. The sequence matters enormously. Proactive disclosure of AI's role in customer-facing decisions, offered before a customer has reason to ask, demonstrates that the organization has nothing to hide. Reactive disclosure, offered only when a customer discovers AI involvement on their own or raises a complaint, suggests that the organization hoped they would not notice.

Customer trust in AI requires transparency at two levels. The first is disclosure: customers should know when AI is involved in decisions that significantly affect their experience or outcomes. The second is recourse: customers should have a clear pathway to request human review of AI-influenced decisions. Organizations that offer both that tell customers AI is involved and give customers a genuine option to engage with a human decision-maker build a qualitatively different kind of customer trust than those that offer only disclosure. The recourse mechanism demonstrates that the organization understands the limits of AI's authority and has preserved the conditions for human accountability.

DIAGRAM 5.6: STAKEHOLDER TRUST MAP

Board and Investor Trust: Governance Maturity as Risk Signal

Boards are increasingly aware that AI governance is a material risk dimension, not an operational footnote. The serious AI leader understands that board and investor trust is built not through optimistic AI narratives but through demonstrated governance maturity. Governance maturity means the board can see that AI deployment decisions are made within a coherent framework, that risk is assessed before deployment rather than discovered after, that accountability is clearly assigned for AI outcomes, and that the organization has a credible response capability when AI systems produce unintended consequences.

Briefing a board on AI is not the same as briefing a board on AI governance. An AI briefing presents capabilities and milestones. An AI governance briefing addresses risk exposure, accountability structures, and the conditions under which AI authority is limited.

Boards that receive only the achievements of AI deployment, without the governance architecture behind them, are being positioned as cheerleaders rather than fiduciaries. The serious AI leader provides both, because boards that understand your governance are far better partners in navigating AI risk than boards that have been sold only the upside.

Regulatory Trust: The Case for Early Engagement

The instinct to minimize regulatory visibility until required is understandable and almost always strategically wrong. Regulators who discover AI deployment through a complaint, an audit finding, or a reported incident approach the organization in an adversarial posture that is difficult to change. Regulators who have been engaged proactively, briefed on deployment plans, consulted on compliance questions before they became violations, and treated as governance partners rather than enforcement threats approach the same organization in a fundamentally different frame.

Early regulatory engagement has a secondary benefit: leaders often overlook that regulators have access to cross-industry pattern data that your compliance team does not. They have seen how similar AI deployments have failed in other organizations, which failure modes have caused the most significant harm, and which governance gaps are most cited in enforcement actions. That intelligence is genuinely valuable and available to organizations that engage regulators early as part of a governance partnership, rather than treating regulatory interactions as a necessary minimum to be managed.

Vendor and Partner Trust: Responsible AI Supply Chains

AI governance does not stop at your organizational boundary. The AI tools your vendors use to process your data, the models your partners rely on to generate outputs that inform your decisions, and the third-party platforms that provide AI capabilities embedded in your products are all part of your AI supply chain. All of them are part of your Stakeholder Trust perimeter. A serious manager who maintains rigorous internal AI governance but lacks visibility into vendor AI practices has built a wall around the front door while leaving the back door unmanaged.

Responsible AI supply chain accountability requires three things in vendor and partner relationships: contractual transparency about AI use and data handling, audit rights that are exercised rather than used as negotiating leverage, and clear accountability provisions for harm resulting from vendor AI failures. Vendors who resist these provisions are telling you something important about their own governance posture. The cost of insisting on them is the occasional loss of a preferred vendor. The cost of not insisting on them is absorbing governance failures that originated outside your organization but that your clients, your regulators, and your board will hold you responsible for, regardless.

The Reputational Calculus

The reputational mathematics of AI governance failure is asymmetric in ways that consistently surprise leaders who have not thought them through in advance. Getting AI governance right before a crisis costs: time in governance design, investment in training and validation infrastructure, and some friction in deployment timelines. Getting it wrong costs: regulatory action, client attrition, media coverage, loss of board confidence, employee retention issues, and years of rebuilding with stakeholders. These costs are neither comparable nor proportional. The organization that proactively invests in Stakeholder Trust is not simply doing the right thing; it is making a sound, risk-adjusted investment. Organizations that treat AI governance as overhead rather than insurance are inefficient. They are self-insuring against risks they have not yet fully priced.

DIAGRAM 5.7:
THE REPUTATIONAL CALCULUS OF AI GOVERNANCE

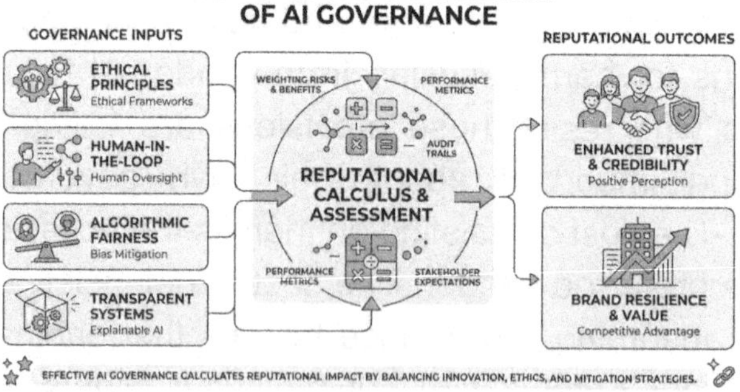

Building Self-Trust as an AI Leader

The Psychological Pressure to Defer

The pressure to defer to algorithmic recommendations is one of the least discussed yet most consequential forces shaping AI governance within organizations. It operates through a combination of social dynamics, cognitive shortcuts, and organizational incentive structures that are individually understandable and collectively corrosive. Socially, overruling an AI recommendation in a meeting requires the leader to absorb the implied accusation of irrationality. The algorithm uses data, you are using intuition, and the culture has been trained to view that distinction as a disadvantage for intuition. Cognitively, algorithms provide a form of decision cover: if the AI recommended it and the outcome was poor, the leader can diffuse accountability across the technology. Organizationally, AI adoption metrics often reward decisions that move quickly with AI support, rather than those that pause to assert human judgment.

None of these dynamics makes algorithmic deference rational. They make it understandable. The serious AI leader understands the distinction and understands that leadership is precisely the practice of acting on what is rational rather than what is socially comfortable. Building Self-Trust requires developing an explicit practice of asserting human judgment, not a heroic act of occasional rebellion, but a disciplined habit of engaging with AI recommendations critically and taking visible ownership of the final decision regardless of whether it aligns with the algorithm.

When the Algorithm Is Right, and You Are Wrong

Genuine Self-Trust includes the humility to course-correct when AI reveals an error in human reasoning. This is not capitulation; it is calibration. The leader who examines an AI recommendation, finds it conflicts with their intuition, investigates why, and concludes that the data genuinely does not support their initial read, has exercised exactly the right combination of skepticism and intellectual honesty. The key is that the conclusion was reached through deliberate engagement with the evidence, not through deference to the algorithm's authority.

Operationalizing this kind of calibration requires practice: when you override an AI recommendation, document the reason. If your override results in a poor outcome, review the documentation. Over time, this creates a record of your decision-making patterns, in which your human judgment reliably adds value that AI cannot capture and reliably introduces error. That record is the empirical foundation of genuine Self-Trust. It is not faith in your own judgment. It earns confidence, based on evidence of where that judgment performs.

DIAGRAM 5.8: THE SELF-TRUST CALIBRATION LOOP

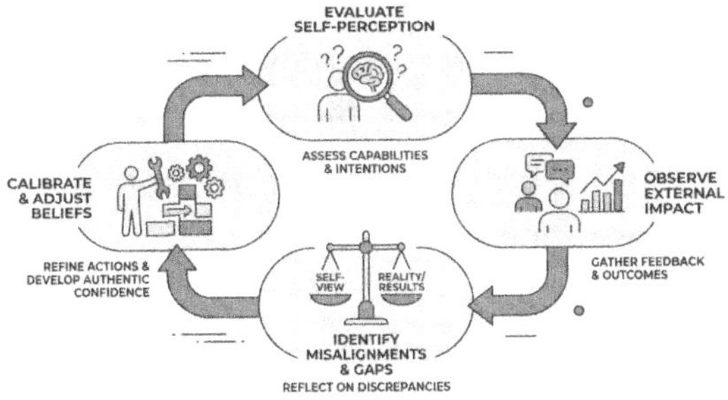

A continuous process of aligning internal self-perception with external reality to build and maintain effective self-trust for leadership.

When You Are Right, and the Algorithm Is Wrong

The courage to assert human judgment over an AI recommendation when the stakes are high and social pressure favors compliance is among the most demanding leadership skills in the AI era. It requires the leader to hold two things simultaneously: genuine intellectual engagement with the AI's reasoning, and confidence that the factors the algorithm cannot see-organizational culture, relationship context, ethical dimension, and strategic ambiguity- are legitimately relevant to the decision at hand.

The Serious Decision Spectrum provides useful scaffolding here. When a decision sits in the Assert quadrant, high stakes, low algorithmic data density, the leader's own judgment is not simply permitted, it is required. The algorithm's role in Assert decisions is to provide supporting analysis and surface considerations the leader may have missed, not to generate the decision. A leader who has internalized the Spectrum can engage with organizational pressure to defer to AI with a clear framework: "This decision belongs in Assert. The algorithm can inform it, but it cannot make it." That is not anti-AI sentiment. It is principled governance.

Self-Trust Without Arrogance

The disciplined posture of the serious AI leader is neither submission to algorithms nor dismissal of them. It is engaged independence, the capacity to take AI seriously as a source of analysis while maintaining clear personal accountability for the decisions that analysis informs. Arrogance in this context looks like dismissing AI outputs because engaging with them feels threatening to leadership identity. Submission appears to be accepting AI outputs because the social cost of disagreement is too high. Neither posture is leadership. Leadership is the consistent practice of deliberate engagement: taking the algorithm's reasoning seriously, adding the context the algorithm cannot access, and owning the outcome.

Self-Trust of this kind is not innate. It is developed through practice, the calibration record described above, peer accountability, and the kind of honest post-decision review that most organizational cultures do not make time for. The serious manager who invests in developing Self-Trust is investing in the leadership capability that underpins every other dimension of the Trust Architecture, because a leader who does not trust their own judgment cannot credibly build a governance environment in which human judgment is genuinely valued.

Accountability as the Foundation of Trust

The One Statement That Destroys Trust Instantly

"The AI decided." These three words represent the single most damaging statement an AI leader can make in a high-stakes situation. They are damaging not because they are false- sometimes the AI did, in fact, make or substantially shape a decision- but because they represent an abrogation of exactly the accountability that leadership requires. Boards, clients, regulators, and teams do not need AI systems to be infallible. They need the humans who deploy those systems to be accountable for their outcomes. When a leader says, "the AI decided," they are claiming an escape from that accountability that no leadership role in a serious organization actually offers.

The correct statement, in every circumstance, is: "We used AI-assisted analysis to inform this decision, and I am accountable for the outcome." This statement is more demanding: it requires that the leader has genuinely understood what the AI contributed, can explain how its outputs were evaluated, and is prepared to own both the decision and its consequences. But it is also the statement that maintains leadership credibility, preserves institutional trust, and demonstrates the governance maturity that external stakeholders need to see.

Diagram 5.9: The Accountability Cascade

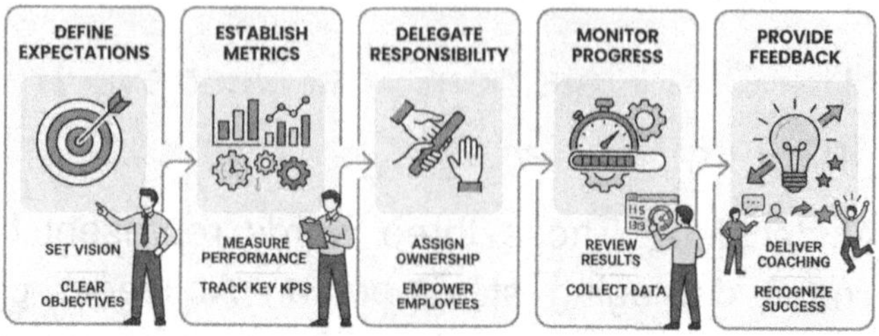

A systemic process for creating a culture of ownership and achieving organizational goals through aligned actions and clear expectations.

Accountability Structures for Opaque Systems

Not all AI systems are explainable. Some of the most powerful AI tools in enterprise use large language models, complex recommendation engines, and deep learning classifiers that produce outputs through processes that even their creators cannot fully audit at the level of individual decisions. This is a governance reality, not a reason to avoid deployment. But it requires a specific accountability architecture: one that does not rely on reconstructing why a given output was generated and that maintains human accountability regardless of the algorithm's opacity.

The accountability structure for opaque systems rests on three governance commitments. First, deployment boundaries: opaque systems are deployed only in contexts where the output's impact on individuals can be reviewed and contested, and where human override is preserved as a structural feature of the workflow rather than an afterthought. Second, output validation: because individual outputs cannot be explained in detail, validation focuses on population-level performance-bias audits, accuracy sampling, and drift monitoring that detect systemic problems even when individual anomalies cannot be traced. Third, consequence ownership: when an opaque system produces a harmful output, the accountability question is not "can we explain this specific output?" It is "did we have adequate governance in place, and what are we changing now?" An answer to the second question is always available, regardless of the first.

Documenting AI Decision Trails

AI governance documentation is organizational memory. It records not only what decisions were made with AI assistance, but also what governance was in place at the time, what human review occurred, who was accountable for the outcome, and what was learned from the result. This documentation has three distinct values. For internal governance, it creates an audit trail that enables organizations to identify systemic patterns in AI decision-making, including errors that individual reviews might miss. For external accountability, it demonstrates to regulators and auditors that governance existed in practice, not just in policy. For organizational learning, it provides the data needed to improve AI deployment decisions over time.

Decision trail documentation does not require elaborate new systems. It requires discipline. A simple governance log maintained at the workflow level, recording which decisions used AI assistance, what review occurred, and who authorized the final decision, is substantially more valuable than a sophisticated governance platform that no one maintains consistently. Operational clarity in documentation matters more than technological sophistication in documentation architecture.

The Trust Recovery Playbook

Trust, once broken, does not repair itself. It requires deliberate, sustained action, and the sequence of that action matters as much as its content. The trust recovery playbook for AI governance follows four stages. Acknowledgment comes first: full, unconditional recognition that the trust failure occurred and that it has caused real harm. Leaders who move directly to explanation, "here is why this happened," before acknowledgment have inverted the sequence, signaling defensiveness rather than accountability. Explanation comes second: a clear, honest account of what failed in the system, the governance, or the judgment that produced the failure of trust. This explanation must be specific enough to be credible and honest about organizational responsibility, including leadership responsibility.

Remediation comes third: concrete, verifiable changes to governance, systems, or practices that address the specific failure. Vague commitments to "do better" are not remediation. Specific changes to validation protocols, disclosure practices, escalation pathways, and accountability assignments are. Transparency about the remediation plan, including timelines and mechanisms for affected parties to verify progress, is what separates performative accountability from the real kind. Demonstration comes fourth and takes the most time: sustained behavior over months and years that proves the changes are embedded. Trust recovered through sustained demonstration is typically more durable than the trust that existed before the failure, because it is now grounded in evidence rather than assumption.

DIAGRAM 5.10: THE TRUST RECOVERY PLAYBOOK

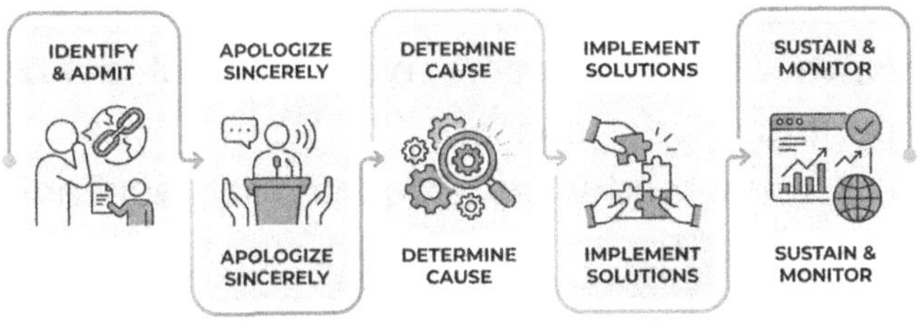

A structured process for leaders to rebuild trust after organizational breaches, focusing on accountability, corrective action, and ongoing validation.

The Trust Architecture Audit

The quarterly audit is the operational mechanism that keeps the Trust Architecture from becoming a theoretical framework. Conducted every ninety days, it asks the same set of diagnostic questions across all four layers, with the explicit goal of identifying which layer has degraded most since the previous audit and what specific action will address that degradation before it triggers a cascade.

System Trust Audit Questions

The System Trust audit covers five core questions. Leaders who cannot answer each question clearly have identified a governance gap that warrants immediate attention.

- Have any AI systems produced outputs that surprised the team in the past ninety days? If so, what was the root cause, and what governance change resulted?
- What is the current sampling protocol for human review of high-stakes AI outputs, and is it being followed consistently?
- Have any AI vendors been contacted about performance concerns? What was the response, and what accountability mechanism is in place?
- Are the deployment boundaries for each AI system in use still appropriate given changes in the operating environment, data inputs, or decision stakes?
- Can every leader who uses AI outputs explain, at an appropriate level, what those systems do, what they do not do, and where human review is essential?

Team Trust Audit Questions

The Team Trust audit focuses on the internal environment in which AI governance signals are sent and received. Honest answers require input from the team, not just self-assessment by leadership.

- Have team members raised AI-related concerns in the past ninety days? If not, is that because there are no concerns, or because the environment does not support raising them?
- Have there been AI-assisted mistakes in the past ninety days? How were they handled, and what did that handling communicate to the team about psychological safety?
- Have team members been given genuine input into any AI policy or workflow decisions in the past ninety days? Has that input been visibly incorporated or explained?
- Is the reskilling investment still visible and accessible to team members, or has delivery pressure displaced it?
- Are team members aware of how AI is used in workforce decisions that affect them, and do they have a clear path to raise concerns about those uses?

Stakeholder Trust Audit Questions

The Stakeholder Trust audit extends the governance perimeter to the external relationships that determine the organization's reputational position on AI.

- Have there been any external inquiries from clients, regulators, or partners about AI use in the past ninety days? How were they handled, and what follow-up is outstanding?

- Has the board received an AI governance update in the past ninety days that addressed risk as well as capability? What questions did they raise, and have those questions been answered?
- Have there been any changes to the regulatory environment relevant to AI that require a governance response? Has that response been initiated?
- Are vendor AI governance provisions being actively monitored, or are they contractual artifacts that have not been reviewed since signing?
- Have any stakeholder-facing disclosures about AI use become outdated as systems or use cases have evolved?

Self-Trust Audit Questions

The Self-Trust audit is the most personally demanding element of the quarterly review. It requires honest reflection on the leader's decision-making patterns over the past 90 days.

- Have there been situations in the past ninety days where I deferred to an AI recommendation that I had genuine reservations about? What drove that deference?
- Have there been situations where I overrode an AI recommendation? Did I document the reasoning? What was the outcome?

- Am I building the calibration record that allows me to distinguish where my judgment adds value from where it introduces error?
- Are the situations that land in the Assert quadrant of the Serious Decision Spectrum being treated as leadership decisions, not AI decisions with human approval?
- Am I modeling the relationship with AI that I want my team to have engaged, critical, accountable, and independent?

Diagram 5.11: The Quarterly Trust Architecture Audit

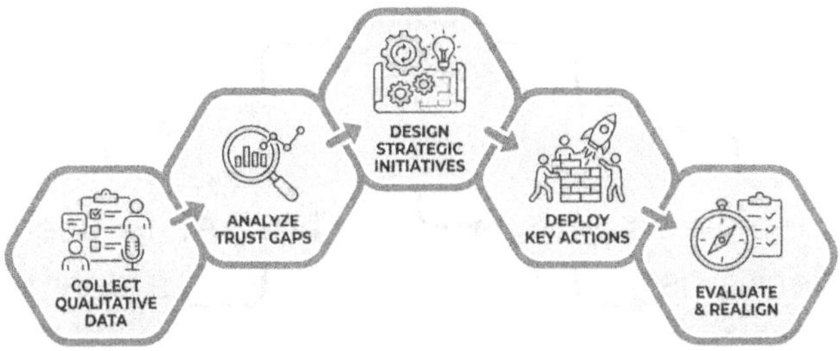

CONTINUOUS PROCESS: Regular assessment, analysis, intervention, and monitoring ensures organizational **integrity** and **leadership trust.**

The Serious Manager's AI Trust Checklist

The behaviors and artifacts in this checklist are the visible expression of a well-governed Trust Architecture. Leaders who can confirm each item have built the infrastructure that makes AI initiatives sustainable.

On System Trust:

- Documented deployment boundaries exist for every AI system in use, specifying where AI authority is appropriate and where human review is required.
- Output validation protocols are defined, assigned, and operational, not aspirational.
- AI vendor contracts include transparency provisions, audit rights, and accountability mechanisms for output failures.
- Leadership can explain AI system failure modes at an appropriate level and has a documented response protocol for when they occur.
- System performance is monitored on a defined cadence, with a clear escalation path when performance degrades.

On Team Trust:

- Employees are aware of how AI is used in decisions that affect them and have a clear path to raise concerns.
- Reskilling investment is current, accessible, and visibly endorsed by senior leadership.
- Psychological safety around AI failure has been assessed through team input, not leadership assumption.
- AI policy development includes genuine team participation with visible feedback loops.
- Leadership response to AI-assisted mistakes has been reviewed to confirm it reinforces rather than undermines a learning culture.

On Stakeholder Trust:

- Customer-facing disclosures about AI use are current, accurate, and include a human review option where appropriate.
- The board has received an AI governance briefing within the past ninety days that addresses risk exposure, not just capability milestones.
- Proactive regulatory engagement is documented and current.
- Vendor AI governance is monitored through active audit, not assumed through contract language.
- A trust recovery protocol exists and has been reviewed since the last deployment.

On Self-Trust:

- A personal calibration record exists, documenting AI alignment and divergent decisions with outcomes.
- The last Assert-quadrant decision has been reviewed to confirm that leadership judgment drove the outcome, not algorithmic deference.
- The quarterly Self-Trust audit has been completed honestly, including input from a trusted peer or coach.
- Leadership development on AI discernment, not just AI literacy, is part of the leader's current development plan.

- The leader can articulate the specific conditions under which their human judgment adds value that AI cannot provide.

Diagram 5.12: Trust Architecture Maturity Levels

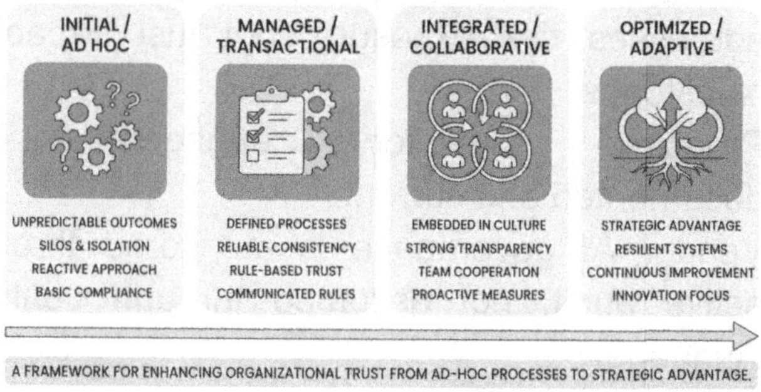

The Serious Leader's Commitment to Trust

Every chapter in this book describes the capability that AI-era leaders need to develop. Chapter 1 provides the technical foundation. Chapter 2 addresses the mindset shift. Chapter 3 equips the leader for better decisions. Chapter 4 gives the language. But capability without trust is potential without purchase; it cannot gain traction in the organization. The leader who understands AI and communicates well about it, but whom their team does not trust to use it fairly, and whose stakeholders do not trust to govern it responsibly, and who does not trust their own judgment enough to assert it when it matters, that leader cannot lead an AI initiative to durable success. They can launch it. They cannot sustain it.

Trust Architecture is not a remediation framework for leaders who have already broken trust. It is a proactive governance infrastructure for leaders who understand that trust does not maintain itself, and that in AI-powered organizations, the cost of trust erosion compounds faster than in conventional operating environments because the systems themselves are less transparent, the failure modes are less intuitive, and the speed of deployment outpaces most governance instincts. Building trust architecture before you need it is not insurance against a remote risk. It is the operating condition for everything else to work.

The AI-CLEAR model's Accountability dimension, owning AI outcomes, not just successes, but errors and unintended consequences, is not a personality trait. It is a structural commitment that is visible in governance documentation, in how leaders communicate during incidents, in how teams are led through AI-assisted mistakes, and in how external stakeholders are treated before, during, and after AI governance failures. Accountability, consistently expressed across all four Trust Architecture layers, transforms technical AI competence into organizational AI leadership.

Chapter 6 moves from the leader's relationship with trust to the harder challenge of aligning an entire executive team around AI, because trust that exists only in one part of the organization is fragile, and AI initiatives that lack genuine executive alignment do not simply move slowly. They generate the organizational contradictions that erode the very trust this chapter has been building. The work continues, and the Trust

Architecture you have built here will be the platform on which it rests.

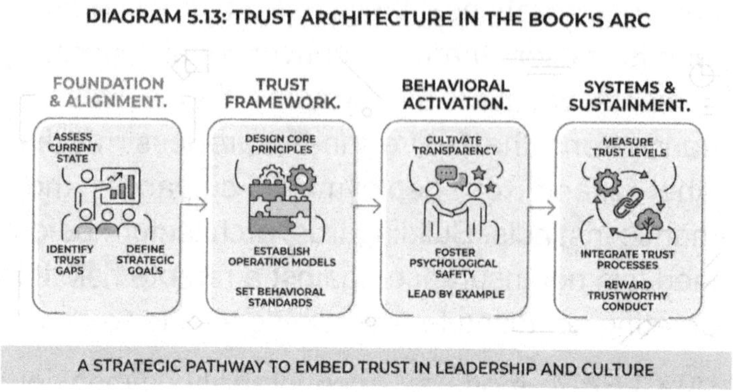

7 Why Agreement Is Not Enough: Getting Leadership Truly Aligned on AI

The Meeting That Looked Like Alignment

The quarterly executive committee meeting at a mid-sized regional financial services company was, by every external measure, a success. The Chief Executive Officer had just presented the company's AI transformation roadmap, eighteen months of pilots, platform investments, and workforce enablement programs, and the room had responded with genuine enthusiasm. The Chief Financial Officer committed her team to participate. The Chief Operating Officer volunteered two process areas for early automation. The Chief Human Resources Officer offered to co-sponsor the AI literacy training initiative. The Chief Technology Officer, who had spent six months preparing the strategy, left the meeting feeling that the hard work of building organizational commitment was done.

It was not done. Within three weeks, the CFO's team had quietly deprioritized their participation in the AI pilot, citing a pending audit cycle that had not come up in the meeting. The COO's two process areas required capital expenditure approvals that had not been factored into the roadmap timeline, stalling implementation by four months. The CHRO's literacy initiative was launched without a budget line because no one had formally included it in the departmental operating plan. And the CTO, now trying to hold the initiative together from the center, discovered that each executive had left the meeting with a subtly different understanding of what the AI transformation was supposed to accomplish.

This is not a story about a bad strategy or incompetent leaders. The executives in that room were experienced, capable, and genuinely supportive of the AI initiative. What they lacked was alignment. Support and alignment are two different organizational conditions, and confusing one for the other is among the most reliable paths to wasted investment, eroded credibility, and AI programs that never reach the scale they were designed for. This chapter is about the difference between those two conditions, why the gap between them persists even in sophisticated organizations, and the specific structures and disciplines that serious AI leaders use to close it.

DIAGRAM 6.1: THE SUPPORT-TO-ALIGNMENT GAP

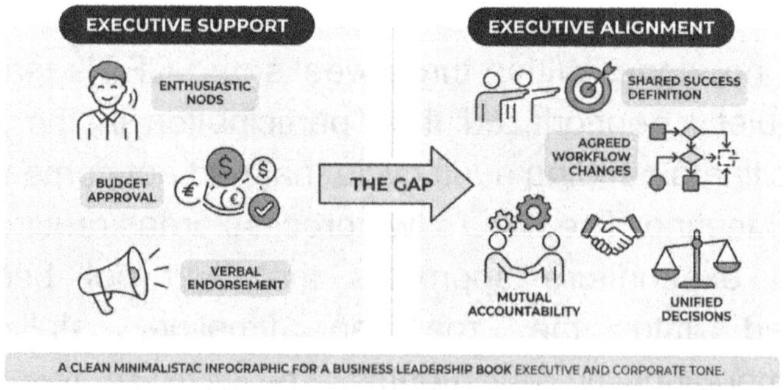

Defining Alignment: The Gap Between Support and Commitment

What Support Looks Like in Practice

Executive support is a posture. It manifests in speeches that frame AI as a strategic imperative, budget approvals for AI infrastructure and talent, enthusiastic participation in vendor briefings, and the visible endorsement of AI initiatives in town halls and all-hands communications. Support is easy to generate. It costs almost nothing in executive time, workflow disruption, or organizational commitment. And it produces almost no durable AI progress because support, without alignment, has no mechanism to sustain itself when priorities compete, and trade-offs become real.

Support is also, paradoxically, easy to measure and easy to report. A leader can point to a funded budget line, a signed charter document, or a photograph of the executive team at an AI launch event and credibly claim that the organization has executive support. This is why support gets reported as alignment. The metrics look the same from a distance. The difference only becomes visible when the initiative encounters its first serious obstacle- a budget freeze, a failed pilot, a departing champion, a competitor making faster moves- and the question of whether executives will hold the line or quietly redirect their attention reveals itself.

What Alignment Looks Like in Practice

Alignment is an operational condition, not a posture. A leadership team that is genuinely aligned with AI shares a clear, consistent definition of what the AI initiative aims to accomplish. They agree on which workflows will change, in what sequence, and at what pace. They have mutual accountability structures: they know who is responsible for which outcomes, what the decision rights are at each level, and how they will escalate when something is not working. And they can speak independently and consistently to employees, customers, board members, and external stakeholders about the organization's AI strategy and why it is the right one.

Operational clarity is an acid test. If you asked each member of your leadership team, separately and without preparation, to describe the top three outcomes your AI initiative will achieve in the next twelve months, and they gave you materially different answers, you have support but not alignment. If you asked them what would constitute failure, what signal would tell them the initiative needed to be restructured or paused, and they could not answer consistently, you have a governance problem that no amount of enthusiasm will solve. Mission-aligned AI leadership requires that the leadership team shares not just the ambition but the definition.

The Alignment Audit: Four Questions Every Leadership Team Must Answer Consistently

Before investing further in AI governance structures, a serious manager should run a simple diagnostic. Pose the following four questions to each member of the senior leadership team separately, and compare the answers. The degree of variance in responses is a precise measure of the alignment gap.

- What is the single most important business outcome our AI initiative will achieve in the next twelve months?
- Which three workflows will be most transformed by AI in that period, and who owns accountability for each transformation?
- What would a successful AI initiative look like to the frontline employees most affected by it?
- At what point would we decide to pause or significantly restructure the initiative, and who would make that call?

These four questions cover the essential dimensions of operational alignment: outcome definition, workflow accountability, stakeholder impact, and decision authority. Organizations with genuine alignment will produce answers that, while not identical, reflect a shared mental model. Organizations with support-not-alignment will produce answers that are consistent on aspiration and divergent on specifics, which is precisely where implementation lives.

Diagram 6.2: The Four-Question Alignment Audit

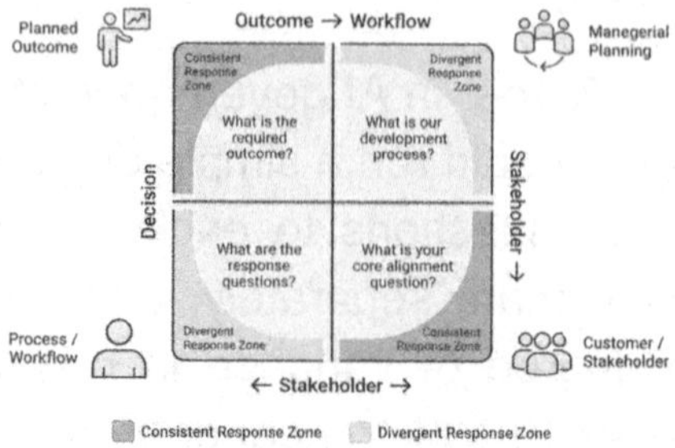

Caption: The four Four-Question Alignment Audit: a business leadership framework for organizational coherence.

Why the Alignment Gap Is So Persistent

The Prioritization Competition

Every executive in a leadership team has a strategic agenda that predates the AI initiative and will outlast it. The CFO is managing cost pressures and regulatory exposure. The COO is running a continuous improvement program that has been underway for three years. The CHRO is navigating a talent market that has not normalized. The Chief Revenue Officer is managing a sales cycle that demands her complete attention every quarter. When an AI initiative competes with these established agendas for executive bandwidth, it rarely wins unless it is structurally embedded within those agendas rather than positioned alongside them.

This is the first source of persistent alignment gaps: AI is positioned as an addition to the executive agenda rather than as a lens through which existing priorities are pursued. When that happens, AI becomes a fair-weather commitment. It receives attention when calendars are clear, and priorities are stable, and it gets deprioritized when the operational demands that define most executive lives crowd back in. The leaders who maintain alignment under these conditions are the ones who have made AI integral to the work, not supplemental to it, whose AI strategy is woven into their operating rhythm rather than scheduled as a separate initiative.

The Definitional Ambiguity Problem

Ask ten senior executives what "AI transformation" means, and you will get ten different answers, not because the executives are confused, but because the phrase is genuinely underspecified. For some, transformation means deploying machine learning to optimize existing workflows. For others, it means building new AI-native products or services. For others still, it means changing the organization's operating model to be data-driven at every level. Each of these is a legitimate interpretation. Each requires a different strategy, investment profile, and success metric. And when a leadership team holds different interpretations of the same phrase, they are not aligned; they are co-existing in a definitional fog that will produce collisions when execution begins.

Serious AI leaders address this by replacing the phrase "AI transformation" with a specific, bound statement of intent: what will change, for whom, by when, and what will be measurably different when it works. That specificity is uncomfortable because it forecloses options, creates accountability, and makes failure legible. It is also the only basis for genuine alignment. Ambitious language without an operational definition is not a strategy; it is an aspiration with a slide deck.

Temporal Misalignment

AI initiatives operate on timescales that do not match the rhythms of most executive accountability structures. A meaningful enterprise AI program, from initial capability assessment through pilot, validation, scaled deployment, and organizational adaptation, typically takes 18 to 36 months to produce measurable workflow-level impact. Most executives, by contrast, are accountable to quarterly results cycles, annual performance reviews, and strategic planning horizons that rarely extend beyond three years in operational detail. This creates a structural tension: the executive team is being asked to sustain alignment on an initiative whose payoff is genuinely long-cycle, while the organizational systems they operate within reward short-cycle thinking.

The response to temporal misalignment is not to pretend the tension does not exist; it is to design AI initiatives with a staged value architecture that produces visible, meaningful outcomes within each accountability cycle, while building toward the longer-term transformation. This means identifying the three to five workflow improvements that can be demonstrated within six months, the organizational capability gains that will be evident within twelve, and the structural changes that the eighteen-to-thirty-six-month program is ultimately designed to deliver. Leaders who can narrate this staged value story to their peers sustain alignment; leaders who ask for patience on a single long-term bet lose it.

The Technical-Business Divide

AI literacy is uneven across most leadership teams, and this asymmetry creates misaligned expectations that, over time, erode alignment. A technology leader who understands how large language models work will have a fundamentally different mental model of what is achievable and at what cost than a business leader who has absorbed AI capability claims through vendor briefings, media coverage, and conference presentations. Neither perspective is wrong, but they create divergent expectations that materialize as conflict at precisely the moments when unified leadership is most needed: when a pilot underperforms, when a capability that seemed straightforward turns out to be technically complex, or when the AI system produces an output that surprises everyone in the room.

The solution is not to turn all executives into technologists, but to establish a shared factual baseline, a common understanding of what AI tools can and cannot currently do, what responsible deployment requires, and what the realistic implementation timeline looks like. Building that shared baseline is itself an alignment activity, and most organizations underinvest in it. The AI steering committee, discussed in the next section, is the right venue for this ongoing literacy work.

Political Dynamics: When AI Becomes a Proxy

In some organizations, AI initiatives become sites for pre-existing political contests over resources, organizational influence, and whose domains expand and whose contracts are cut. When this happens, alignment becomes structurally impossible because the executives involved are not actually debating AI strategy: they are using it as a medium for a different negotiation. The signals that political dynamics are contaminating AI alignment discussions include disproportionate debate about governance structures relative to outcome goals, resistance that tracks organizational boundaries rather than substantive concerns, and alignment that appears to hinge on who proposed the initiative rather than what it will accomplish.

Experienced AI leaders recognize these dynamics and address them directly through one-on-one conversations that separate substantive concerns from political positioning, through governance designs that distribute rather than concentrate influence, and, when necessary, through escalation to the CEO or the board when political obstruction materially slows strategic progress. The Accountability dimension of the AI-CLEAR model, the leader's willingness to own outcomes and name problems, is particularly relevant here. Political dynamics do not resolve themselves. They require leaders with standing and the willingness to call them by their right name.

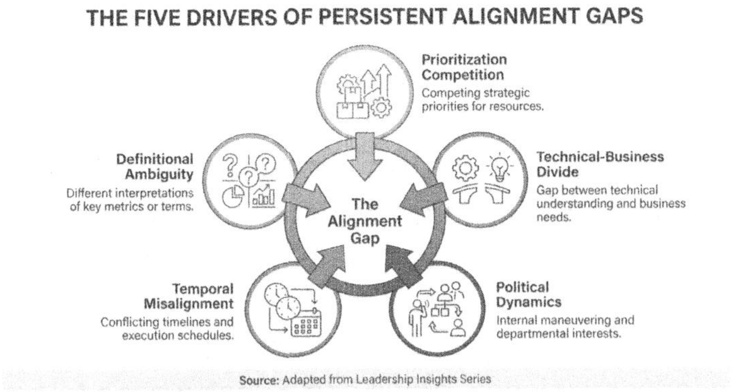

Building an AI Steering Committee That Actually Works

Why Most AI Governance Bodies Fail

An AI steering committee that holds meetings without making decisions is not governance; it is theater. And the theater is expensive. It consumes executive time, creates the appearance of oversight without substance, and provides a convenient organizational structure to blame when things go wrong. Most AI governance bodies fail because they were designed to represent stakeholders rather than to produce decisions. They are assembled with an eye toward inclusion, ensuring that every function has a seat, every perspective is heard, and that this is done without regard to authority. Representatives without decision-making power can inform but not commit. They can flag concerns but not resolve them. They can achieve consensus on recommendations that then go elsewhere for actual approval, adding time and friction while providing no accountability.

A steering committee that works is designed around decisions, not representation. It has a clear mandate that specifies what it decides versus what it informs. It has members with the organizational authority to make commitments on behalf of their functions, not advisors who must take everything back for approval. It meets on a cadence determined by the decision load, not by calendar convenience. And it has a chair whose role is to drive decisions, not to facilitate discussion. The distinction matters: facilitation produces conversation; governance produces commitments.

Composition: Who Must Be in the Room

The membership of an effective AI steering committee follows a simple principle: every function whose workflows, workforce, or risk profile will be materially affected by the AI initiative must be represented by a leader with the authority to commit that function. In most enterprise organizations, this means the committee includes the Chief Technology Officer or Chief Information Officer, the Chief Data Officer or equivalent, the Chief Financial Officer or a delegated deputy with capital authority, the Chief Operating Officer, the Chief Human Resources Officer, and the Chief Risk Officer or General Counsel. At the chair position sits either the CEO or a senior executive who reports directly to the CEO and carries explicit authority to arbitrate disputes and elevate unresolvable conflicts.

The committee should be small enough to make decisions, typically seven to ten members, and should include no more than one or two external advisors, whose role is to provide perspective rather than to vote. Representation from business unit leaders should rotate based on which units are most directly engaged in current AI initiatives, ensuring that the committee maintains operational contact with the work rather than becoming an abstract governance layer that loses touch with implementation reality.

Chartering the Committee: Mandate, Authority, and Cadence

The committee charter is the document that converts organizational goodwill into accountable governance. A well-designed charter specifies four things precisely: the committee's mandate (the scope of AI initiatives it governs), its authority (the decisions it makes versus those it informs or recommends), its accountability (what it is responsible for producing and on what timeline), and its cadence (how often it meets, under what conditions it convenes emergency sessions, and how decisions are recorded and communicated).

On authority, clarity is essential, and ruthlessness is appropriate. The charter should specify, without ambiguity, which categories of AI investment the committee approves versus which it reviews. It should name the escalation path for decisions that exceed the committee's authority. And it should include a standing authorization for the chair to make time-sensitive decisions between sessions, with a defined notification protocol. Governance bodies that require full committee approval for every decision are slow and lose the confidence of the leaders doing the actual implementation work. Governance bodies whose approval process is unclear produce decisions that get relitigated; alignment is destroyed not by disagreement but by the absence of a final answer.

Decision Rights: What the Committee Decides Versus What It Informs

Decision rights, the clear specification of who decides what, are the structural backbone of effective AI governance. Without them, every significant AI decision triggers a negotiation over who has authority, creating delay, ambiguity, and exactly the kind of political dynamics described in the previous section. The steering committee should maintain a living decision rights register that categorizes AI decisions into three tiers.

- Tier 1 Committee Decides: New AI initiatives above a defined investment threshold; changes to AI governance policy; decisions that materially affect workforce structure or customer-facing systems; initiative pause or termination decisions.
- Tier 2 Committee Informs: Vendor selection below a defined threshold; pilot design and

methodology; AI model evaluation criteria; team-level implementation decisions made by accountable executives.

- Tier 3 Committee Reviews in Retrospect: Operational AI decisions made within approved parameters; model updates within defined performance bounds; budget reallocations within approved ranges.

This tiering ensures that the committee's attention is focused on decisions that genuinely require cross-functional alignment, while freeing operational leaders to move quickly on decisions that are theirs to make. The Serious Decision Spectrum introduced in Chapter 3 is directly applicable here: the committee's role is to handle decisions in the Assert and Augment quadrants, where human stakes are high, and the organizational implications require senior judgment. Routine, well-defined operational decisions should flow through normal management channels, not through the steering committee.

Running Effective Alignment Meetings

An effective steering committee meeting is not a presentation session; it is a decision session. Every agenda item should be categorized as either a decision item or an information item, and the ratio of decision items to information items should be at least 2:1. Before each meeting, the committee chair should circulate a pre-read that gives members the information they need to arrive ready to decide, not to spend meeting time being briefed. Meeting time is decision time.

Structured disagreement is a productive feature, not a dysfunction to be managed away. Alignment is not unanimity; it is the ability to reach a decision that everyone commits to implementing, even if not everyone preferred it. Effective chairs create deliberate space for dissenting perspectives before calling for commitment, then hold the line on commitment once it is given. Documented decisions written in plain language, distributed within twenty-four hours, and accessible to the committee members who need to act on them are the mechanism by which alignment meetings produce alignment. A meeting that produces conversation but not documentation produces nothing durable.

DIAGRAM 6.4: THE AI STEERING COMMITTEE STRUCTURE

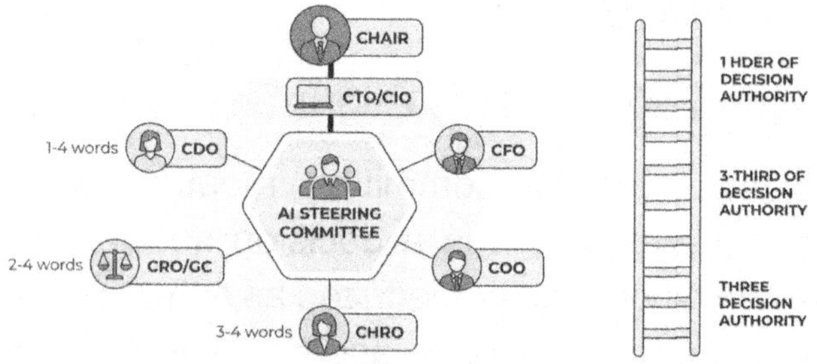

Caption: The infographic node accepts to the laweor for business leadership book.

The AI Champion: Your Most Important Alignment Asset

AI Champions Versus AI Sponsors and Why Both Matter

Organizational AI programs routinely distinguish between sponsors and champions, but the distinction is rarely explained with the precision it deserves. An AI sponsor is an executive who provides formal authority and resources to the senior leader whose name appears on the initiative charter, whose budget covers the investment, and whose organizational standing lends the program credibility. Sponsorship is transactional in the best sense: it is the formal organizational commitment without which serious AI programs cannot get off the ground.

An AI champion is something different and, in many ways, more powerful. The champion is the leader who actively advances alignment across formal governance touchpoints, who talks about the AI initiative in one-on-one meetings, in team settings, and in informal conversations in ways that sustain shared understanding and organizational energy. Champions do not need to be the most senior person in the room. They need to be the most credible, the most connected across organizational boundaries, and the most genuinely committed to the initiative's success. The sponsor provides the license; the champion provides the momentum. Both are necessary. Neither is sufficient except for the other.

Identifying the Right AI Champion

Four characteristics define an effective AI champion, and they are rarely all present in the same person, which is why champion identification deserves deliberate attention rather than default appointment. The first is organizational influence, both informal and formal, the ability to change minds through conversation rather than through authority alone. The second is cross-functional credibility: the champion's perspective is respected across organizational silos, not just within their own domain. The third is AI literacy sufficient to speak knowledgeably and confidently about what the initiative is doing and why, not at the technical level of an engineer, but at the conceptual level of a senior leader who understands the tools and their implications. The fourth and most important is genuine conviction: the champion believes in what the initiative aims to accomplish and cares whether it succeeds.

This last characteristic is non-negotiable. Appointed champions who do not genuinely believe in the initiative are worse than no champion at all. They communicate their ambivalence through the texture of their advocacy, in the qualifications they insert, and in the moments when they stay silent rather than speak. An effective champion is visibly excited about the work, personally engaged with the outcomes, and willing to spend their relational capital to defend the initiative when it is under pressure.

The AI Champion's Toolkit

Between formal steering committee meetings, which typically occur monthly or quarterly, the alignment they produce can erode silently. An effective AI champion actively maintains alignment through a set of ongoing practices. First, regular informal communication: brief, candid conversations with each executive stakeholder that surface emerging concerns before they calcify into positions. These are not update calls; they are alignment checks, intended to catch divergence early, when it is still easy to address.

Second, visible celebration of progress: the champion ensures that milestones, pilot successes, and workflow improvements are communicated across the organization in ways that reinforce the initiative's value and maintain leadership confidence. This is not spin; it is the deliberate management of the organizational narrative, which leaders often neglect in favor of technical execution. Third, proactive escalation: when the champion senses that a peer's commitment is wavering, they address it directly rather than waiting for it to surface in a governance meeting, where dynamics are more constrained and the stakes are higher. Alignment is maintained in the corridor, not just the conference room.

Building Alignment Resilience: When the Champion Leaves

One of the most common causes of AI initiative collapse is the departure of a key AI champion due to promotion, restructuring, or a shift in organizational priorities. When the champion leaves, the informal alignment work they were doing becomes visible in its absence, and the initiative can lose coherence faster than the governance structures can compensate. Serious AI leaders build for this contingency from the beginning, not as crisis planning but as organizational design.

Alignment resilience means distributing the champion role across at least two to three leaders who collectively cover the champion's cross-functional reach and informal authority. It means documenting the alignment work, decisions made, concerns addressed, and commitments given, so that alignment is encoded in organizational memory rather than residing in an individual's relationships. And it means developing what might be called local champions at the operational level: the product owners, department heads, and team leaders who carry the AI initiative's values and direction into day-to-day work without requiring the senior champion's constant attention.

The Product Owner as Local AI Champion

At the operational layer, where AI tools meet actual workflows and actual people, the product owner or equivalent role is the most critical alignment node in the organization. This is the leader who translates executive alignment into team-level practice: who decides which AI capabilities the team uses and how to use them, who maintains the feedback loop between frontline experience and senior governance, and who serves as the first line of response when AI systems produce unexpected results.

Product owners who are empowered, informed, and connected to the AI governance structure are the mechanism by which enterprise alignment becomes an operational reality. Product owners who are left out of the alignment conversation become bottlenecks: they implement without understanding, escalate without context, and become the source of the very misalignment that governance structures are designed to prevent. Building AI literacy, decision-making authority, and governance access for product owners is not a training activity; it is a structural investment in the pilot-to-production pathway that every AI initiative ultimately depends on.

DIAGRAM 6.5: THE AI CHAMPION NETWORK

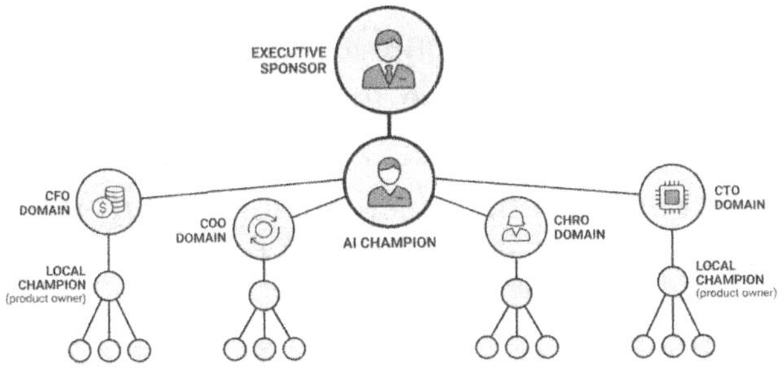

Corporate tone: This corporatœrship who a business leadership to leaderships executive and corporate tone.

Aligning Vision with Execution

The Strategy-Execution Translation Problem

The gap between AI strategy and AI execution is not primarily a technology problem. It is a translation problem. Executive leadership teams produce vision statements, roadmaps, and investment theses that are necessarily abstract; they operate at the level of organizational intent rather than implementation detail. The teams responsible for building, deploying, and operating AI systems work at the level of specific decisions, workflows, and technical constraints. Between these two levels sits a translation layer that, in most organizations, is underdeveloped, under-resourced, and underappreciated.

The translation problem manifests in a characteristic pattern: an AI strategy that is ambitious and coherent at the executive level becomes fragmented and inconsistent at the operational level, as different teams interpret high-level direction through the lens of their own constraints and priorities. A supply chain team and a customer service team, each implementing AI under the same organizational mandate, will make fundamentally different choices about vendor selection, data governance, change management, and success metrics, not because they disagree with the strategy, but because no translation mechanism connects strategic intent to operational specifics.

OKR-Based AI Alignment

Objectives and Key Results, when applied with discipline and specificity to AI initiatives, are among the most effective tools available for closing the strategy-execution gap. An AI-specific OKR structure connects the organizational vision to measurable team-level outcomes through a clear cascade: the organizational objective states the AI transformation goal in outcome terms; the key results at the leadership team level specify the observable changes in capability, workflow, or stakeholder experience that will indicate progress; the team-level OKRs translate those leadership-level indicators into specific, time-bound, measurable actions.

Critical discipline in AI OKR design is resisting the temptation to use technology activities as key results. "Deploy an AI chatbot to customer service" is an activity. "Reduce customer service resolution time by twenty-three percent while maintaining satisfaction scores above four-point-five" is a key result. The distinction matters because activity metrics track what is being done, while outcome metrics track whether it is working. Alignment built around activity metrics produces organizations that are busy but not effective. Alignment built around outcome metrics produces organizations that are focused on the right things and able to recognize when a particular approach is not delivering.

The 10-20-70 Principle in Action

Enterprise AI investment is typically distributed in a 10-20-70 ratio: roughly 10% for algorithms and models, 20% for data and technology infrastructure, and 70% for people, processes, and organizational change. The arithmetic of this distribution has important implications for executive alignment.

If the leadership team's attention is calibrated to the investment, seventy percent of executive attention on AI should be focused on the organizational change dimensions, such as how workflows are being redesigned, how employees are being supported through the transition, how management practices are being updated, and how accountability structures are being maintained. In practice, the opposite is usually true: leadership attention focuses on technology, platform choices, model performance, and infrastructure architecture, while organizational dimensions receive residual attention once technical decisions are made. This inversion is one of the primary reasons AI initiatives succeed in pilots and fail at scale. Pilots are predominantly technology problems. Scale is predominantly an organizational problem.

Serious AI leaders use the 10-20-70 framework as an alignment diagnostic: if technology updates dominate the steering committee's agenda, the governance body is focused on the wrong ten percent. Rebalancing the agenda to reflect the organizational weight of the people-and-process dimension is a structural intervention that drives alignment changes by forcing the conversation toward the dimensions where alignment is needed.

Managing the Expectation Curve

Every AI initiative passes through what might be called the valley of disappointment, the period between the early enthusiasm of a successful pilot and the organizational reality of enterprise-scale deployment, when progress is slower than expected, and obstacles are more complex than anticipated. The distance between where the organization is and where it was supposed to be becomes acutely visible to every executive involved in the original commitment. This period is the highest-risk moment for alignment: it is when sponsors quietly reduce their attention investment, when champions lose confidence in their own advocacy, and when skeptics who had been silenced by early success find their voice again.

Leaders who anticipate the valley of disappointment rather than discovering it manage it fundamentally differently. They brief their executive peers before the valley arrives, setting expectations for the period of complexity, naming the specific challenges they anticipate encountering, and framing those challenges as normal phases of transformation rather than as signals of strategic failure. They maintain visible engagement with the initiative during the valley, demonstrating through their own behavior that leadership commitment does not fluctuate with the difficulty curve. And they identify the leading indicators that, even in the valley, signal the initiative is on the right trajectory: early capability gains, workforce adoption rates, and operational metrics moving in the right direction, even if the headline outcome is still emerging.

Tempo as an Alignment Tool

Organizational attention follows organizational rhythm. AI initiatives that produce regular, visible milestones more effectively maintain leadership attention than initiatives structured as single long-horizon bets. This is not simply a communications strategy; it is a structural design choice. Serious AI leaders design their initiative cadence so that meaningful decision points, demonstrable progress markers, and alignment-affirming moments occur frequently enough to keep the leadership team engaged and the organizational narrative coherent.

A ninety-day initiative rhythm, with a defined milestone at the end of each quarter for the full leadership team to review and respond to, sustains alignment in a way an annual roadmap review cannot. The ninety-day cadence creates the conditions for what alignment requires: regular shared exposure to the same information, the opportunity to course-correct before drift becomes deviation, and the repeated reinforcement of shared commitments through collective decision-making. Tempo, designed deliberately, is an alignment infrastructure.

Diagram 6.6: The Vision-to-Execution Alignment Bridge

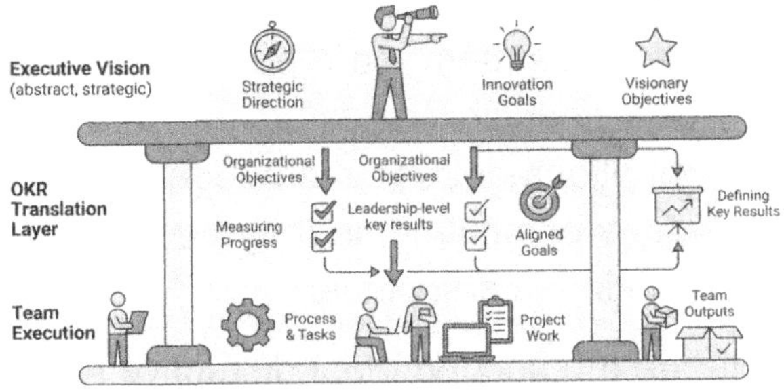

A minimiset infographic infographic designed ballon leadersa for business **/corporate tone**

Navigating Competing Priorities and Misalignment Events

The Most Common Alignment-Breaking Events

Alignment is not a state that an organization achieves and then maintains passively. It is an active equilibrium that requires continuous maintenance and is vulnerable to predictable disruptions. Understanding those disruptions in advance, knowing what they look like, how they unfold, and what responses are most effective, is essential preparation for any leader responsible for sustained AI progress.

Budget conflicts are the most common alignment-breaking event, and they follow a characteristic pattern: an organizational budget pressure emerges that was not anticipated when the AI initiative was scoped, and the AI investment suddenly becomes visible as a candidate for reduction. Leaders who are genuinely aligned absorb this pressure without losing their shared commitment to the outcome; they work together to identify where investment can be maintained and where it can be responsibly adjusted. Leaders who had support but not alignment use the budget pressure as cover to withdraw commitments they were never fully comfortable with in the first place.

Failed pilots are the second most disruptive alignment event. Every serious AI program will have pilots that do not perform as expected. This is not a risk to be avoided but a reality to be managed. What determines whether a failed pilot breaks alignment or strengthens it is the quality of the leadership response. Leaders who have established shared expectations about the experimental nature of pilot work, have built psychological safety into their governance culture, and respond to failure with analysis rather than attribution can absorb pilot failures without organizational fracture. Leaders who have not done this work discover that failed pilots become political events rather than learning events.

The Misalignment Early Warning System

Alignment erodes before it collapses, and the signals of erosion are legible if a leader is paying attention. The first signal is narrative divergence: the language different executives use to describe the AI initiative begins to differ in emphasis, optimism, and the specifics they highlight. When the CFO is describing the initiative primarily in terms of cost efficiency, while the CTO is describing it in terms of capability development, and the COO is describing it in terms of workforce impact, the leadership team has stopped sharing a story, which means they have already begun to drift from a shared strategy.

The second signal is meeting behavior: the quality and quantity of participation in AI governance meetings decline, with executives sending deputies rather than attending themselves, engaging with their phones rather than the agenda, or leaving early with increasing regularity. The third signal is decision lag: decisions that should be made in a governance session are repeatedly deferred, with no clear reason and no escalation. Decision lag is almost always a symptom of unspoken disagreement; someone in the room does not want to commit to the direction implied by the decision but is not yet willing to surface that concern explicitly.

The AI champion's most valuable function is operating this early warning system, staying close enough to the informal life of the leadership team to detect these signals before they become crises, and taking corrective action when correction is still relatively low-cost. The Trust Architecture from Chapter 5 is the relevant framework here: the champion must maintain sufficient Team Trust with each executive peer to have honest conversations when alignment is fraying, and sufficient Self-Trust to raise those concerns even when the organizational culture inclines toward optimism and positive framing.

Re-Alignment Protocols: Resetting Without Losing Momentum

When alignment has eroded to the point where it requires explicit intervention, a formal realignment process, rather than the informal corrections described above, the first imperative is to address the underlying cause rather than the surface symptoms. Alignment cannot be restored by scheduling an additional meeting, commissioning another presentation, or asking executives to reaffirm their commitment to a strategy that the realignment process has revealed they understand differently. Those interventions treat the symptoms of misalignment and inconsistent behavior without addressing the cause: usually a divergent understanding of what the initiative is for, who is accountable for what, or what success looks like.

A structured realignment session begins with an honest diagnostic: each executive briefly, without crosstalk, shares their current understanding of the initiative's top priority, the biggest obstacle they see, and the one decision they believe the leadership team needs to make that it has not yet made. This diagnostic almost always reveals the specific dimensions on which alignment has broken down. It creates the conditions for a targeted reconstruction of shared understanding, rather than a general recommitment to a strategy that everyone agrees to in the abstract.

When Alignment Cannot Be Achieved

There are circumstances in which executive alignment on an AI initiative cannot be achieved, and the underlying disagreements about strategy, risk tolerance, organizational readiness, or resource allocation are genuine and irreconcilable with the current leadership team and organizational context. This is a difficult reality to acknowledge, because it requires naming a conclusion that most organizations are culturally inclined to avoid. But the cost of pursuing an AI initiative without the alignment to sustain it is high: wasted investment, eroded credibility, organizational cynicism, and the specific harm done to the employees whose workflows and roles were disrupted by an initiative that was then abandoned.

Serious AI leaders are willing to have an honest conversation about organizational readiness when the evidence demands it. The escalation decision, the choice to pause an AI initiative because leadership alignment is insufficient to support it, is one of the most consequential decisions a leader in this space will make, and one of the least discussed. It requires the Accountability dimension of the AI-CLEAR model in its fullest expression: the willingness to own the outcome of a difficult judgment, to communicate it with clarity and without defensiveness, and to use the pause as an opportunity to address the root causes of misalignment before the initiative is restarted under better conditions.

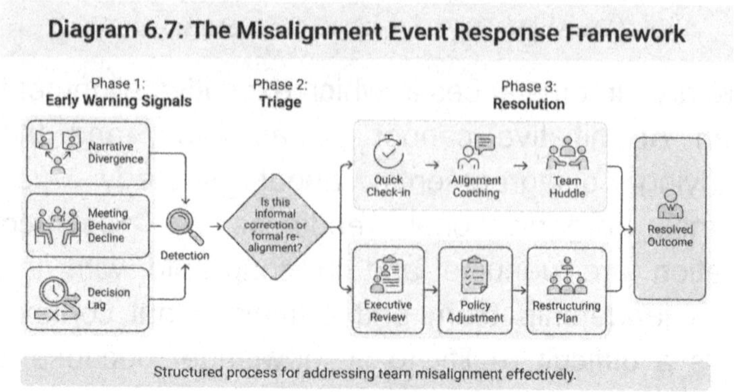

Cross-Functional Alignment: Beyond the C-Suite

Why C-Suite Alignment Is Necessary but Not Sufficient

Executive alignment creates conditions for AI success, but it does not guarantee it on its own. The decisions made in a steering committee meeting become organizational reality only when they are translated into action by the middle managers, team leaders, department heads, and individual contributors who run the day-to-day operations of an enterprise. And this translation is not automatic. A leadership team that is genuinely aligned on AI strategy can still find its initiatives stalled, circumvented, or quietly bypassed at the operational level because middle-management alignment is a separate problem that requires its own attention.

Middle managers occupy the most difficult position in any organizational transformation: they are accountable for operational performance while simultaneously being asked to change the processes that produce it. In AI initiatives, this tension is acute. A department head who is being measured on quarterly productivity targets while also being asked to invest time, attention, and workflow disruption in an AI implementation that will pay off in eighteen months faces a structural conflict that executive alignment, on its own, does not resolve. Addressing that conflict requires deliberate investment in the middle management layer's understanding of the AI initiative, their ability to translate it into team practice, and their performance management structures, which must be aligned to reward AI adoption rather than penalize the short-term disruptions it inevitably creates.

Building AI Alignment Cascades

Alignment cascades are the organizational mechanism by which a shared executive understanding of AI strategy flows down to the team level in a form that is specific, actionable, and grounded in the realities of day-to-day work. A cascade is not a communication plan; it is a structured process by which each level of the organization translates the alignment from the level above into its own operational language and surfaces the questions and constraints that need to flow back upward for executive consideration.

In practice, an alignment cascade works through sequential, structured conversations: the executive team aligns the strategy and translates it into three to five outcomes for each function. Each functional head convenes with their department leaders to translate functional outcomes into department-level priorities and success metrics. Each department leader does the same with their team leaders. At each level, the translation creates an opportunity to surface mismatches between the executive strategy and the operational reality mismatches that, if not surfaced, will become implementation failures. The cascade makes alignment visible and makes misalignment correctable before it becomes costly.

The Role of Shared AI Literacy

Alignment across organizational levels is only possible if the people at each level share a sufficient common language and understanding of what they are being asked to align around. In AI initiatives, this shared literacy cannot be assumed; it must be built deliberately, at scale, and with attention to the different literacy needs of different roles. An executive needs to understand AI's strategic implications and governance requirements. A middle manager needs to understand how AI changes the workflows they are responsible for and what their accountability for AI outcomes looks like. A frontline worker needs to understand how the AI tools they will use function, what they can and cannot do, and how to escalate concerns when systems behave unexpectedly.

Building this layered organizational literacy is itself an alignment activity. When employees at every level share a factual, calibrated understanding of what AI tools do and why they have been deployed, the organizational narrative about AI coherence that executive alignment is trying to sustain becomes much easier to maintain. People who understand what is happening are far less likely to fill information vacuums with anxiety, resistance, or informal workarounds that undermine official initiatives. Organizational AI literacy is not primarily about technical education; it is about the shared understanding that enables aligned action.

Product, Engineering, and Business Alignment on AI Features

At the operational layer, where AI is most intensively developed and deployed, a specific, recurring alignment challenge arises among product teams, engineering teams, and business stakeholders. This is not a personnel problem; it is a structural one. Product teams prioritize user experience and feature velocity. Engineering teams prioritize technical quality, scalability, and maintainability. Business stakeholders prioritize outcome metrics, cost management, and regulatory compliance. All three perspectives are legitimate. None is complete. And when they operate without a shared alignment protocol, they produce the classic failure patterns of enterprise AI: technically excellent systems that solve the wrong problem, business-aligned features that create technical debt, and products that satisfy no one because they represent a political compromise rather than a genuine solution.

A practical alignment protocol for product, engineering, and business teams on AI features begins with a shared definition of success, a statement of the specific user or business outcome the AI feature is intended to produce, written in language that all three groups can evaluate against. It continues with a structured process to surface and resolve cross-functional constraints before they become blockers during implementation. And it includes a regular cadence of joint reviews in which all three perspectives are present simultaneously, rather than sequentially, because sequential reviews produce documents that travel between teams, losing context and accumulating misunderstandings at each handoff. Simultaneous review produces conversations that resolve misalignment in real time.

DIAGRAM 6.8: THE AI ALIGNMENT CASCADE

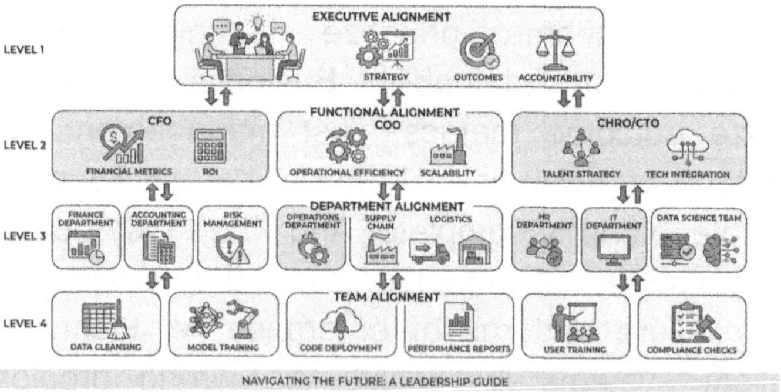

The Serious Manager's Alignment Checklist

The following checklist translates the frameworks and practices in this chapter into specific behaviors, artifacts, and decisions that a leader responsible for AI alignment can act on immediately. This is not a one-time assessment; it is a recurring governance discipline, calibrated to the ninety-day initiative rhythm described in the section on tempo.

Diagnosing Alignment

- Run the four-question alignment audit with each member of the senior leadership team separately, in a conversation rather than a survey. Compare responses for material variance.
- Map the five drivers of alignment gaps against your current organizational context. Identify which one or two are most active in your situation.
- Ask the AI champion to give you an honest assessment of where alignment is strongest and where it is most at risk. Pay attention to the qualifications, not just the headline.

Governance Structure

- Confirm that the AI steering committee charter specifies mandate, authority, accountability, and cadence with operational precision, not just a conceptual description.
- Review the decision rights register and confirm that every significant category of AI decision is

clearly assigned to one of the three tiers. Address any categories that are currently ambiguous.

- Evaluate the meeting agenda ratio: are at least two-thirds of agenda items decision items rather than information items? Restructure if not.
- Confirm that every committee member has the authority to perform their function, not just to advise or represent.

Champion Network

- Identify the current AI champion and assess their effectiveness against the four criteria: informal influence, cross-functional credibility, AI literacy, and genuine conviction.
- Identify at least two additional leaders who could serve as co-champions or successors and invest in building their understanding and connection to the initiative.
- Ensure that product owners and operational team leads have access to governance information, decision context, and escalation pathways, not just implementation directives.

Vision-Execution Connection

- Review the AI initiative's OKRs and confirm that key results are framed as outcomes, not activities. Revise any activity-based key results to reflect measurable organizational change.
- Assess the current distribution of leadership attention against the 10-20-70 principle. If

attention is concentrated on technology rather than people and process, rebalance the steering committee agenda.

- Brief the executive team on the initiative's current position on the expectation curve, where you are, including if you are in the valley of disappointment, and provide the leading indicators that signal continued progress.

Maintaining Alignment Under Pressure

- Establish the misalignment early warning system: assign the AI champion responsibility for monitoring the three signal categories, narrative divergence, meeting behavior, and decision lag, and for reporting concerns on a defined cadence.
- Prepare a realignment protocol in advance: know how you will structure the conversation if alignment breaks down significantly, who will facilitate it, and what decisions it needs to produce.
- Have an honest conversation about organizational readiness if the evidence warrants it, including, if necessary, the decision to pause rather than continue without sufficient alignment to sustain the initiative.

Diagram 6.9: The 90-Day AI Alignment Review Rhythm

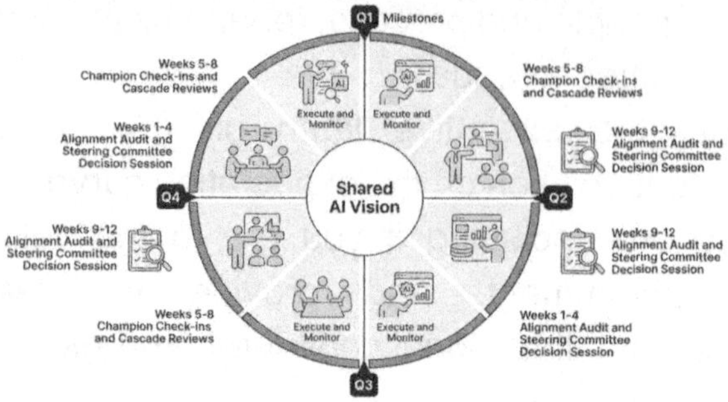

What Alignment Actually Requires

The leadership teams that sustain AI progress over multi-year transformation timelines share a common characteristic: they have done the unglamorous work of building actual alignment, not just generating visible support. They have conducted diagnostic conversations that reveal what each executive understands the initiative aims to accomplish. They have built governance structures with real authority and real accountability, not consultative bodies that provide cover without commitment. They have invested in AI champions who actively maintain a shared understanding between formal meetings and in alignment cascades that carry that understanding from the boardroom to the frontline. And they have developed the organizational discipline to address misalignment early, before it becomes a crisis that consumes the political capital that the initiative needs to survive.

This work connects directly to everything that has come before in this book. The mindsets introduced in Chapter 2, particularly the AI-CLEAR model's intellectual curiosity and strategic readiness, are prerequisites for the honest diagnostic conversations that alignment requires. The decision frameworks from Chapter 3 provide the structure that governance bodies need to be genuinely decisive rather than perpetually deliberative. The communication disciplines from Chapter 4 enable the clarity of shared language on which alignment depends. And the Trust Architecture from Chapter 5, particularly Team Trust between executive peers and Self-Trust in individual leaders, is the relational infrastructure on which every alignment structure ultimately rests.

Chapter 7 extends this foundation into the workforce dimension: once leadership is genuinely aligned, the organization's attention must turn to the people who will execute the aligned strategy, the teams whose capability, motivation, and structural positioning will ultimately determine whether AI ambition becomes AI performance. Alignment is not the end of the leadership work. It is the beginning of the condition under which the harder, more consequential work of human-AI teaming can succeed.

The organizations that get AI right are not the ones with the most sophisticated technology or the largest AI budgets. They are organizations where the people responsible for decisions, from the boardroom to the team level, share a coherent, honest, and operational understanding of what they are trying to accomplish.

That shared understanding is what alignment is. And it is available to any organization willing to do the work of building it.

8 Building the Team That Can Lead Alongside AI

A Leader Confronts the Readiness Gap

The Chief Information Officer of a regional financial services company had spent eighteen months building the strategy. The AI roadmap was thorough: natural language processing for document review, predictive models for credit risk, and a generative AI assistant for the relationship management teams. The board had approved the budget. The technology vendors were contracted and implementation-ready. And then the rollout began.

Within six weeks, the CIO was fielding uncomfortable questions. Adoption rates within the relationship management team were stuck below 15%. The credit risk team was running the AI model in parallel with its old spreadsheet workflow, using neither output to make decisions. Three senior analysts have submitted internal transfer requests. And in a candid conversation that the CIO would later describe as the most important of the year, a twenty-year employee told her plainly: “Nobody told us what this means for our jobs. Nobody asked us if we knew how to use it. And nobody has made it safe to say it’s not working.”

The CIO had built a technically capable AI program and an organizationally unprepared workforce to receive it. The gap between what the technology could do and what the team was ready to do with it had become the primary constraint on the entire initiative. She had done what most executives do: solved the technology problem first and assumed the people would follow. They did not.

This chapter is about closing that gap before it opens. It addresses the most consequential leadership challenge in AI adoption: building, developing, and sustaining the human team that operationalizes AI strategy. Technology without capable, confident, psychologically supported people is not a business advantage. It is an expensive capability that sits unused on a server.

DIAGRAM 7.1: THE AI READINESS GAP

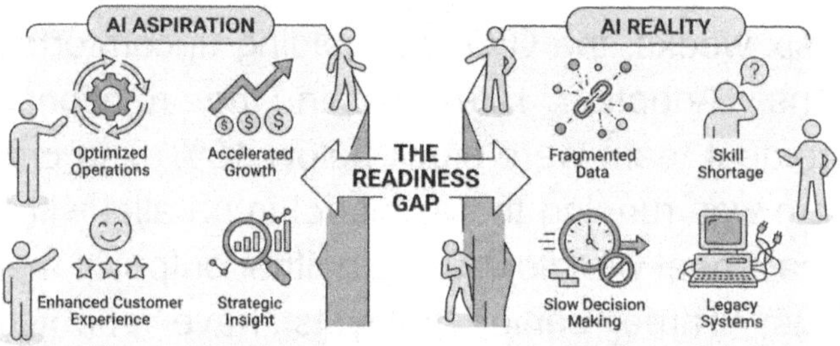

THE READINESS GAP REPRESENTS THE CHALLENGE OF BRIDGING THE DIFFERENCE BETWEEN ORGANIZATIONAL AMBITION FOR AI ADOPTION AND THE PRACTICAL REALITY OF CAPABILITIES, RESOURCES, AND CULTURE REQUIRED TO SUCCESSFULLY IMPLEMENT.

Why Workforce Readiness Is the Most Neglected Variable in AI Strategy

Most AI transformation programs allocate investment in roughly the same pattern: technology infrastructure first, governance second, workforce development third, or not at all. This sequence is backward. The organizations that achieve durable workflow-level impact from AI are not the ones with the most sophisticated tools. They are the ones whose people know how to direct, interpret, question, and improve those tools. Technology is a multiplier: an unprepared base multiplies low capability, while a strong base turns the multiplier into a genuine competitive advantage.

The stakes are not limited to productivity metrics. When workforces are unprepared for AI, the consequences cascade in three directions. First, adoption fails quietly: people find workarounds, revert to familiar processes, and the AI investment delivers a fraction of its projected value. Second, errors go uncaught when people do not understand what an AI system is doing, and they are not equipped to recognize when it is wrong. The judgment that catches AI failure requires the same depth of domain knowledge that reskilling programs must build. Third, the best talent leaves when skilled professionals see no development pathway or organizational investment in their AI capabilities, and they will go to organizations that offer one.

The Trust Architecture introduced in Chapter 5 is instructive here. Team Trust, the second layer that covers the leader-to-human-team relationship, depends specifically on employees believing that AI will augment their work rather than undermine it. That belief does not emerge from policy announcements. It is built on visible investment, transparent communication about role evolution, and psychological safety to enable honest engagement with the technology. Neglecting workforce readiness does not just slow AI adoption. It erodes Team Trust in ways that take years to repair.

The AI-CLEAR Leadership Model from Chapter 2 places Empowerment at its center for exactly this reason. The Empowerment dimension measures whether a leader creates the conditions for their team to work effectively alongside AI, including skill development, clear role boundaries, and permission to experiment without fear. Organizations that struggle with AI adoption almost universally score low on Empowerment. The leader may be Curious, may understand Leverage, and may hold themselves Accountable. But if the team has not been empowered, none of that individual leadership strength translates into organizational performance.

AI Readiness Assessment: Knowing Where Your Team Stands

Why Most Organizations Overestimate Their Workforce AI Readiness

Ask a room of senior executives whether their teams are ready for AI, and the majority will say yes, or at least "mostly." Ask the teams themselves, and the answer is consistently and significantly different. The executive layer tends to conflate tool access with capability, completion of a mandatory training module with genuine skill, and the absence of loud complaints with psychological comfort. None of these equivalences holds.

The overestimation problem has a structural cause: the people best positioned to assess readiness, frontline employees who perform the actual workflows, also have the least organizational incentive to disclose their gaps. In most corporate cultures, admitting unfamiliarity with a new tool is coded as a performance risk. Gaps stay hidden until they surface as adoption failures, costly errors, or quiet attrition. A serious readiness assessment creates conditions for honest self-reporting and supplements it with behavioral observations rather than relying on self-certification alone.

The Four Dimensions of Team AI Readiness

A practical readiness assessment examines four distinct dimensions, because capability in one does not imply capability in the others. An organization can have technically literate analysts who still cannot integrate AI outputs into actual workflows. It can have strong workflow integrators who lack the judgment to know when to override the model. Mapping all four dimensions reveals where the real constraints are.

- Technical Literacy: Does the team understand, at a working level, what the AI systems they are using do? This is not a requirement to understand the underlying mathematics. It is the ability to articulate what data the system uses, what it optimizes for, what its known limitations are, and what types of errors it is prone to making. Technical literacy is the prerequisite for all informed use of AI.

- Workflow Integration: Can team members embed AI tools meaningfully into their existing work processes? Many organizations discover that employees have access to tools but no workflow; they can open the system but have not developed the habit, the prompt discipline, or the process design to use it productively. Workflow integration is where adoption lives or dies.
- Judgment Capability: Can team members recognize when AI outputs should be trusted, when they require scrutiny, and when they should be overridden? This is the most strategically important dimension and the one most likely to be underdeveloped. Judgment capability requires domain expertise, contextual awareness, and what might be called calibrated skepticism, neither blind acceptance nor reflexive dismissal.
- Adaptive Capacity: Can team members learn, adjust, and update as the AI landscape evolves? This is the meta-skill: the ability to improve at improving. Organizations that invest only in current-tool proficiency find themselves conducting the same reskilling exercise every eighteen months. Adaptive capacity, properly cultivated, compounds over time.

Diagram 7.2: The Four Dimensions of Team AI Readiness

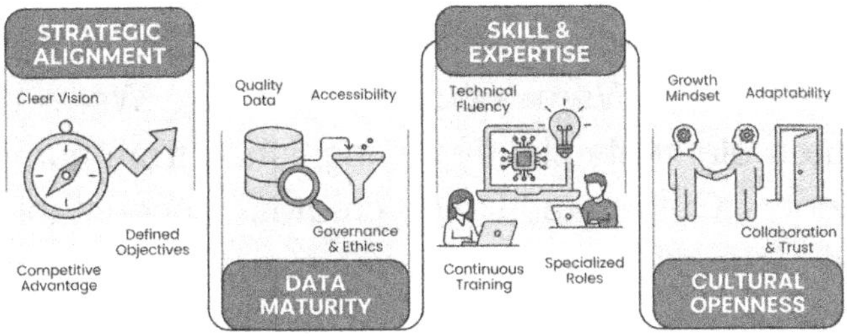

A framework for assessing and developing the essential capabilities for effective team-level AI implementation.

Running a Practical Readiness Assessment

A useful readiness assessment, rather than one that merely produces reassuring numbers, combines three measurement approaches. The first is a structured self-assessment, administered to individuals rather than teams, with questions that probe specific behavioral capability rather than general confidence. Questions like "describe how you verified the last AI-generated recommendation before acting on it" reveal far more than "rate your confidence in using AI on a scale of one to five."

The second approach is workflow observation: watch how work gets done. Which steps involve the AI tool? At what points does an employee bypass it? Where do delays occur? Observation reveals the gap between stated capability and demonstrated behavior. It also reveals workflow design problems that no amount of training will fix, instances where the AI tool has been inserted into a process that was not designed to use it.

The third approach is output auditing: examine a sample of work products that involved AI assistance. How well did the employee integrate AI outputs? Were errors caught? Were outputs verified? Were AI-generated elements clearly distinguished from human judgment? Output auditing creates accountability without surveillance; it measures results, not keystrokes.

Mapping the Readiness Gap and Prioritizing Investment

A readiness assessment is only useful if it produces actionable segmentation. After assessment, the team typically breaks into three meaningful categories. Those who score well across all four dimensions can become internal champions and peer coaches. Those with specific gaps in one or two dimensions can be developed efficiently with targeted investment. Those with fundamental literacy gaps require foundational development before more advanced skills can be built.

The prioritization decision is not simply about sequencing the third group first. Capability investment should be matched to strategic need. If your AI strategy depends heavily on judgment capability because the workflows involve high-stakes decisions where AI is in the Augment quadrant of the Serious Decision Spectrum, then developing judgment must be the priority, even if it means temporarily deprioritizing technical literacy programs for roles that are less central to that strategy. Operational clarity about which capabilities unlock the most strategic value is the leader's job, not the learning and development departments.

Reskilling Programs That Actually Work

Why Most Corporate Reskilling Programs Fail

The organizational graveyard of AI transformation is littered with reskilling programs that looked comprehensive in the planning deck and produced almost nothing in the field. The failure modes are consistent: mandatory online courses completed in the minimum possible time without content retention; training delivered in isolation from actual work that never transfers to workflow; programs designed to check a compliance box rather than change behavior; and cohort-based learning that begins with great momentum, loses participants to competing priorities by week three, and concludes with high satisfaction survey scores and no behavioral change.

What works is learning embedded in work, not adjacent to it. Reskilling programs with documented workflow-level impact share a common design logic: they teach skills at the moment and in the context where they will be applied; they use real work products rather than hypothetical cases; they build repetition over weeks rather than concentrating it in a two-day workshop; and they include a social accountability mechanism a peer group, a manager check-in, or a visible output that sustains engagement after initial momentum dissipates.

The Spectrum of AI Skills

Not everyone on the team needs the same AI skills, and treating the entire workforce as though they do is a waste of resources and a source of resentment. The skill spectrum runs from AI literacy to the broadest level to deep technical capability at the narrowest, and different roles require different positions on that spectrum.

- AI Literacy for All: Every member of the team, regardless of role, needs a working understanding of what AI systems are, what they can and cannot do, and how to engage with them critically. This is the foundation layer. It takes approximately four to six hours to deliver well and should be designed for someone who has never used an AI tool at work, rather than for someone who already has strong opinions about it.
- Workflow Proficiency for Practitioners: Employees who use AI tools regularly in their work need hands-on proficiency in the specific tools they use, calibrated to the specific workflows where those tools appear. This layer is role-specific and cannot be delivered generically. A credit analyst using an AI risk model needs a different level of workflow proficiency than a procurement officer using a contract analysis tool.
- Judgment and Oversight Competency for Decision Makers: Anyone whose role involves

acting on AI outputs or approving AI-informed recommendations needs specific development in judgment and oversight. This means understanding model limitations, recognizing common failure modes, and developing the professional confidence to push back when outputs do not make sense in the domain.

- Technical and Integration Capability for Specialists: A smaller group needs the technical depth to configure, evaluate, and improve AI systems. These are the prompt engineers, AI project leaders, governance specialists, and analytics professionals whose jobs are substantially defined by AI work. Their development pathway is longer, more specialized, and more expensive, but also more leveraged.

DIAGRAM 7.3: THE AI SKILL SPECTRUM

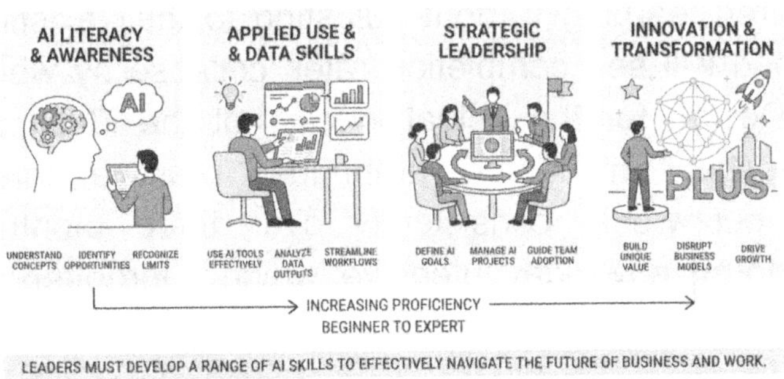

Building Learning Pathways That Fit Real Constraints

The honest constraint for most organizations is not budget; it is time. Managers already report that their teams operate at or above capacity. Adding a reskilling program to that load without removing something else or genuinely integrating learning into the flow of work increases the pressure on already-stretched teams.

The most effective design approach is the pilot-to-production learning pathway: start with a small cohort, measure actual behavioral outcomes rather than satisfaction scores, adjust based on what drives real capability change, and scale only then. Sponsors who want to announce enterprise-wide transformation immediately resist this approach. But programs scaled before validation produce large volumes of completed modules and minimal actual changes in capability. The small, rigorously evaluated cohort outperforms the enterprise rollout with measurement theater.

Learning pathway design must also address the practical reality of competing priorities. Programs that ask employees to spend four hours per week on structured learning without adjusting to their existing workload will see completion rates collapse by week four. Design for the actual week, not the idealized week. Thirty minutes of embedded practice, three times per week, consistently over three months, outperforms a two-day intensive, which is forgotten by the end of the following week.

The Manager's Role in Reskilling

The single most powerful variable in the success of reskilling programs is not curriculum quality, delivery format, or investment level. It is whether the direct manager actively supports the development.

Employees read managerial behavior precisely. A manager who makes time in team meetings to discuss new skills, asks about AI application in one-on-ones, and visibly adjusts their own behavior based on AI learning signals that reskilling is a genuine organizational priority. Absence from the process, or pulling employees out of learning sessions for competing demands, does the opposite.

This places a specific obligation on senior leaders: middle managers must themselves be developed before they can develop their teams. The manager who is asked to be an AI adoption champion but has not been given the skills, time, or permission to develop their own AI capability cannot play that role credibly. Investing in middle-manager AI capabilities is a prerequisite for workforce reskilling at scale, not a follow-on activity.

The Changing Role of the Middle Manager

Why AI Amplifies the Importance of Middle Management

There is a persistent and largely unfounded narrative that AI will reduce the need for middle management. The argument goes: if AI can aggregate information, generate reports, monitor performance, and flag exceptions, then the middle manager whose primary function is to relay information and supervise tasks becomes redundant. This argument mistakes the description of bad management for the description of all management.

The middle manager whose value is defined entirely by information relay, who passes directives down and status updates up, is indeed being displaced by AI. But that manager was not creating much value to begin with. The middle manager, whose value lies in team capability development, contextual judgment, relationship maintenance, and organizational translation, is not made redundant by AI. It makes them more important. As AI takes over routine tasks, the cognitive bandwidth previously consumed by task monitoring and report generation becomes available for genuinely complex human work that only effective managers can do.

The most significant shift is that AI changes what middle managers are accountable for. They are no longer accountable primarily for managing tasks. They are accountable for managing the capabilities of the humans who direct those tasks and, by extension, for the quality of every human-AI interaction within their team. This is a higher-order accountability, and it requires a different skill set.

Diagram 7.4: The Evolving Middle Manager Role

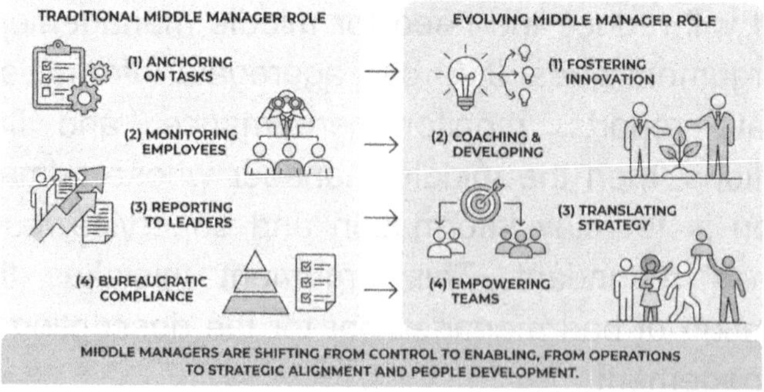

The New Middle Manager Skill Set

The AI-era middle manager operates across four primary functions, each of which demands competencies that traditional management development has emphasized.

- Orchestration: The manager coordinates across human and AI contributors, designing workflows that allocate tasks appropriately between the two. This requires a precise understanding of what AI systems do well, what they do poorly, and where human judgment is irreplaceable. Orchestration is not just process design; it is constant calibration as both AI capabilities and human skill levels evolve.
- Translation: The manager translates strategic AI direction from senior leadership into specific, actionable workflow changes for frontline employees. This translation requires fluency in both the language of executive strategy and the practical reality of day-to-day operations. The middle manager who cannot translate does not amplify strategy; they absorb it and let it disappear.
- Coaching: The manager develops individual team members' AI capabilities through ongoing coaching rather than episodic training. Coaching in this context means working through specific AI application challenges in real-world situations, providing feedback on how AI outputs were interpreted and acted upon, and

building judgmental capability that no online course can replicate.

- Escalation: The manager recognizes when an AI-related problem, an error pattern, an adoption failure, an unintended consequence, or an ethical concern is beyond the team's ability to resolve and routes it appropriately. Effective escalation is a skill, not a reflex. It requires knowing what escalation-worthy is and where to send it.

From Task Supervisor to Capability Builder

The shift from task supervisor to capability builder is the central transformation in the middle manager's role, and it requires specific organizational support to happen. Capability building takes time that was previously consumed by task monitoring. Organizations that want their middle managers to make this shift must do three things: redefine what success looks like for the manager role, reduce the administrative and reporting burden that currently consumes manager time, and provide coaching and development that enables managers to execute the new role rather than simply declaring it.

The Empowerment dimension of the AI-CLEAR model applies directly here. Senior leaders who want capable middle managers must create the conditions for middle-manager development with the same intentionality they expect those managers to apply to frontline teams. The cascade of Empowerment must be deliberately built from the top down, not assumed to emerge spontaneously.

Organizational Design Implications

As middle managers evolve toward the orchestration-and-coaching model, organizational design must evolve with them. Spans of control that made sense when the manager's primary activity was task supervision may be too wide when the manager's primary activity is coaching individual capability. Decision rights centralized in the manager role may need to be distributed to AI-capable frontline employees, who can now access information and analysis that previously required managerial mediation.

The organizations that navigate this most effectively approach it as a deliberate redesign rather than an organic drift. They map current managerial activities, identify which are being displaced by AI and which are expanding in importance, and redesign the role accordingly. This is a significant organizational investment, but it is substantially smaller than the cost of leaving middle managers in roles that no longer fit the work they are being asked to do.

Hiring for AI-Era Competencies

What AI-Era Hiring Actually Looks Like

The most common mistake in AI-era hiring is conflating technical familiarity with AI readiness. Candidates who have used generative AI tools are not necessarily better equipped for AI-augmented work than those who have not. The competencies that matter are not primarily technical. They are cognitive and behavioral, substantially harder to assess in an interview than Python fluency.

This does not mean technical capability is irrelevant. Roles that involve configuring, evaluating, or governing AI systems require genuine technical depth. But for most roles where AI augments existing professional work knowledge, client-facing roles, analytical roles, and operational roles, the critical differentiators are learning agility, systems thinking, comfort with ambiguity, and what might be called collaborative judgment. These are the competencies that determine whether someone will thrive in a working environment continuously reshaped by changes in AI capabilities.

DIAGRAM 7.5: AI-ERA HIRING COMPETENCY FRAMEWORK

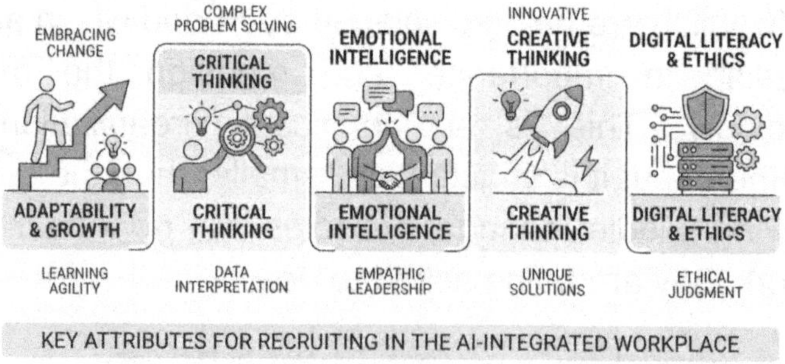

The Competencies That Matter Most

Learning agility is the capacity to acquire new skills and update mental models quickly in response to changing environments. In an AI context, it means learning a new

AI tool, developing effective use patterns, and then updating those patterns when the tool changes or a better approach emerges. Learning agility is not raw intelligence; it is the openness to unlearning and relearning that intelligence alone does not guarantee.

Systems thinking is the capacity to understand how parts of a system interact, revealing the consequences and feedback loops that are invisible in a narrow view. In an AI context, it means understanding how outputs from one workflow affect downstream decisions, how changes in model behavior ripple through dependent processes, and how an AI recommendation that appears locally optimal might be globally suboptimal. Systems thinkers catch integration errors that specialists miss.

Comfort with ambiguity is the capacity to make sound judgments and take decisive action without full information. AI does not eliminate ambiguity; it changes its shape. The worker who needs complete certainty before acting is not well-positioned in an environment where AI provides probabilistic outputs, incomplete datasets, and confidence scores that require interpretation. Comfort with ambiguity is not the absence of rigor. It is the disciplined capacity to work with incomplete information without becoming either paralyzed or reckless.

Collaborative judgment is the capacity to integrate AI recommendations into a broader decision framework that includes domain expertise, organizational context, stakeholder relationships, and ethical considerations. It is the skill of neither dismissing nor deferring to AI, of treating AI as a sophisticated input while retaining the final authority of the human decision-maker. This is the competency that the Serious Decision Spectrum was designed to develop: the discernment to know which quadrant a decision belongs in and to act accordingly.

Evaluating AI Competency in Interviews

When used correctly, behavioral interview questions provide a more reliable signal of AI-era competencies than any technical assessment. The key is to probe the behavioral pattern rather than the candidate's opinion of AI.

- For learning agility: "Tell me about a time when a tool or system you relied on changed significantly. How did you adapt? What did you have to unlearn?"
- For systems thinking: "Describe a decision you made that had unintended downstream consequences. How did you discover them? What did you change?"
- For comfort with ambiguity: "Describe a situation where you had to act on incomplete information. How did you decide what you knew enough to proceed, and how did you manage the risk of what you did not know?"
- For collaborative judgment: "Tell me about a time when a quantitative model or analysis pointed in one direction and your professional judgment pointed in another. How did you navigate that?"

These questions do not presuppose AI experience. They probe cognitive and behavioral patterns that translate into AI competency, regardless of the candidate's familiarity with current tools. A candidate who demonstrates strong collaborative judgment with a spreadsheet will do the same with an AI system. A candidate who shows no capacity to question quantitative outputs will not develop that capacity because the outputs now come from an AI model.

Cognitive Diversity as a Performance Requirement

The business case for cognitive diversity in AI teams is not primarily ethical, though the ethical case stands on its own. It is operational. Homogeneous teams share the same blind spots, so they tend to fail in similar ways. They ask the same questions, which means they make the same errors. They make the same assumptions about what the AI model is measuring, which means they apply its outputs in systematic, inappropriate ways.

Diverse teams, with different analytical styles, different domain backgrounds, and different comfort levels with AI, catch more errors, ask more varied questions, and produce more robust collective judgment. Mission-aligned AI leadership actively builds this diversity into the team structure, not as a compliance obligation but as a deliberate strategy for building judgment capability that no individual possesses alone.

The Build-Versus-Buy Talent Decision

Organizations face a genuine tension in AI talent strategy: the skills needed are in high demand externally, external hiring is costly, and external hires without organizational context often fall short of expectations. Meanwhile, internal development takes time and produces uneven results. The honest answer is that most organizations need both, and the strategic question is where each approach applies.

Build internally when competencies are primarily behavioral, when organizational context is critical to performance, when talent exists but requires investment, and when the risk of attrition from external hiring is high. But externally, when technical depth does not exist internally and cannot be developed in the relevant timeframe, when a new capability needs to be seeded quickly, or when an external hire can accelerate internal talent development through demonstrated practice. The mature talent strategy deliberately uses both pathways.

Psychological Safety as AI Adoption Infrastructure

Why Psychological Safety Is Foundational

Psychological safety, the shared belief that the team environment is safe for interpersonal risk-taking, is not a cultural amenity. In an AI context, it is operational infrastructure. When people do not feel safe raising concerns about AI outputs, errors go unreported. When they do not feel safe admitting they do not understand a tool, capability gaps go invisible. When they do not feel safe failing in an experiment with a new AI application, nobody experiments, and the organization loses the iterative learning that produces genuine gains in capability. The absence of psychological safety makes every other AI workforce investment less effective.

Chapter 5's Trust Architecture makes clear that Team Trust is the layer that covers the leader-to-human-team relationship, and it depends specifically on employees believing that AI will not be used against them. Psychological safety is the mechanism through which that belief is either built or destroyed. A team where AI performance data is used to surveil individual behavior, where AI adoption is treated as a compliance metric with consequences for low scores, or where leaders respond to AI-related mistakes with blame rather than with investment in learning, will not produce the open, experimental engagement that AI adoption requires. It will produce a performance-theater appearance of adoption without any underlying capability.

The Fear Landscape: What People Are Actually Afraid Of

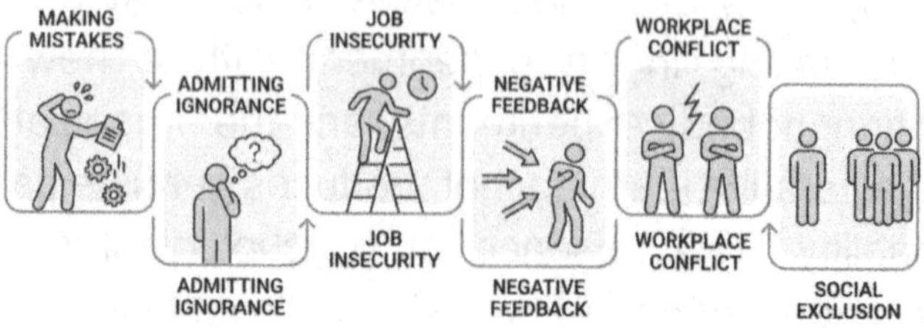

DIAGRAM 7.6

The Fear Landscape

Understanding what people are afraid of when AI enters the workplace is the prerequisite for addressing it productively. The fears are not uniform, and responses that work for one type of fear can amplify another. Leaders who treat all AI anxiety as a single phenomenon, "fear of change," miss the specificity required to respond effectively.

The fear of job displacement is the most visible but not always the most operationally significant. Many employees have mitigated this fear by assessing which parts of their work are likely to be automated and which are not. What they have not moderated is the fear of skill obsolescence, the worry that they are falling behind in a skills race they did not sign up for and cannot pace adequately while holding a full-time job. This fear is addressed by genuine, accessible development investment, not a catalog of online courses, but a clear, supported pathway.

The fear of performance surveillance is among the most corrosive and the least discussed. Employees who suspect AI tools are being used to monitor their behavior disengage from honest use of AI. They optimize for being seen as using AI rather than actually using it to improve their work. This fear is addressed by transparency: be explicit about what is being measured, why, and by whom. The principle of responsible-by-design applies to internal workforce measurement as directly as it does to customer-facing AI systems.

The identity threat, the fear that AI will devalue professional expertise, requires the most sophisticated response. Many professionals have built their identities around competencies that AI now appears to demonstrate. The response is not reassuring that their expertise is still valued; employees see through that. The response is a genuine reframing: their expertise is precisely what enables them to direct, question, and improve AI. The machine can pattern-match. Only the expert can tell the machine what matters when its patterns are missing.

Building Safety Through Transparency

Transparency is the primary tool for building psychological safety in an AI context, and it must be specific rather than general. General statements, such as "AI will make your work better," lack credibility because they are neither actionable nor verifiable. Specific transparency does four things: it explains how AI will affect each role category, not just the organization; it describes how performance will be evaluated in an AI-augmented context; it communicates how AI adoption will factor into career development; and it creates a feedback channel through which employees can report AI-related concerns without professional risk.

The most effective transparency mechanism is a direct conversation between a manager and an individual employee about what AI means for their specific role, skills, and career. No enterprise communication strategy reaches every employee at the level of detail and trust that a well-equipped manager can in a twenty-minute one-on-one. This reinforces the need for middle manager capability development to precede, or at a minimum accompany, any broad AI deployment. Managers who cannot speak credibly about AI's impact on their team cannot be the transparency vehicle that psychological safety requires.

Creating Permission to Experiment

Organizations that want employees to develop genuine AI capabilities must grant explicit permission to experiment and accept that experiments fail. The culture that punishes AI-related mistakes produces employees who use AI only when already certain of the outcome, which is precisely the low-risk scenario where AI adds the least learning value.

Permission to experiment is not the absence of accountability. It is a specific governance structure: experiments are bounded, expected outcomes are defined in advance, failure is analyzed rather than attributed, and learning is captured and shared. The organization that treats an AI experiment failure as an intelligence asset, a concrete data point about what does not work and why, builds a learning culture that compounds in capability over time. The organization that treats it as a performance liability gets the organizational behavior it has signaled: caution, conformity, and minimal risk-taking.

The Leader as Coach

The shift from directing work to developing people who direct AI is the most significant behavioral change required of leaders at every level of the organization. In a task supervision model, the leader's value is in having the answers, knowing how the work should be done, and ensuring it is done that way. In a capability-building model, the leader's value lies in developing the people who will develop and apply better answers than any single leader could.

Coaching here is not a soft skill. It is a specific behavioral practice: asking questions that develop the employee's own judgment rather than providing the answer; creating space for the employee to work through AI application challenges before intervening; providing feedback on the quality of the employee's AI oversight rather than just the quality of the output; and modeling learning behavior being visible about your own gaps, questions, and development in AI capability. Leaders who ask "how did you decide to trust that output?" teach an entire team to ask themselves the same question.

Managing Resistance Without Dismissing It

Why Resistance to AI Is Often Rational

The executive response to AI resistance is often a category error: treating rational concern as irrational fear and responding to it with communication campaigns rather than substantive engagement. This response fails because it addresses the wrong problem. In many organizations, AI resistance is not primarily emotional; it is a sophisticated professional judgment that the current AI deployment has real problems that are not being acknowledged.

The middle manager who resists adopting an AI-generated performance assessment framework is not necessarily afraid of change. They may have a well-founded concern that the model's training data does not adequately represent the range of roles in their team, that the performance metrics it optimizes are not the ones that actually predict long-term employee success, or that using it without modification will produce assessments that damage trust with the people they manage. That resistance is intelligence, not obstruction. Dismissing it as change aversion loses the most valuable feedback the organization could receive about a deployment with genuine flaws.

DIAGRAM 7.7: THE THREE SOURCES OF AI RESISTANCE

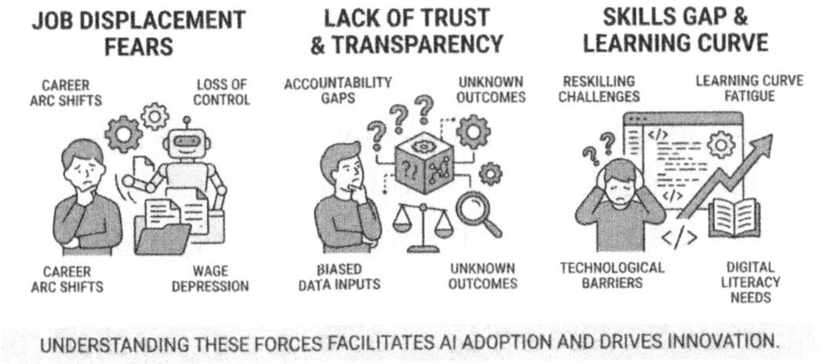

The Three Sources of Resistance

Effective resistance management begins with accurate diagnosis. Resistance that comes from different sources requires different responses, and a response designed for one source can actively worsen another. The three primary sources are capability gaps, trust deficits, and identity threats.

Capability gap resistance is the most straightforward to address and the most misdiagnosed. An employee who resists using an AI tool because they do not understand it well enough to use it confidently will not announce that limitation; they will generate other objections. The strategic objection ("this tool doesn't fit our workflow"), the quality objection ("the outputs aren't reliable enough"), or the timing objection ("this isn't the right time to introduce this change") may all be rationalizations for an underlying capability gap. The diagnostic test is simple: offer genuine, non-judgmental developmental support and observe whether the objections persist.

Trust-deficit resistance reflects a specific failure in organizational credibility. When employees do not trust that leadership will honor commitments regarding AI's impact on jobs, evaluations, or career development, they resist adoption as a rational protective measure. Trust deficit resistance is addressed by closing the credibility gap through visible behavior that demonstrates commitments are real and being kept. Communication strategies that are not backed by behavioral change intensify rather than resolve resistance to trust deficits.

Identity threat resistance is the most complex and requires the most sustained engagement. When AI challenges the competencies through which a professional has built their identity and their reputation, the threat is not hypothetical, and the response is not irrational. The senior analyst who spent 15 years developing a judgment capability that an AI system now appears to replicate faces a genuine disruption to their professional identity. Addressing it requires a reframing that is credible, not "your expertise is still valued" as a consolation, but "your expertise is what makes you capable of doing what this system cannot: directing it, improving it, and knowing when to override it." The reframing must be followed by a concrete workflow redesign that places the expert in a higher-order role, not just a new label for the same tasks.

Converting Skeptics Into Contributors

The most powerful tool for converting skeptics is not persuasion. It is experience, specifically early wins, that demonstrates value to the skeptic themselves. The employee who resists an AI tool until they discover it saves them three hours of preparation on a tedious task is not convinced by the argument that AI is valuable. The experience of value converts them. Design the early adoption experience to generate that discovery for the skeptic, not just to confirm it for the enthusiast.

Visible proof is the second powerful converter: when a colleague, the skeptic, respects not a technology evangelist, but a recognized domain expert, visibly adopts and benefits from an AI application, the social signal is far stronger than any executive communication. This is why investing in the first cohort of adopters is strategically important beyond that cohort's individual contribution. The early adopter who becomes a credible peer advocate is worth dozens of enterprise communication campaigns.

When Resistance Signals a Real Problem

The most mission-aligned response to AI resistance is to treat it systematically as a potential source of intelligence about the deployment. Not all resistance signals a real problem, but some of it does, and the organizations that cannot distinguish between the two take on the risk of scaling flawed deployments past the point where correction is affordable. A formal mechanism for capturing, analyzing, and acting on employee concerns about AI applications is not a concession to resistance; it is responsible governance.

Patterns of resistance that focus on specific roles, workflows, or team contexts should trigger a structured review of the deployment in that area. If the professionals most expert in a domain consistently find AI outputs unreliable for that domain, that finding deserves investigation rather than dismissal. If the teams with the highest psychological safety, where people feel safest raising concerns, are producing the most AI-related complaints, that may mean the AI has real problems that other teams are experiencing but not reporting. Leadership that creates channels for honest feedback and takes that feedback seriously builds a workforce that is invested in making AI work rather than either performatively compliant or silently disengaged.

Sustaining Team Capability in a Moving Landscape

Why AI Workforce Development Is Continuous

The most important design assumption for an AI workforce strategy is that it will never be complete. Organizations that treat AI capability development as a transformation project with a beginning, a budget, and an endpoint find themselves perpetually behind. The AI landscape does not stop evolving when the reskilling program concludes. Tools change, use cases expand, governance requirements shift, and the competitive context moves. Workforce capability must move with it.

This does not mean the workforce must sprint indefinitely. It means the organization must build systems for continuous learning that do not depend on heroic effort or constant executive sponsorship. The goal is not a workforce that is always in training. It is a workforce that is always learning through the structure of their work, their peer relationships, their feedback mechanisms, and their access to practical insight into what is actually changing and why it matters.

Diagram 7.8: The Continuous AI Capability Development System

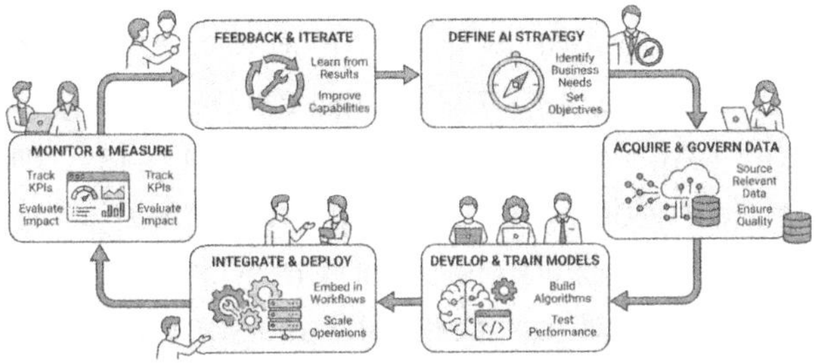

A continuous, cyclical process to build organizational AI capability, driving sustained value and competitive advantage.

Building Organizational Learning Systems

Organizational learning systems for AI capability have three essential components. The first is an ongoing sensing mechanism, a regular, lightweight process for identifying what is changing in the AI capability landscape relevant to the organization's work, and what the operational implications are. This does not require a dedicated intelligence function. It requires that a person or a small group be accountable for maintaining current awareness and translating it into practical guidance.

The second component is a knowledge management infrastructure that captures what the organization learns from its AI deployments. Most organizations invest heavily in deploying AI and almost nothing in capturing what they learn from those deployments. The team that discovered a reliable approach for a specific workflow has developed organizational knowledge worth sharing. The team that found a consistent failure mode has developed intelligence worth distributing. Without a capture mechanism, that learning evaporates when team composition changes.

The third component is a governance structure that reviews workforce capability implications whenever a significant AI deployment decision is made. Responsible-by-design in workforce terms means that no deployment decision is complete without an explicit assessment of workforce readiness requirements.

Communities of Practice and Peer Learning

Communities of practice, informal groups of practitioners who share a domain and meet regularly to exchange practical knowledge, are among the most effective and least expensive learning infrastructure an organization can build. In an AI context, they serve three functions: creating a forum for sharing domain-specific AI applications, which yields more relevant guidance than any general training program; sustaining social accountability for ongoing learning; and surfacing frontline AI experiences, including failures and concerns, to the leaders who need to know.

Peer learning is particularly well-suited to the rapid, iterative nature of AI capability development. The person who discovered a better way to use an AI tool last week is a more current source than any course designed six months ago. Building peer learning mechanisms into the flow of work through brief sharing at team meetings, after-action reviews of AI-involved projects, and peer coaching pairs compounds learning across the organization without requiring proportional increases in formal training investment.

Retention Strategies for AI-Capable Talent

AI-capable employees are among the most mobile in the labor market. The competencies that define effectiveness in AI-augmented work- learning agility, systems thinking, and judgment capability- are highly portable and in strong demand. Leaders who invest in developing those competencies without investing equally in retaining the people who develop them are building the competitor pipeline.

Retention for AI-capable talent operates on a different logic than retention for more specialized technical roles. The AI-capable knowledge worker is not retained solely by compensation, though compensation must be competitive. They are retained by the quality of the work, the pace of learning, the caliber of colleagues, and the clarity of their growth pathway. They are particularly sensitive to stagnation in organizational learning in environments where the work no longer develops their capabilities. Ironically, the worst retention outcome is an organization that develops AI capabilities in its people and then provides no outlet for those capabilities in meaningful work.

The retention strategy that works is the same as the development strategy: create challenging work that requires AI-era competencies, provide visibility into the learning pathway, invest in people who have demonstrated capability, and give them genuine authority over the AI workflows they are responsible for. The Empowerment dimension of the AI-CLEAR model is as much a retention mechanism as it is a development mechanism. People stay where they are growing and where their judgment is trusted.

The Long Game: Building an Organization That Gets Better at Getting Better

The ultimate measure of an AI workforce strategy is not the level of capability achieved at any single point in time. It is the rate at which the organization develops capability relative to the pace of change in the AI landscape. An organization that builds strong capabilities in current AI tools but lacks adaptive capacity will find itself in a persistent catch-up cycle. An organization that builds adaptive capacity, the meta-skill of learning how to learn with AI, will find that each new AI development is less disruptive because the organizational muscle for integration already exists.

Building adaptive capacity at the organizational level requires the same level of intentionality as at the individual level. It requires leadership that models learning behavior rather than certain performance, governance structures that treat workforce capability as a strategic asset, and investment decisions that prioritize development over time. And it requires the psychological safety infrastructure discussed earlier in this chapter because organizations learn fastest when people are willing to share what is not working, not just what is.

This feeds directly into Chapter 8's discussion of stewardship. Leaders who build genuine capability in their people and create conditions for them to thrive alongside AI earn the moral authority to lead AI responsibly. Stewardship is not just about governance structures and ethics frameworks. It is about the commitment, demonstrated in every workforce decision, to use AI in ways that develop rather than diminish the people the organization depends on. And for Chapter 9's 90-day integration plan to become operational, this chapter's workforce foundation is the prerequisite.

Manager's Checklist: Building the Team That Can Lead Alongside AI

Use this checklist to assess your current position and identify your highest-leverage development priorities.

AI Readiness Assessment

- Have you assessed your team on all four readiness dimensions: technical literacy, workflow integration, judgment capability, and adaptive capacity?

- Can you identify the three to five individuals whose readiness gaps are most likely to constrain your AI strategy?
- Do you have a mechanism beyond self-reporting, workflow observation, or output auditing to validate readiness assessments?
- Have you matched your development investment priorities to the readiness dimensions that most directly affect your strategic objectives?

Reskilling Program Design

- Are your reskilling programs embedded in actual work, or conducted in isolation from it?
- Have you started with a small, rigorously measured pilot before scaling any learning program?
- Have your middle managers developed an AI capability before being asked to champion AI adoption in their teams?
- Do you have a mechanism for measuring behavioral capability change, not just course completion?

Middle Manager Development

- Have you explicitly redefined the middle manager role to reflect the shift toward orchestration, translation, coaching, and escalation?

- Have you reduced the administrative burden on middle managers to create time for the higher-order work the new role requires?
- Are reporting structures and decision rights designed for AI-augmented teams, or are they inherited from a pre-AI operating model?

Hiring and Talent

- Are your interview processes designed to assess learning agility, systems thinking, comfort with ambiguity, and collaborative judgment, not just technical familiarity?
- Does your team have sufficient cognitive diversity to catch the errors and blind spots that homogeneous teams consistently miss?
- Do you have an explicit build-versus-buy framework for AI talent decisions, or are you defaulting to external hiring for technical roles and internal development for behavioral ones?

Psychological Safety and Culture

- Have you explicitly communicated what AI means for each role category on your team, not just the organization?
- Have you been transparent about how AI performance data will and will not be used in performance evaluation?
- Have you created explicit permission and governance for AI experimentation, including a process for capturing learning from failed experiments?

- Are you modeling learning behavior by being visible about your own AI capability development and questions rather than performing certainty?

Resistance and Feedback

- Do you distinguish between the three sources of resistance capability gaps, trust deficits, and identity threats- and respond to each appropriately?
- Do you have a formal mechanism for capturing, analyzing, and acting on employee concerns about AI deployments?
- Have your highest-skilled domain experts been positioned in roles that direct and improve AI rather than compete with it?

Continuous Development

- Do you have an ongoing sensing mechanism for identifying AI capability changes relevant to your organization's work?
- Do you have a knowledge management infrastructure that captures and distributes what the organization is learning from its own AI deployments?
- Does your workforce strategy assess the capability development requirements of any new AI deployment before implementation, not after?

Diagram 7.9: The AI Workforce Development Maturity Model

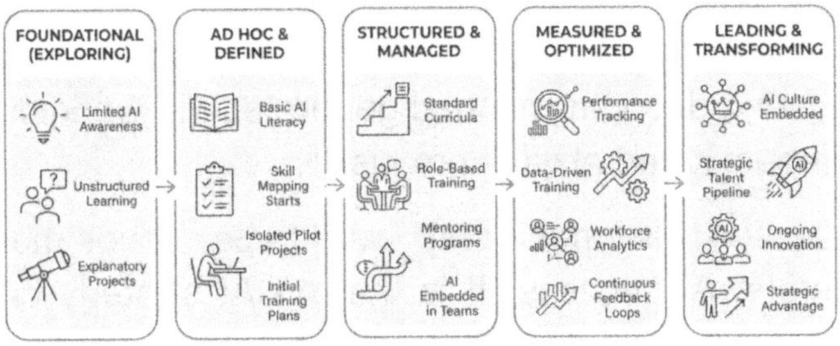

A progression framework for organizations to build capability and leverage AI across the workforce, shifting from initial exploration to strategic transformation.

What Serious Leaders Take From This Chapter

Every AI strategy eventually encounters the same irreducible constraint: it depends on people. Technology can be sophisticated, governance rigorous, and executive alignment complete, yet the strategy still stalls if the workforce is not ready, willing, and supported. That readiness does not emerge without investment, and that investment is not primarily financial. It is leadership attention, organizational design, and the sustained creation of conditions where people can learn, experiment, and grow alongside tools that are themselves changing.

At the beginning of this chapter, the CIO built a technically capable program on an organizationally unprepared foundation. Her recovery began when she made workforce readiness a strategic priority rather than treating it as an HR function. When she ran the readiness assessment, restructured the middle manager role, established feedback mechanisms, and granted her teams explicit permission to engage honestly with what was not working, adoption rates doubled. Within two quarters, adoption rates had doubled. Within a year, the program that had been at risk of being decommissioned generated the workflow-level impact it had always promised.

The lesson is not that workforce investment guarantees AI success. It is that no AI strategy can succeed without it. The organizations that outperform their peers in AI adoption are not consistently those with the most sophisticated technology; they are the ones whose people have been genuinely equipped, genuinely supported, and genuinely empowered to use it.

This chapter covers the assessment, development, and cultural infrastructure that makes that possible. Chapter 8 extends the discussion to the broader obligation of leadership: the stewardship that transforms AI capability from a competitive advantage into a responsible exercise of organizational power. The workforce investment described here is itself an expression of stewardship, the commitment to develop rather than diminish the people who will ultimately determine whether AI serves or undermines the mission that organizations exist to advance.

DIAGRAM 7.10: THE AI WORKFORCE READINESS FLYWHEEL

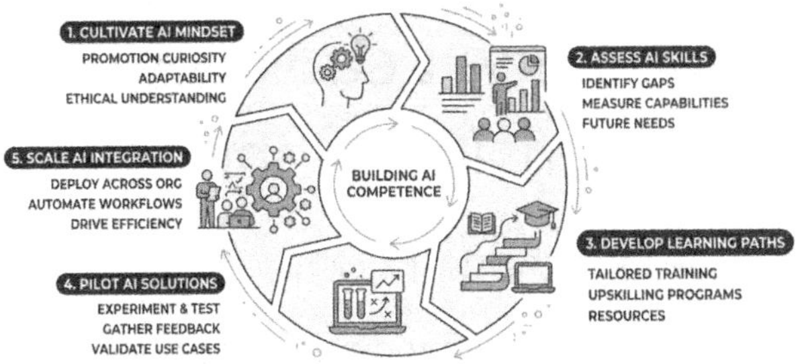

A continuous loop driving sustainable **workforce preparation**, **digital transformation**, and **sustained competitive advantage** in an AI-driven business environment.

9 The Obligation Behind the Opportunity: Leading AI With Responsibility and Care

A Question of Ownership

The CHRO of a regional financial services firm reached out to her CEO eleven months after her company went live with an AI-powered performance management platform. The vendor had promised an objective system that evaluated employee output against measurable targets, free from the subjectivity of individual managers' bias. What the vendor had not disclosed clearly enough, and what the organization had not examined carefully enough, was that the model had been trained on data from a workforce far larger, far less diverse, and operating in a very different market than theirs. Within two quarters, the system consistently flagged employees in certain branch roles for underperformance while assigning high ratings to others whose work was structurally different but scored similarly against the training data's underlying patterns.

No single person had made a bad decision. The procurement team had followed standard vendor evaluation protocols. The technology team had correctly integrated the system. The HR team had launched the rollout with appropriate training materials. Legal has reviewed the contract. And yet, when the CHRO sat across from the CEO with a preliminary analysis in her hand, the question in the room was both obvious and unanswered: who was responsible for this?

The scenario is not unusual. What makes it instructive is not the specific failure mode of AI systems producing biased outputs, which is a documented, well-studied problem, but the organizational vacuum that allowed it to persist for eleven months before anyone named it. No one had been assigned accountability for monitoring the system's real-world impact on real people. No one had a protocol for what to do if outcomes diverged from intent. No escalation pathway existed. And now the organization was managing both a workforce trust crisis and potential regulatory exposure, all while trying to understand what had gone wrong in a system that none of the leaders fully understood.

Stewardship is the discipline that prevents this scenario. Not governance documents sitting on an intranet. Not a checklist completed at the time of procurement. Stewardship as a living, operational practice; a posture that leaders maintain continuously; a structure that persists beyond the initial deployment; and a cultural commitment that makes accountability automatic rather than after-the-fact.

DIAGRAM 8.1: THE ACCOUNTABILITY VACUUM

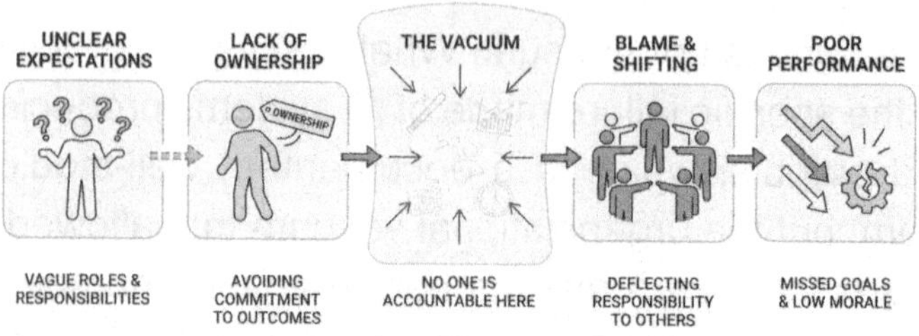

A failure to establish clear accountability leads to operational inefficiencies, missed opportunities, and a disengaged workforce.

Why Stewardship Is the Culmination, Not the Addendum

Every preceding chapter in this book builds toward this one. The mindsets from Chapter 2 determine whether a leader sees responsible AI as a genuine obligation or a compliance checkbox. The decision frameworks in Chapter 3 are where stewardship is enacted through decisions, in the actual choices about what AI is permitted to do and what requires human authority. The communication capability in Chapter 4 is the mechanism by which stewardship is made visible to teams, stakeholders, and the workforce whose work is being reshaped. The Trust Architecture from Chapter 5 is what good stewardship produces over time and what poor stewardship destroys. Executive alignment in Chapter 6 makes organization-wide stewardship structurally possible. And the team-building work of Chapter 7 determines whether the leader has the people around them to execute stewardship with real capability rather than procedural theater.

None of these capabilities functions without stewardship as its organizing ethic. A brilliant decision framework applied without accountability produces clean analysis and diffuse responsibility. Trust without stewardship is fragile; it holds until the first consequential failure, at which point its absence is catastrophic. Communication without stewardship is messaging, not commitment. Stewardship is not the final topic in the book because it is less important than the others. It is the final topic because it is the frame that holds everything else together.

The business case for responsible AI is frequently framed in terms of regulatory compliance as a floor to stay above rather than a ceiling to reach toward. Serious managers reject this framing. Organizations that govern AI well earn competitive advantages that their less disciplined peers cannot replicate: a talent pool that trusts their employer's AI practices enough to engage with full energy rather than self-protective wariness; a customer base that associates the brand with trustworthy data practices; a regulatory posture that anticipates scrutiny rather than reacts to it; and a governance infrastructure that scales as AI capabilities expand. Responsible-by-design AI programs scale. Programs that layer governance on after the fact break under the weight of their own accumulated technical and ethical debt.

Reframing Stewardship: From Constraint to Competitive Advantage

The Custodian Mindset

The most important conceptual shift a leader can make in approaching AI governance is from the owner mindset to the custodian mindset. Owners optimize for current use. Custodians optimize for sustained integrity. The distinction matters because AI systems are not static assets; they evolve, drift, and produce downstream effects that were not fully predictable at the time of deployment. An AI model trained on last year's data is already operating on a different population than the one it was evaluated on. An AI system that performed fairly in its first six months may perform unfairly in month eighteen as the operational context has shifted. Stewardship requires the ongoing attention that custodianship implies: not just deploying AI responsibly but maintaining that responsibility through the system's entire operational life.

This mindset maps directly onto the Accountability dimension of the AI-CLEAR Leadership Model introduced in Chapter 2. A leader who scores low on Accountability and treats outcomes as the algorithm's responsibility rather than their own is not a steward. They are a liability. The leader who understands that AI outputs bear their name, regardless of how much of the process was automated, is building an organizational culture in which accountability is structural rather than episodic.

The Cost of Governance Failure

Ungoverned AI does not simply underperform. It compounds. A bias in a hiring algorithm, left unexamined, becomes a pattern across thousands of decisions before it surfaces. A customer-facing AI model that handles complaints differently based on demographic signals may take 18 months to generate enough internal data to reveal the disparity. By that point, the reputational and legal exposure is already real. If a vendor's AI uses your proprietary data beyond what's stated in the contract, you may face unexpected intellectual property and privacy liabilities.

Each of these failure modes shares a common structure: a gap between the point of deployment and the point of accountability—leaders who maintain governance as an ongoing practice close this gap continuously. Leaders who treat governance as a procurement event discover the gap when the damage is already done. The pattern is consistent enough across industries that it functions less like a risk and more like a certainty: ungoverned AI, deployed at scale, will eventually produce a harmful outcome. The only real variable is whether governance is in place to catch it before it becomes a crisis.

Governance as the Infrastructure of Scale

There is a practical asymmetry that serious managers internalize early in their AI governance work: governance is cheap at the design stage, expensive at the remediation stage. Adding a bias audit protocol to an AI procurement process takes days. Conducting a bias audit after an AI system has been making consequential decisions for 18 months, while managing the workforce fallout and regulatory inquiry that triggered the audit, takes months and costs far more in every measurable dimension.

This asymmetry is not just about cost. It is about what scales. An organization with a robust governance infrastructure can expand its AI portfolio with confidence. Each new deployment follows established patterns: accountability is assigned, monitoring is built in, escalation pathways are defined, and workforce impact is assessed before and after. An organization without this infrastructure hits a ceiling. Each new deployment adds more ungoverned complexity, and the risk surface grows faster than the leadership team's capacity to manage it. Governance is not the brake on AI ambition. It is the prerequisite for sustainable AI ambition.

Diagram 8.2: The Governance Scale Curve

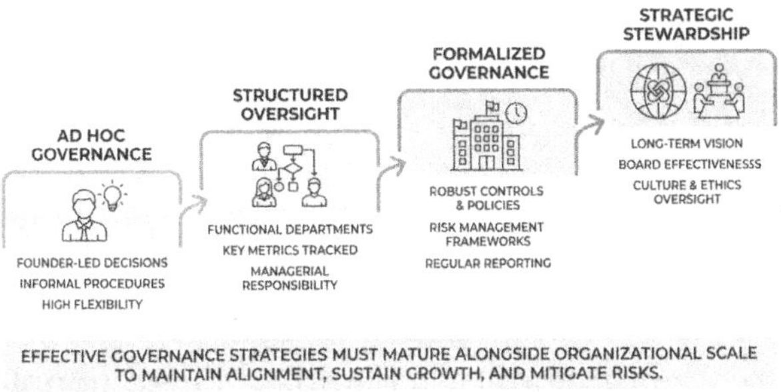

Responsible AI Principles: Making Them Operational

The Principle-to-Practice Gap

Most organizations of meaningful size now have responsible AI principles in place. They appear in annual reports, on corporate websites, and in executive keynotes. They cover the expected terrain: fairness, transparency, accountability, safety, and privacy. They are, by and large, well-intentioned. And for most organizations, they sit largely unused at the level where AI operates in procurement decisions, model validation processes, vendor negotiations, and the design of operational workflows.

Principles that live only at the executive communication level are not governance. They are reputation management with an ethical wrapper. The serious manager's job is to close the gap between what the organization says it believes about AI and what the organization does when AI deployment decisions are made at speed, under budget pressure, and without the convenient clarity of a showcase announcement.

Five Operational Principles and What Each Demands

Fairness requires that AI systems not systematically disadvantage any group of people, employees, customers, or communities in ways not justified by legitimate operational criteria. Operationalizing fairness means testing models for disparate impact before deployment, not just during development; establishing ongoing monitoring for demographic performance differentials; building decision rights that require human review when AI outputs produce material consequences for individuals; and having a clear, pre-established process for addressing unfair outcomes when they are identified.

Transparency requires that the people affected by AI decisions have meaningful access to the process by which those decisions were made. This does not mean exposing proprietary model architecture. It means that an employee who receives an AI-generated performance assessment can understand the criteria used to evaluate them. It means that a customer whose loan application was assessed by an algorithm can access a plain-language explanation. Transparency is not a technical disclosure; it is a human communication obligation.

Accountability requires that a named human being, not the algorithm, not the vendor, not the organization in the abstract, is responsible for the outputs of every AI system in operational use. This sounds self-evident and is persistently violated. Accountability diffuses naturally in complex organizations with layered technology stacks. Operationalizing accountability means explicitly assigning it: who owns this system's outcomes, who is notified when those outcomes produce harm, and who has the authority and obligation to act.

Safety requires that AI systems not expose the organization or the people it serves to operational, physical, or psychological harm. For most enterprise AI deployments, safety does not mean preventing catastrophic failure; it means building in the human oversight mechanisms that can catch consequential errors before they become consequential. No AI system is reliable enough to operate without structured human review at the points where errors would matter most.

Privacy requires that the personal data on which AI systems operate is handled in ways that the individuals it represents would recognize as legitimate. This is both a regulatory obligation and a trust obligation. People who learn that their personal data was used in ways they did not understand or consent to do not differentiate between legal compliance and ethical behavior. Privacy stewardship builds trust; privacy failure destroys it, often permanently.

The Responsible AI Review

The most practical governance mechanism a mid-to-large organization can build is the responsible AI review: a structured checkpoint applied to every significant AI system before deployment and at regular intervals during operation. The review is not a full audit; it is a fifteen to thirty-minute governance ritual that surfaces the critical accountability questions before operational momentum makes them harder to answer honestly.

A well-designed responsible AI review asks six questions. First: who is accountable for this system's outcomes, by name? Second: what are the highest-stakes decisions this system influences, and what human oversight exists at each of those points? Third: what does the data this system uses represent, and whose interests might that data systematically under-reflect? Fourth: How will we know if this system produces unfair, inaccurate, or harmful outputs once it is operational? Fifth: What is the escalation pathway if something goes wrong? Sixth: Has the impact on the affected workforce been assessed and communicated?

These questions do not require technical expertise to ask or answer. They require the organizational commitment to ask them before launch rather than after harm. The leader who builds responsible AI review into standard deployment practice is not slowing AI adoption; they are building the governance infrastructure that makes scale possible.

Diagram 8.3: The Responsible AI Review Checkpoint

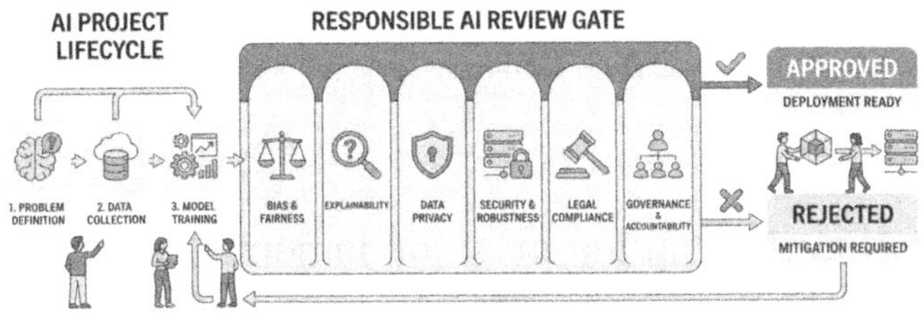

A RIGOROUS PROCESS TO ENSURE ETHICAL, FAIR, AND COMPLIANT AI DEPLOYMENTS.

When Principles Conflict

Serious managers encounter genuine tensions among responsible AI principles that no single principle can resolve. The most common conflicts involve transparency versus safety (full disclosure of model inputs could expose proprietary methodology or enable gaming), fairness versus accuracy (group-specific fairness adjustments may reduce aggregate predictive performance), and privacy versus accountability (investigating harm requires accessing data collected under confidentiality expectations).

These conflicts do not have universal answers. They have context-dependent answers that require the Serious Decision Spectrum from Chapter 3 applied with deliberate care. When a decision falls in the Assert quadrant, high stakes, values-laden, limited clean data, and no optimization model are the factors that resolve it. A leader must decide, own the decision, and be accountable for the consequences. The governance infrastructure's job is to ensure that these conflicts are surfaced and decided deliberately rather than resolved by default through inaction or expedience.

Data Stewardship in the AI Era

Data Is the Accountability Chain

Every AI system, in the most fundamental sense, is a transformation of data into decisions. The quality, representativeness, provenance, and governance of that data determine not just the performance of the system but the character of its impact. A leader who does not understand what data their AI systems are built on, where that data came from, who it represents, and how it was assembled does not understand the AI system, regardless of how technically sophisticated their understanding of the model architecture might be.

Data lineage, the documented chain of custody from source to operational deployment, is not a technical documentation requirement. It is a leadership accountability tool. When an AI system produces a harmful outcome, the investigation almost always begins with the data. What was it trained on? Were the people it affects represented in that training? Were there systematic biases in how the data were collected, labeled, or filtered? A leader who cannot answer these questions is not equipped to manage the accountability conversation, let alone prevent a recurrence.

Privacy as a Leadership Obligation

Data privacy has evolved from a legal requirement to a competitive and cultural differentiator. Organizations that take privacy seriously attract customers who care about how their data is used, a population that is growing in every market segment and demographic. They attract employees who are increasingly attentive to how their employer handles data. And they develop the governance muscles that protect them from the compounding exposure caused by poor data practices as AI systems become more capable and consequential.

Privacy stewardship in the AI context requires leaders to understand several distinctions that their predecessors did not need to navigate. Data collected for one purpose, customer service interactions, may be used to train or fine-tune AI systems in ways the customer did not expect or authorize. Personal data processed by a third-party AI vendor may be retained, used for model improvement, or exposed to additional parties under terms that are technically disclosed but practically invisible. An AI system that synthesizes many data points about an individual may infer sensitive characteristics that the individual never disclosed directly. Each of these scenarios creates obligations that responsible leaders address proactively, not after a data protection authority inquiry arrives.

The Data Sharing Dilemma

One of the most consequential decisions a leader makes in AI governance is whether, how, and under what terms organizational data is shared with AI vendors for training, fine-tuning, or model improvement. The value proposition is real: vendor models trained on your specific operational data may perform better for your use cases than generic models. The risks are equally real and frequently underweighted at the point of decision.

Organizational data shared with a vendor may be incorporated into that vendor's training dataset, potentially benefiting competitors that use the same platform. Confidential operational data, internal process descriptions, unpublished strategic plans, and personnel information may be processed and retained in ways that create regulatory exposure. And once data has been incorporated into a model's weights, the ability to audit or remove it is limited. Responsible data sharing decisions require a clear understanding of vendor contractual terms, a risk assessment of the data categories involved, and explicit leadership accountability for the decision, not just IT or legal sign-off.

Building a Data Governance Culture

Data governance that functions only as an IT process is governance in name only. The organization where every team understands that data quality is a leadership responsibility, where data decisions are made with the same deliberateness as financial decisions, is the organization whose AI systems benefit from high-quality inputs rather than suffering from accumulated data debt. Building this culture requires leaders to model the behavior: asking questions about data provenance during operational reviews, making data-quality investments visible in resource allocation, and treating data-governance failures with the same seriousness as financial-control failures.

DIAGRAM 8.4: THE DATA STEWARDSHIP CHAIN

A RESPONSIBLE AND EFFICIENT DATA STEWARDSHIP PROCESS ENSURES DATA ACCURACY, COMPLIANCE, AND VALUE FOR BUSINESS DECISION-MAKING.

Algorithmic Accountability: Who Is Responsible for What AI Does

The Accountability Diffusion Problem

In traditional process failures, accountability is traceable: a decision was made, someone made it, and the chain of responsibility is visible. AI-assisted or AI-driven decisions distribute responsibility across a longer and less visible chain: the data scientists who built the model, the vendor who supplied the platform, the IT team that integrated it, the manager who approved the deployment, the executive who set the strategic context, and the AI system itself, which produces outputs that no single person explicitly chose. This distribution does not create shared accountability. It creates the illusion of accountability while producing an accountability vacuum where it matters most.

The accountability vacuum is not accidental. It is a natural byproduct of organizational complexity amid technical opacity. Most managers who deploy AI systems cannot fully explain how they work. When an output causes harm, the instinct is to point at the complexity as a defense. The serious manager resists this instinct. AI outputs carry the name of the leader who deployed the system, just as financial reports carry the name of the CFO who signed them. Technical complexity is an explanation, never an excuse.

Assigning and Holding Algorithmic Accountability

The structural solution to accountability diffusion is explicit assignment: for every AI system in operational use, a named individual is responsible for the system's outcomes. This person is accountable for monitoring, escalation, remediation, and communication with affected parties when the system produces a harmful or unexpected result. They do not need to understand every technical dimension of the system. They need to understand the system's purpose, its likely failure modes, its real-world impact, and the governance mechanisms in place to manage that impact.

Algorithmic accountability assignment should be formalized as a governance document: the AI system register. This is a living inventory of every AI system in operational use, each entry specifying the accountable owner, the decision domains the system operates in, the data it uses, the monitoring protocol in place, and the escalation pathway for anomalies. Organizations without an AI system register do not know what they have deployed and cannot manage what they cannot see. The register is not an administrative burden; it is the foundation of operational clarity in AI governance.

Auditing for Bias, Drift, and Unintended Harm

AI systems do not remain static in their operational performance. They drift as the population they serve evolves away from the population on which they were trained. They amplify biases that were present but not identified in the training data, as those biases compound over thousands of decisions. They produce unintended interactions with organizational processes that were not fully mapped during the design phase. Responsible governance requires systematic auditing at regular intervals, not just at deployment.

For non-technical leaders, auditing feels like a technical task. In practice, the most important audit activities are well within the capability of an operationally experienced manager. Comparing AI-assisted outcomes across demographic groups reveals disparate impacts without requiring knowledge of the model's internals. Tracking the rate at which human reviewers override AI recommendations reveals whether the system is drifting from calibrated performance. Interviewing frontline employees who work alongside the AI system reveals workflow-level impacts that no monitoring dashboard captures. The leader who builds these practices into their quarterly governance rhythm is auditing effectively without a data science background.

Diagram 8.5: Algorithmic Accountability Assignment

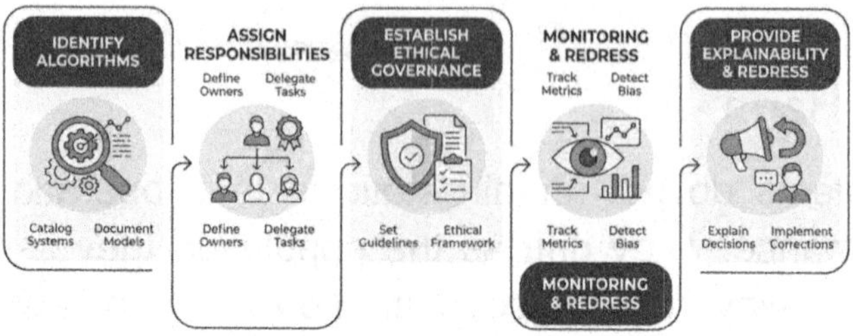

Captione minimalist infographic diagram for a business leadrdership book tona for algorithms in an organization.

Vendor Accountability in AI Procurement

An AI vendor's contractual commitment to responsible AI is not equivalent to the organization's accountability for outcomes. Many vendors offer responsible AI certifications, ethical AI audits, and governance documentation as part of their sales materials. These are inputs to a procurement decision, not substitutes for organizational governance. The organization that deploys a vendor's AI system is accountable for that system's outcomes in its specific operational context, regardless of what the vendor's general documentation says about model fairness.

Responsible AI procurement goes beyond standard vendor risk management. It requires: explicit contractual terms governing how the vendor uses your data; clarity on who bears accountability when model outputs produce harm; access rights to audit or independently validate model performance; vendor disclosure obligations when significant model updates occur; and exit protocols that include data recovery, model transition support, and continuity planning. Leaders who negotiate these terms before procurement have leverage. Leaders who realize they are missing them after deployment do so at a moment of maximum disadvantage.

Workforce Stewardship: Your Responsibility to the People AI Is Transforming

The Ethical Core of AI Leadership

Of all the stewardship responsibilities that attach to AI leadership, workforce stewardship is the most human and the most consequential. AI is reshaping work not in the abstract, future-tense sense that fills conference keynotes, but in the immediate, day-to-day sense that affects the people on every team you lead. Roles are narrowing. Workflows are restructuring. The skills that earned someone a place on a high-performing team two years ago may be losing organizational value in real time, with no guarantee that the skills the organization now needs are ones the person can easily develop. The leader who is not thinking clearly about what they owe the people whose work is being transformed on their watch is not a responsible AI leader; they are a participant in a transformation they have not fully reckoned with.

The Trust Architecture from Chapter 5 is most at risk in the workforce stewardship domain. Team Trust: the conviction employees hold that AI will not be used against them is the layer that deteriorates fastest when leaders fail to communicate clearly, invest visibly in skill development, and protect their people from AI-enabled exploitation or degradation of work. Once the team trust fractures over AI, rebuilding it is genuinely expensive: the loss of engagement, the departure of high performers who are mobile enough to leave, and the cultural residue of betrayal all compound in ways that show up in performance data long after the precipitating events.

Reskilling as Stewardship

Reskilling is not a benefit program or an HR initiative. It is a stewardship obligation. When an organization deploys AI systems that materially change what its workforce needs to do, it assumes responsibility for providing the development pathways that enable its people to evolve alongside those changes. This is not a legal requirement in most jurisdictions. It is a leadership ethic: the acknowledgment that the people who helped build what the organization is today deserve to be part of what it is becoming.

Reskilling as a stewardship investment requires more than making learning resources available. It requires actively identifying which roles are most significantly affected, mapping the skill evolution those roles require, designing accessible development pathways that account for different learning styles and time constraints, and providing management support that enables people to use those pathways rather than completing compliance training at midnight. It requires leaders who model the behavior, who are visibly learning alongside their teams, who make time for development conversations, and who recognize the reskilling journey as part of full performance rather than an add-on.

DIAGRAM 8.6: THE WORKFORCE STEWARDSHIP INVESTMENT FRAMEWORK

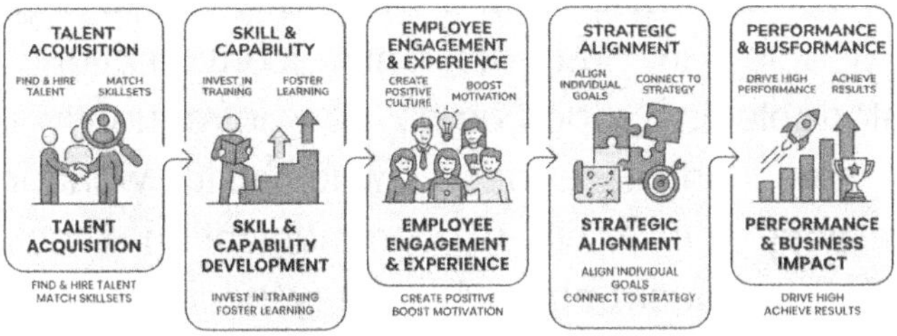

A HOLISTIC APPROACH TO ATTRACTING, DEVELOPING, ENGAGING, AND LEVERAGING HUMAN CAPITAL FOR SUSTAINED SUCCESS.

The Psychological Contract and AI

Every employment relationship carries an implicit psychological contract, an unspoken set of mutual expectations about what the organization and the employee owe each other. For most knowledge workers, this contract has included the expectation that good performance is recognized; that the organization invests in employees' growth; that change is communicated with adequate notice; and that employees' contributions to the organization's success are valued and reciprocated. AI-driven workforce transformation places each of these elements under pressure simultaneously.

When an AI system changes the nature of someone's work by automating the components they find most meaningful, elevating the components they find most stressful, and generating performance metrics they did not agree to be evaluated against, the psychological contract is being renegotiated, whether the leader acknowledges it or not. Responsible leaders acknowledge it. They communicate what is changing and why, what the organization is committing to in support of the transition, and what they are asking of their people in return. This conversation is uncomfortable in proportion to how infrequently the leader has had it. Leaders who build workforce transparency into their AI communication practice rarely find it catastrophic when they need to have a hard conversation. Leaders who have avoided it find that the accumulated weight of unacknowledged change makes the conversation much harder.

The Manager as Workforce Advocate

The most underappreciated element of workforce stewardship is the manager's role as advocate, the person in the organizational structure who can see both the AI system's impact and the individual human experience simultaneously, and who has both authority and the obligation to push back when the combination is harmful. AI-enabled degradation of work, the systematic deskilling of professionals, the reduction of meaningful judgment to AI approval or rejection, and the surveillance of human behavior at a granularity that erodes dignity and autonomy do not announce themselves. It accumulates, tool by tool and policy by policy, until the work that once engaged talented people no longer does.

The serious manager monitors not just what their AI systems produce, but what they do to the people working alongside them. They ask: Has this system reduced or expanded the meaningful judgment exercised by my team? Has it freed them to do more valuable work, or has it reduced them to QA reviewers of algorithmic outputs? Does AI monitoring serve operational quality or surveillance? These are not anti-technology questions. They are questions of stewardship that any responsible leader in any technological era would recognize as essential.

Governing Agentic AI: The New Frontier of Stewardship

Why Agentic AI Requires a Different Governance Posture

The governance frameworks that have served organizations well for AI tool systems that respond to queries, generate outputs, and augment human decisions require significant evolution when applied to agentic AI systems. An AI agent is not a tool that produces outputs for human review. It is a system that takes actions in digital environments, across organizational systems, in interaction with external parties, with meaningful autonomy and the capacity to initiate further sequences of actions. The human oversight model for an AI tool is: I generate, you decide. The human oversight model for an AI agent must be: we define the boundaries, monitor the process, and catch exceptions, because the agent is making decisions and acting without a human in the loop.

This is a governance challenge of a different order. Organizations operating at the frontier of agentic AI deployment are reporting that their existing governance frameworks, built on the assumption of human decision points at each consequential juncture, are insufficient for systems that can traverse hundreds of decision points in the time it takes a human to read an email. Research on leading agentic AI organizations indicates that the majority expect their governance structures to require fundamental redesign within three years, and that AI decision-making authority is expected to grow dramatically as agentic capabilities mature. The serious manager who is not already building governance infrastructure for agentic AI is already behind.

Defining Decision Rights for Autonomous Systems

The critical governance question for agentic AI is not whether to allow AI systems to act autonomously; the efficiency case for agentic automation is genuine and growing, but precisely where to define the boundaries of that autonomy. Decision rights architecture for agentic AI requires leaders to explicitly, in writing, answer which categories of action this system is authorized to take without human approval. What triggers an escalation to human review? What is the override mechanism, and how quickly can it be invoked? What happens when the system encounters a situation outside its defined scope?

This architecture maps directly and practically onto the Serious Decision Spectrum from Chapter 3. Actions in the Automate quadrant, with high data density and low human stakes, are natural candidates for agentic execution with monitoring-only oversight. Actions in the Augment quadrant, with high data density and high human stakes, require agentic assistance with structured human review at the decision point. Actions in the Assert quadrant are not appropriate for agentic autonomy, regardless of how capable the agent becomes. The spectrum gives leaders a principled framework for drawing boundaries rather than defaulting to either excessive restriction or excessive permissiveness based on how impressive the demonstration looked.

DIAGRAM 8.7: AGENTIC AI DECISION RIGHTS ARCHITECTURE

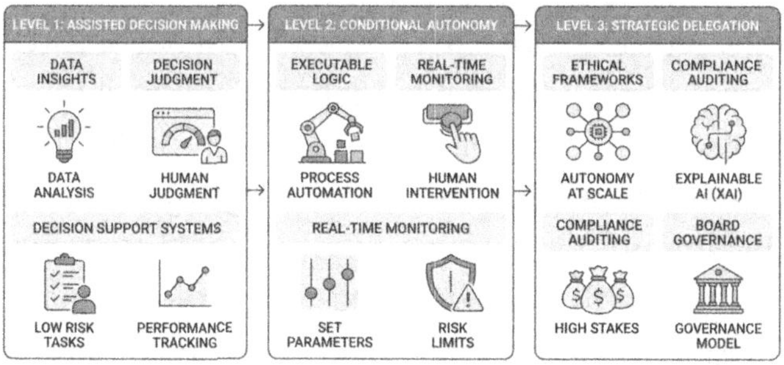

ESTABLISHING CLEAR ACCOUNTABILITY AND OVERSIGHT FOR AGENTIC AI WITHIN THE CORPORATE FRAMEWORK.

Building Governance Infrastructure Before Deployment

The single most consequential governance decision an organization makes regarding agentic AI is whether to build governance infrastructure before or after deployment. The organizational pressure almost always favors the following: the efficiency gains from agentic deployment are immediate and compelling; governance work is unglamorous; and the harm scenarios feel hypothetical until they happen. Leaders who resist this pressure and treat governance infrastructure as a prerequisite for deployment rather than a follow-on responsibility build organizations that can scale their agentic capabilities with confidence.

Pre-deployment governance for agentic AI includes: complete documentation of the agent's authorized scope of action; a human escalation pathway with defined response time obligations; a logging and audit capability that captures agent actions in auditable form; a rollback protocol that can reverse agent actions in the categories where reversal is technically possible; and a stakeholder communication plan for both normal operation and failure scenarios. Organizations that build this infrastructure once as a reusable framework gain significant governance leverage across subsequent agentic deployments. Organizations that improvise governance for each deployment add fragility with every new agent they launch.

The Agentic Manager Skill Set

Managing alongside autonomous AI agents requires a genuinely new skill set. It combines the analytical orientation of someone comfortable reading monitoring dashboards with the operational judgment of someone who knows when a pattern in those dashboards signals a real problem versus normal variation. It requires the ability to define scope boundaries with precision to describe, in terms that an agent can act on, where its autonomy ends. It requires the discipline of communication to maintain transparency with stakeholders about what AI agents are doing on the organization's behalf. And it requires self-trust, the fourth layer of the Trust Architecture, to override an agent's action when judgment and context signal that the right response is a human assertion rather than an algorithmic continuation.

Leaders who develop this skill set are building capability that will become increasingly valuable as agentic AI expands its operational footprint. The "agentic manager" is not a technical specialist. They are excellent leaders who have extended their accountability posture to encompass systems that act with meaningful autonomy and who hold that posture with the same rigor they would apply to a team of capable but unsupervised staff.

Long-Term Stewardship: The Multi-Generational Responsibility

Beyond the Current Deployment

AI stewardship operates across multiple time horizons simultaneously. The immediate horizon, the deployment currently in review, the incident currently under investigation, and the reskilling program currently being designed are where most governance attention appropriately sits. But serious managers also maintain a longer view: what kind of AI-using organization are they building? What patterns of behavior and accountability are being established now that will shape how the organization navigates AI challenges that cannot yet be anticipated? What precedents are being set about who bears accountability, how workforce impact is managed, and what governance is worth in the actual currency of organizational decision-making?

This longer horizon is not an abstraction. The organizations that will lead in AI five years from now are not the ones moving fastest today, regardless of governance. They are the ones building the governance muscles alongside the technical capabilities that establish accountability norms, monitoring practices, workforce investment commitments, and regulatory relationships that will allow them to operate at scale with sustained trust. Stewardship as a long-term investment yields returns disproportionate to those of stewardship as a compliance exercise.

The Precautionary Principle for AI

Responsible AI leadership requires holding a tension that is genuinely difficult to manage: the urgency of AI opportunity versus the caution that consequential uncertainty demands. The precautionary principle- the idea that when potential harm is significant and not fully understood, the burden of proof shifts toward demonstrating safety before proceeding- is not a counsel of AI avoidance. It is a counsel of proportionality. The strength of governance required before deployment should be scaled with the magnitude of potential harm from failure.

A generative AI tool for internal content drafting warrants a governance posture appropriate to its risk profile: useful but low stakes. An AI system that makes consequential decisions about employee compensation, customer creditworthiness, or healthcare resource allocation warrants a governance posture appropriate to its risk profile: significant, irreversible, and affecting vulnerable individuals. The serious manager who applies the same governance intensity to both, either treating all AI as equally low-risk or equally high-risk, is not exercising proportional judgment. They are applying a rule requiring leadership.

AI, ESG, and the Emerging Accountability Framework

Environmental, Social, and Governance frameworks are increasingly incorporating AI as a material consideration for organizational disclosure. The social dimensions of enterprise AI workforce impact, data privacy, algorithmic accountability, and equitable access sit squarely within the "S" of ESG reporting. The governance dimensions board oversight of AI risk, accountability structures, audit practices, and regulatory compliance sit within the "G." Organizations that are already building robust AI governance infrastructure will find that the emerging ESG-AI reporting requirements confirm and reward what they are already doing. Organizations that have not will find that the externally imposed accountability structure is both more demanding and less flexible than what they would have designed for themselves.

The serious manager who builds governance practices now, with an eye to their ESG dimensions, is not anticipating regulatory requirements so much as building the kind of organization that takes its obligations seriously across the full range of stakeholders with a legitimate interest in how AI is deployed on their behalf.

Building an AI Legacy

The most durable frame for long-term stewardship is the question of legacy. What kind of AI-using organization do you want to have built in five years? What will your employees say about how AI was introduced on your watch? What will your customers believe about how their data was used? What will your industry peers recognize about the governance standards your organization upheld when the choices were genuinely difficult, and the pressure to cut corners was real?

These are not rhetorical questions. They are the organizing questions for the governance decisions you are making now, in real time, under pressure, without the advantage of hindsight. The leader who holds these questions continuously and treats stewardship not as a governance burden but as a defining expression of their leadership character is building an AI legacy that will outlast any single deployment and compound in value in ways that cannot be fully anticipated today.

DIAGRAM 8.8: LONG-TERM STEWARDSHIP TIME HORIZONS

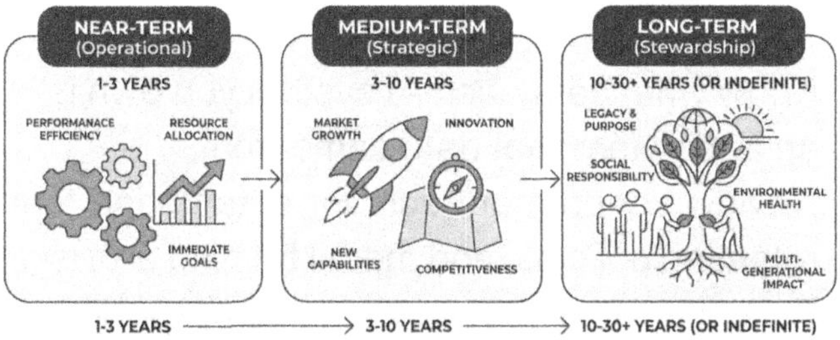

INTEGRATING TEMPORAL PERSPECTIVES FOR SUSTAINABLE CORPORATE LEADERSHIP AND RESPONSIBLE DECISION-MAKING.

Chapter 8 Manager's Stewardship Checklist

Use this checklist to evaluate your current stewardship posture and identify the highest-leverage governance investments for the next quarter.

Governance Infrastructure

- Maintain a live AI system that maps every AI system in operational use to a named accountable owner.
- Conduct a responsible AI review for every new AI deployment before go-live.
- Review and update the AI system register at least quarterly.
- Assign escalation ownership for every AI system by name, with defined response time expectations.
- Establish a rollback and remediation protocol for agentic AI deployments.

Data Stewardship

- Know what data each AI system you own is built on and where that data came from.
- Review vendor contracts for data usage terms, retention policies, and model training provisions.
- Establish a data governance checkpoint in the AI procurement process.
- Audit data quality as part of AI system performance reviews, not just model accuracy.
- Ensure all AI systems in operation comply with applicable privacy regulations and organizational data policies.

Algorithmic Accountability

- Compare AI-assisted outcomes across relevant demographic groups every quarter.

- Track the rate at which human reviewers override AI recommendations and treat significant changes as a monitoring signal.
- Interview frontline employees who work alongside AI systems as part of governance reviews.
- Negotiate vendor accountability provisions in AI procurement contracts before signing.
- Document and communicate the escalation pathway for AI-produced harmful outcomes.

Workforce Stewardship

- Assess which roles on your team are most materially affected by AI deployment and build development pathways accordingly.
- Communicate clearly and proactively when AI changes the nature of work; do not allow the change to accumulate unacknowledged.
- Protect team members from AI-enabled degradation of work and evaluate whether AI systems are expanding or contracting meaningful human judgment.
- Model reskilling behavior visibly; your own learning signals to your team that development is taken seriously.
- Conduct a team trust assessment related to AI at least twice annually, using the Trust Architecture framework.

Agentic AI Governance

- Define decision rights for every autonomous agent in deployment in writing, before launch.
- Build logging and audit capability into agentic deployments as a non-negotiable infrastructure requirement.
- Maintain human override mechanisms and test them regularly.
- Classify agentic actions using the Serious Decision Spectrum before authorizing autonomous execution.
- Conduct quarterly governance reviews of agentic deployments, including scope drift analysis.

Diagram 8.9: The Stewardship Posture Assessment

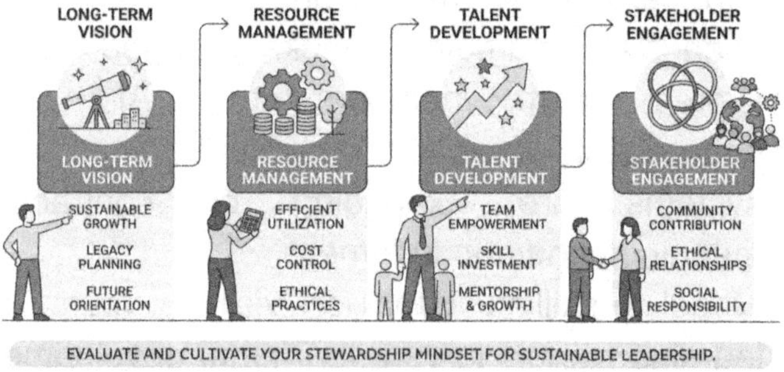

The Obligation That Defines the Opportunity

Stewardship is not the last topic in the serious AI leader's education because it is the easiest to defer. It is the last topic because it requires everything that came before it to function: the mindsets that make accountability genuine rather than performative; the decision frameworks that make governance practical rather than aspirational; the communication capability that makes stewardship visible to the people and institutions that depend on it; the trust architecture that responsible governance protects and poor governance destroys; and the team-building discipline that ensures the leader has the human capability alongside them to execute stewardship at the scale AI now demands.

The obligation behind every AI opportunity is this: when you deploy systems that make or influence consequential decisions, use personal data, reshape work, and act with increasing autonomy, you are not simply leveraging a technology. You are assuming stewardship of the consequences. The AI-CLEAR Leadership Model's Accountability dimension names this directly: AI outcomes belong to the leader who deployed the system, not to the system itself. The Trust Architecture's four layers reveal where that accountability expresses itself in the systems you deploy, the teams you lead, the stakeholders who depend on you, and your own judgment when it diverges from the algorithm.

The leaders who will be remembered well for their AI stewardship by their employees, their customers, their organizations, and the broader professional communities they are part of are not the ones who deployed AI most aggressively or most cautiously. They are the ones who deployed it most responsibly: with governance infrastructure that matched the stakes, with workforce investment that matched the transformation, with transparency that matched the trust they were asking for, and with the accountability to own the outcomes when the system fell short of the standard they had set.

Chapter 9 brings all these threads together: the mindsets, the frameworks, the communication practices, the trust architecture, the executive alignment, the team-building capability, and the stewardship posture that gives them coherence. The serious AI leader is not someone who has mastered each of these domains in isolation. They are someone who holds them together under pressure, in service of the mission, and who leads with the seriousness that the opportunity and the obligation both require.

DIAGRAM 8.10: THE STEWARDSHIP FLYWHEEL

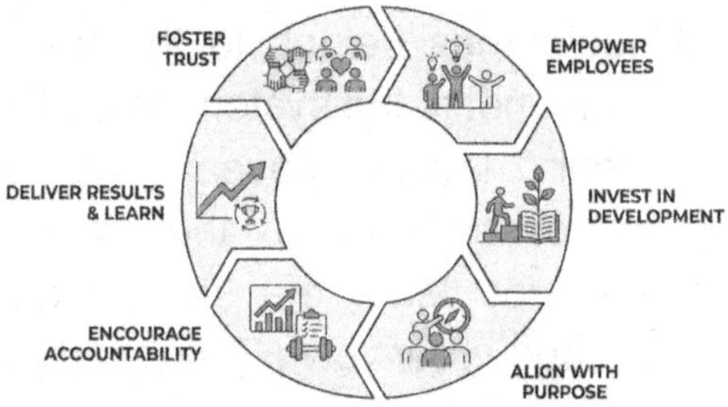

A continuous loop where steward leadership builds trust, empowers teams, and drives sustainable organizational success and momentum.

10 The Serious AI Leader's Compass: When All the Pieces Work Together

The Morning Everything Came Together

Miriam Chen had been running the enterprise technology division of a global financial services firm for four years. She had lived through two failed AI pilots, a bruising data governance incident that attracted regulatory attention, and a workforce anxiety crisis that had cost her three of her best senior managers. By the time she sat down with her leadership team on a Tuesday morning in March, she was not in the mood for another framework presentation.

What she got instead was a moment she would describe, months later, as the clearest she had ever felt in her professional life.

Her team was evaluating a proposal to deploy an AI-driven risk-scoring system across the firm's commercial lending portfolio. The stakes were high: the system would influence decisions affecting hundreds of business customers. The data was dense but imperfect. The vendor's transparency regarding the model's mechanics was, at best, partial. And three members of her leadership team had unresolved concerns about how the system would interact with the firm's existing underwriting culture.

What happened in that room was not a technological miracle. It was a miracle of prepared leadership. The Chief Risk Officer applied the Serious Decision Spectrum without being reminded that she had internalized it from her team's work in the prior quarter. She mapped the lending decision as a clear Augment case: high data density, but the human stakes of commercial credit decisions affecting jobs, communities, and the firm's reputation placed it firmly in the quadrant where AI would inform but never replace human judgment.

The Chief People Officer, who had spent the previous six months building out the AI readiness competency framework the firm had adopted after Chapter 7's workforce planning work, raised the question of whether the frontline underwriters had the psychological safety to push back on AI recommendations they disagreed with. This was not abstract; she had data from a recent team-readiness survey showing that forty percent of underwriters were uncertain whether voicing disagreement with an AI output was culturally acceptable.

Miriam herself had spent the previous year conducting quarterly Trust Architecture audits. She knew exactly where each layer of trust stood. System Trust in the proposed vendor platform was provisional; the team had not yet completed a model transparency review. Team Trust was strong, but the behavioral data from the people survey required attention before deployment. Stakeholder Trust with the firm's regulators was carefully maintained and could not be risked on an insufficiently reviewed system. And her own Self-Trust, her confidence in overriding the vendor's deployment timeline recommendations when her judgment told her the organization was not ready, was at its clearest.

The AI-CLEAR assessment she completed two weeks earlier indicated she was high on Leverage and Accountability, but that her Empowerment dimension needed work; specifically, she was not yet creating enough structured space for her team to challenge AI recommendations without it feeling like a leadership confrontation. She had a specific development action on that item.

Within ninety minutes, the team reached a decision that none of them could have reached two years earlier: conditional approval to proceed with a controlled pilot involving a defined set of loan categories, with mandatory human review of all AI-influenced recommendations, a transparent communication plan for underwriters, a clear escalation protocol, and a firm go/no-go review at sixty days. Not a no. Not blind, yes. A mission-aligned, responsible-by-design decision made with the full weight of integrated AI leadership capability.

Miriam told her team afterward: "That is what all the work was for."

This chapter is about how leaders like Miriam get there and how you can build the same coherence, integration, and operational clarity in your own organization. The frameworks are in place. The journey now is to make them work together.

DIAGRAM 9.1: THE INTEGRATED AI LEADERSHIP DECISION

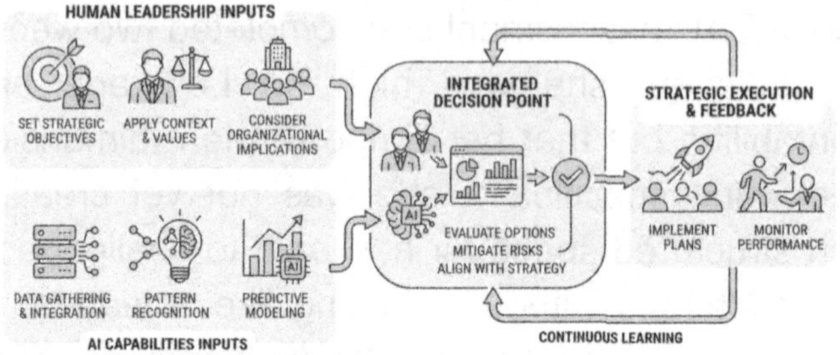

A CYCLICAL PROCESS COMBINING HUMAN JUDGMENT, EXPERIENCE, AND ETHICS WITH AI INSIGHTS, DATA, AND MODELING FOR OPTIMIZED LEADERSHIP DECISIONS.

Why Integration Is the Hardest Part

Most leadership frameworks fail at the same place: the transition from learning to integration. A leader can read eight chapters on AI leadership, understand every concept, score well on every self-assessment, and still struggle to deploy those capabilities simultaneously under real conditions. The reason is not intellectual; it is structural. Individual skills learned in isolation do not automatically become integrated capabilities. They require practice, reflection, and the kind of organizational infrastructure that makes multiple capabilities available simultaneously.

This is why Chapter 9 exists. Not to introduce new frameworks; everything you need has been covered across Chapters 1 through 8. But to show you how those capabilities function as a system, what that system looks like when it is working, and what specific actions will move you from individual proficiency to integrated AI leadership mastery.

The cost of failing to integrate is not theoretical. When leaders apply strong decision-making skills without strong communication skills, they make good decisions that organizations do not follow through on. When they build genuine trust without the alignment structures from Chapter 6, they create pockets of excellent AI culture that die at the boundary of the next business unit. When they are skilled in workforce development but do not connect it to stewardship principles, they build capable teams that operate without the ethical grounding needed to prevent AI deployments from causing harm. The gaps between capabilities are where organizations lose the value that AI leadership could have created.

Integration is also what separates AI leaders who are still effective five years from now from those who are perpetually catching up. Technology will continue to change. The regulatory landscape will shift. New capabilities, new risks, and new workforce realities will emerge at a pace that makes any single framework insufficient on its own. What sustains effective AI leadership over time is not any one tool; it is the mental architecture that allows a leader to bring multiple capabilities to bear on any new situation as soon as it arises. That architecture is what this chapter builds.

Introducing the Serious AI Leader's Compass

The Serious AI Leader's Compass is an integrating framework, not a new set of concepts. Still, a map of how the six core AI leadership capabilities relate to each other, reinforce each other, and, when one is weak, pull the others off course.

The six directions of the Compass correspond directly to the six core capabilities this book has developed:

- North Mindset: The AI-CLEAR Leadership Model from Chapter 2. The orientation point. All other capabilities depend on whether the leader is operating from a mindset of genuine curiosity, disciplined leverage, authentic empowerment, real accountability, and continuous readiness.
- East Decisions: The Serious Decision Spectrum from Chapter 3. The practical engine. The direction that converts orientation into action. Strong decision-making without a strong mindset yields efficient but unprincipled choices.
- South Communication: The translation capability from Chapter 4. The amplification direction. Even perfect decisions, made with an exemplary mindset, create no organizational value until they are communicated in ways that teams understand, trust, and act on.
- West Trust: The Trust Architecture from Chapter 5. The foundation direction. The Compass loses its ability to provide accurate readings when trust is compromised in systems,

teams, stakeholders, or the leader's own judgment.

- Northeast Alignment: The executive alignment structures from Chapter 6. The coordination direction. The point where individual leadership capability becomes organizational capability. Without alignment, even excellent individual AI leadership creates fragmentation.
- Southeast Stewardship: The responsible AI principles from Chapter 8, grounded in the workforce investment of Chapter 7. The sustainability direction. Stewardship ensures that capabilities in other directions are deployed with the care, accountability, and long-term thinking that make AI leadership genuinely durable.

The Compass deliberately uses a metaphor of a compass. Unlike a ladder, which implies that leaders must master one level before ascending to the next, the Compass acknowledges that all six directions are simultaneously present and active. A leader is always operating across all six dimensions. The question is not whether they are, but how consciously and how well they are.

DIAGRAM 9.2: THE SERIOUS AI LEADERS COMPASS

A strategic framework for C-suite executives and managers to guide successful and responsible AI implementation within the organization.

How the Six Directions Interact

The Compass is not merely additive; the six capabilities have specific reinforcing relationships that multiply effectiveness when aligned and create specific vulnerabilities when misaligned. Understanding these relationships allows a leader to diagnose problems with precision rather than vague concern.

Mindset and Trust form the deepest partnership. A leader's AI-CLEAR self-awareness, particularly in the Accountability and Self-Trust dimensions, enables honest maintenance of trust relationships when AI systems produce unexpected results. A leader who lacks the Accountability dimension of the AI-CLEAR Model will instinctively protect their image when an AI deployment goes wrong, exactly when transparent Trust Architecture maintenance demands the opposite.

Decisions and Communication have a critical dependency that most leaders underestimate. The Serious Decision Spectrum gives a leader the right framework for structuring a decision. Still, the value of that structured decision is lost if the leader cannot articulate to their team why a particular decision belongs in the Augment quadrant rather than the Automate quadrant. The leader who makes the right call but communicates it poorly generates exactly as much organizational confusion as the leader who makes the wrong call with confidence.

Alignment and Stewardship form the governance partnership. Executive alignment structures in Chapter 6 determine whether responsible AI principles are operationalized at scale or remain aspirational statements that individual business units interpret as they see fit. A stewardship commitment without alignment infrastructure is a values document. A stewardship commitment backed by strong alignment is an organizational norm.

The Workforce development capability in Chapter 7 sits at the intersection of all directions. Teams that lack AI readiness undermine decision quality by misapplying AI tools. They erode trust by using AI systems in ways that generate errors or raise ethical concerns. They break communication because they lack the shared vocabulary needed to participate in AI leadership conversations. And they make stewardship aspirations impossible to achieve because responsible-by-design AI requires human judgment at every point in the system, which, in turn, requires a capable, ready workforce.

DIAGRAM 9.3: REINFORCING LOOPS WITHIN THE COMPASS

CONTINUOUS MOMENTUM & GROWTH

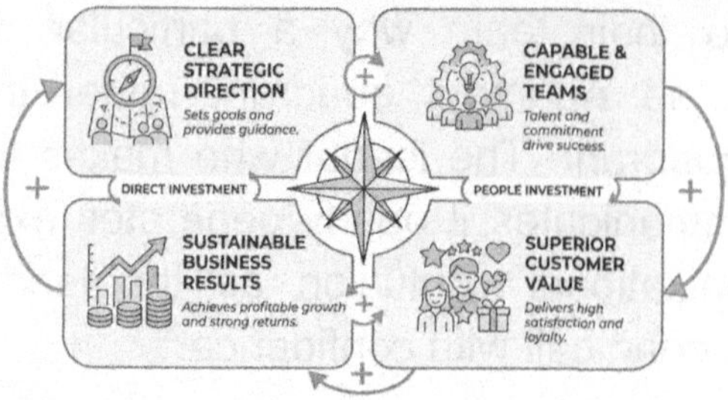

*LEADERSHIP DIAGRAM: Visualizing how key business elements interconnect in a positive reinforcing cycle for sustained organizational success.

The Compass as Diagnostic Tool

The most powerful use of the Compass is diagnostic. When an AI initiative is producing suboptimal results, adoption is stalling, stakeholder confidence is eroding, and governance reviews keep surfacing the same problems, the Compass gives leaders a structured way to identify which direction is pulling the organization off course.

In practice, the diagnostic question for each direction is specific and testable. For Mindset: are leaders across the organization genuinely curious about AI, or are they performing enthusiasm while privately resistant? For Decisions: Are the organization's three most consequential AI choices being made with explicit Spectrum mapping, or are they defaulting to Automate when they belong in Augment or Assert? For Communication: when AI decisions are announced, do teams ask clarifying questions to understand them, or do they comply without engaging because they never expected to be genuinely informed? For Trust: in the last ninety days, has any layer of the Trust Architecture eroded, and if so, has the leader taken active steps to rebuild it, or managed the appearance of trust while the underlying relationship weakened? For Alignment: Do the leaders in your AI governance body genuinely share a purpose, or are they present in the room but pursuing organizational interests that diverge as soon as they return to their business units? For Stewardship: Are responsible AI principles visible in daily operational decisions, or do they only surface during formal governance reviews and regulatory inquiries?

The answers to these questions are not always comfortable. The leader who takes the Compass seriously will, at least once in every diagnostic cycle, find a direction that is significantly weaker than they thought it would be. That is the point. A compass is only useful if it tells the truth.

When the System Is Working: Integration in Practice

A Story of Integrated Success

Consider what happens when all six Compass directions are operating at full strength. A regional hospital network launched an AI-driven patient triage prioritization system across its emergency departments. The project was large, technically complex, and carried extraordinary human stakes: the system would influence decisions about which patients received immediate attention.

The Chief Medical Officer leading the initiative had completed an AI-CLEAR self-assessment the previous year and identified Empowerment as her weakest dimension. She had a specific leadership development action: create structured forums where frontline clinical staff could challenge AI triage recommendations without social cost. She acted on it before deployment, not after. She established clinical AI review rounds: weekly 30-minute sessions in which emergency physicians and nurses could surface cases in which the AI recommendation had been overridden and discuss whether the override was appropriate, inappropriate, or uncertain. These sessions generated the psychological safety that made the entire system trustworthy to the people who operated it.

Before a single deployment decision was made, the team used the Serious Decision Spectrum to map every decision point in the triage workflow. The results were illuminating. Automated assignment of patients to waiting priority categories based on vital signs fits cleanly in the Automate quadrant, with high data density and low direct stakes for that specific micro-decision. But the decision to escalate a borderline case to immediate physician evaluation fell squarely within Assert territory: the data was often ambiguous, and the human stakes were as high as they could be. The team built the system architecture around these quadrant assignments rather than treating every step of the process the same way.

The communication strategy was designed before deployment began, not as an afterthought. Frontline staff received a plain-language explanation of exactly what the system did, what it did not do, and what their authority was when their clinical judgment disagreed with it. That authority was explicit, documented, and backed by leadership. No one had to wonder whether overriding the AI would be held against them.

The Trust Architecture audit, conducted sixty days before go-live, revealed a specific Team Trust deficit: nurses were uncertain whether the system's triage recommendations would be used to evaluate their performance. The CMO addressed this directly in writing, in a staff meeting, and in a protocol document before the system went live. System Trust was earned gradually through a phased rollout that started with the lowest-stakes triage categories and expanded only after clinical staff felt genuinely confident in the system's reliability. Stakeholder Trust with the hospital network's board and external accreditation bodies was maintained through proactive governance documentation prepared in advance by the leadership team.

At 90 days post-deployment, the triage system was operating effectively, with clinical override rates consistent with the team's expectations, nurse satisfaction scores that had improved rather than declined, and zero serious adverse events attributable to AI-influenced triage decisions. The Chief Medical Officer attributed none of the success to the technology itself. She attributed it to the leadership infrastructure her team had built.

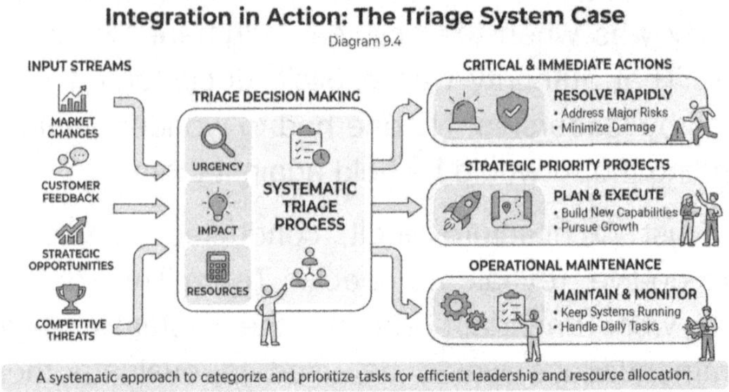

A Story of Preventable Failure

The inverse story is equally instructive. A large retail organization deployed an AI system for workforce scheduling that optimized shift assignments for several thousand store employees. The system was technically sophisticated and operationally sound by every metric the technology team measured. It was also a damaging failure.

The Compass diagnosis of what went wrong is exact. The VP of Store Operations, who led the initiative, had strong Leverage and Readiness scores on the AI-CLEAR model. She understood AI capability and was current on the technology, but her Empowerment and Accountability dimensions were underdeveloped. She never created the infrastructure for store managers to raise scheduling concerns. She was not visible as the accountable leader when problems emerged. When the system began generating schedules that violated informal team agreements that managers had built over the years, store managers did not escalate; they worked around the system, generating inconsistent applications that undermined both the AI's optimization goals and the team trust that the scheduling process had previously maintained.

The decision architecture failure was precise: the team had correctly identified shift optimization as an Automate decision (high data, relatively low individual-decision stakes), but had failed to recognize that the aggregate effect of thousands of automated decisions restructuring long-standing work patterns across entire store communities created a human stakes profile that required human review and a communication strategy that treated the workforce as stakeholders, not just optimization inputs.

Communication was the most visible failure. The system was rolled out with a technical briefing for IT and a memo for regional managers. There was no plain-language explanation for frontline employees about how the system worked, what criteria it used, or how they could raise concerns. The first time many employees knew about the new scheduling logic was when their shift patterns changed in ways they had not been warned about and did not understand. The damage to trust was immediate, significant, and almost entirely preventable.

The lesson is not that the scheduling AI was wrong. For routine shift optimization within clearly defined parameters, AI scheduling can generate genuine workforce-level impact and operational efficiency. The lesson is that even technically sound AI deployments fail when they lack leadership. Technology did what it was designed to do. The leadership system did not.

DIAGRAM 9.5: THE PREVENTABLE FAILURE PATTERN

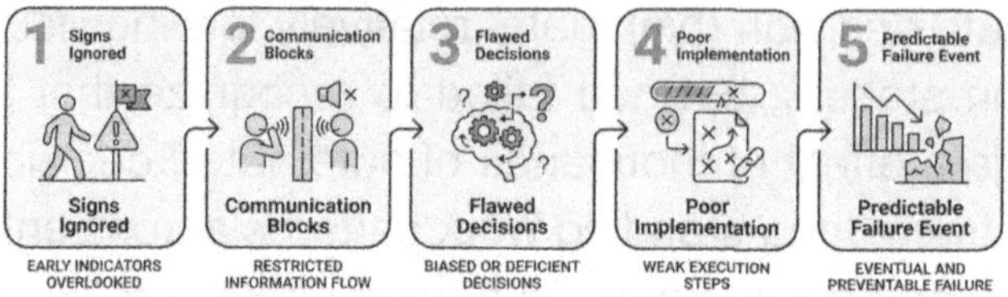

KEY TAKEAWAY: Proactive leadership identifies and addresses systemic weaknesses before they lead to failure.

The Compound Return on AI Leadership Investment

One of the most important dynamics in the Compass system is that capability in one direction genuinely accelerates development in others. This is not an optimistic assertion; it is the observable pattern among organizations that have consistently invested in AI leadership development.

Leaders who develop strong communication capability find that their trust relationships deepen naturally, because transparency is the primary trust-building mechanism. Leaders with strong Trust Architecture maintenance see their decision-making improve because the architecture's self-trust dimension specifically reinforces the willingness to make difficult calls when AI recommendations point in the wrong direction. Leaders who invest in workforce AI readiness, as Chapter 7 describes, find that their alignment conversations become more substantive because the organizational AI vocabulary has expanded beyond the C-suite.

The practical implication is that your development investment is not purely additive; it is compounding. When you strengthen your weakest Compass direction, you generate acceleration in the directions adjacent to it. The AI-CLEAR self-assessment helps you identify which investment will produce the largest return not just in that dimension, but across the system.

The Serious AI Leadership Maturity Assessment

Before a 90-day plan can be meaningful, a leader needs an honest baseline. The Serious AI Leadership Maturity Assessment gives you that baseline across all six Compass directions. It is not designed to be flattering. It is designed to be accurate.

The assessment uses a five-level scale for each direction, with behavioral anchors at each level. The anchors are designed to be as observable as possible, not what you believe about your capability, but what you and others can see in your leadership behavior.

Maturity Scale Anchors

Level 1 Awareness: The leader understands the concept intellectually but has not yet developed consistent behavioral practices in this area. In Mindset terms, a Level 1 leader can articulate the AI-CLEAR model but does not apply it self-critically. In Trust terms, a Level 1 leader knows the four layers exist but has not conducted a Trust Architecture audit.

Level 2 Application: The leader applies the capability in structured contexts when prompted, during formal reviews, or in high-stakes situations where the process is explicitly defined. A Level 2 Decision leader uses the Serious Decision Spectrum when a formal decision review process calls for it, but defaults to intuition in less formal settings.

Level 3 Consistency: The leader applies the capability as a default behavior, not just in formal settings. A Level 3 Communication leader does not wait for a formal change management process to communicate about an AI initiative; they maintain ongoing transparent communication as a standard practice.

Level 4 Integration: The leader applies multiple capabilities simultaneously and fluidly. They no longer think of Mindset and Decisions as separate capabilities; they bring the AI-CLEAR model to every Spectrum mapping conversation as a matter of course. The six Compass directions are starting to function as a unified posture.

Level 5 Leadership: The leader develops this capability in others. They design organizational systems that build capability across the team. A Level 5 Alignment leader does not just execute strong alignment practices themselves; they have built governance structures, facilitation protocols, and organizational norms that produce alignment even when they are not in the room.

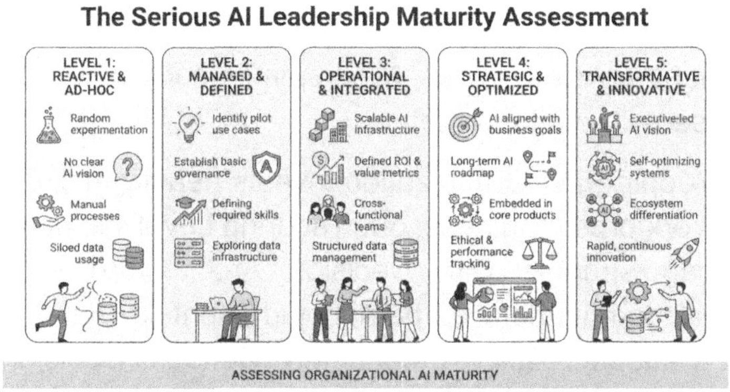

Common Organizational Patterns

Years of AI leadership consulting reveal that organizations tend to cluster into a small set of maturity patterns, each with characteristic strengths and predictable blind spots.

The Technology-Forward Organization typically scores Level 4 or above on Decision capability; the technical leaders are sophisticated users of AI decision frameworks, but often scores Level 2 or below on Communication and Empowerment. The AI capability is real but inaccessible to most of the organization because the people who built it have not invested in making it comprehensible, trustworthy, and useful to those who need to operate within it.

The Governance-Heavy Organization scores strongly on Alignment and Stewardship. The governance processes are robust and regularly reviewed, but often score Level 2 on Mindset Readiness because the governance rigor creates risk aversion that crowds out the intellectual curiosity needed to stay current as technology evolves. These organizations often have excellent policies about AI systems that no longer represent the state of the art.

The People-First Organization invests heavily in Trust and Workforce readiness, often scoring Level 4 in both, but can struggle with Decision Architecture. The cultural commitment to human judgment is genuine and valuable. Still, without the Serious Decision Spectrum discipline, it sometimes extends to decisions that would benefit significantly from greater AI authority, placing avoidable cognitive burden on teams and slowing execution.

The Balanced Organization, the one that Miriam Chen's team was building by the time of the Tuesday morning meeting, as this chapter opens, does not score highest in any single direction. Instead, it maintains Level 3 or higher across all six directions and actively prevents any direction from falling below that threshold. This is the profile that sustains AI leadership effectiveness over time.

Team and Organizational Assessment

The most powerful use of maturity assessment is not individual but collective. When a leadership team completes the assessment independently and compares results, the gaps between individual perceptions often reveal exactly the organizational dynamics that are limiting AI leadership effectiveness.

A common finding: the most senior leaders systematically overestimate their communication maturity, while frontline managers and individual contributors underestimate the Trust Architecture being maintained on their behalf. This perception gap is itself a leadership finding: it tells the senior leader that their communication is not reaching the organization the way they believe it is, and that the trust investments they are making are not yet visible to the people who need to feel them most.

When conducting a team-level maturity assessment, the facilitating leader should do three things: share their own results first and honestly, create a process in which all participants can share without comparing their scores to the leader's, and specify what organizational action will follow from the results. A maturity assessment that produces a strategy document no one acts on is worse than no assessment at all; it generates cynicism about the entire AI leadership development process.

Diagram 9.7: Team Maturity Assessment Facilitation Process

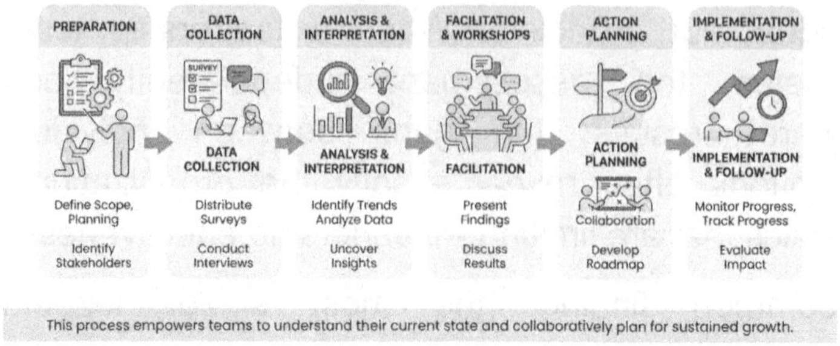

The 90-Day Action Plan

Leadership capability changes through repeated behavioral practice, not through understanding alone. The 90-day action plan that follows is structured around this principle. It is not a learning curriculum. It is a behavioral action plan, a specific set of leadership behaviors to practice, decisions to make, and organizational structures to build over the next ninety days.

The 90-day horizon is deliberate. It is long enough for organizational change to become visible and short enough for accountability to remain real. Each phase of the plan targets a different layer of AI leadership development: foundation, structure, and culture, and corresponds directly to the chapter content that grounds it.

Days 1 through 30: Foundation

The first thirty days are about honest inventory and priority setting. You cannot build forward from a false baseline.

- Complete the AI-CLEAR self-assessment from Chapter 2. Identify your lowest-scoring dimension and write one specific behavioral action you will take in the next thirty days to develop it. Do not choose the action that sounds most impressive; choose the one that will have the most direct impact on your actual day-to-day AI leadership.
- Complete a Trust Architecture audit using the four-layer framework from Chapter 5. For each layer- System Trust, Team Trust, Stakeholder Trust, and Self-Trust- write a one-sentence current-state assessment and identify whether that layer has strengthened, held steady, or weakened in the past ninety days.
- Conduct the executive alignment audit from Chapter 6. Identify the one alignment gap in your leadership team's AI governance that is most likely to create operational problems in the next six months. Do not manage this finding; address it directly with the relevant leader within the first thirty days.
- Complete the Serious AI Leadership Maturity Assessment for yourself and, if possible, facilitate a team-level completion with your direct reports. Use the results to identify which

two Compass directions represent your highest-priority development opportunities.

- Review the AI initiatives currently in flight in your organization. For each one, identify which quadrant of the Serious Decision Spectrum it primarily occupies and whether the current governance approach matches that quadrant assignment.

By Day 30, you should have: a completed AI-CLEAR assessment with one active development action, a Trust Architecture audit with at least one concrete maintenance action in progress, a named alignment gap with a plan to address it, and a maturity baseline for yourself and your team.

DIAGRAM 9.8: THE 90-DAY AI LEADERSHIP ACTION PLAN

Days 31 through 60: Structure

The second phase builds the organizational structures that turn individual leadership capability into institutional capability. This is where personal practice becomes organizational infrastructure.

- Establish or substantially rechart your AI governance body, using the alignment principles from Chapter 6. The governance body should have a clear charter, defined decision rights, and a regular meeting cadence. If a governance body already exists, assess whether it has a genuine shared purpose or is performing alignment without achieving it.
- Apply the Serious Decision Spectrum from Chapter 3 explicitly to your organization's three most consequential current AI decisions. Convene the relevant decision-makers, map each decision on the two-axis grid, and document the appropriate level of AI authority for each one. If any decision has been implicitly treated as Automate when it belongs in Augment or Assert, correct that classification before the next decision cycle.
- Build an AI communication calendar for the next quarter. Using the communication principles from Chapter 4, identify the key AI updates, milestone announcements, and stakeholder briefings that need to happen over the next sixty days and assign specific owners and formats to each one. The communication calendar should

exist as a visible artifact, not a mental model, so that it can be reviewed and updated as conditions change.

- Assess your workforce AI readiness using the four-dimensional framework from Chapter 7: technical literacy, workflow integration, judgment capability, and adaptive capacity. Identify which readiness dimension shows the largest gap between the current state and your AI strategy's requirements. Commit to a specific reskilling investment, however modest, that closes part of that gap within the next sixty days.
- Conduct a stewardship review of your current AI deployments using the responsible AI principles from Chapter 8. For each deployment, assess whether data governance is documented. Is there a clear accountability owner? Is there an escalation protocol for harmful outputs? If any deployment fails any of these three questions, address the gap before proceeding to the Culture phase.

By Day 60, you should have: a functioning governance body with a clear charter, Spectrum-mapped decisions for your three most consequential AI choices, a visible communication calendar, a named workforce readiness investment in progress, and a completed stewardship review with gaps documented and assigned.

Days 61 through 90: Culture

The third phase targets the deepest and most durable layer of organizational change: culture. Culture does not change through policy. It changes through visible leadership behavior repeated consistently until it becomes the norm.

- Launch a team AI literacy initiative, using the reskilling principles from Chapter 7. The initiative does not need to be large or expensive. What makes it culturally significant is that it is visible, leader-sponsored, and connected to real work. The leader who participates in AI literacy development alongside their team sends a stronger signal than any policy document.
- Complete a responsible AI review of every current AI deployment using the governance framework from Chapter 8. By this phase, the stewardship review from Day 31–60 has identified gaps that need to be closed. Every deployment should have a documented accountability owner, a data governance statement, and an active escalation protocol before the 90-day period ends.
- Publish your personal AI leadership principles. These are not corporate policy; they are your own articulation of how you lead in the context of AI: what you believe about human-AI collaboration, what you will and will not permit AI to decide on your behalf, and what you owe your team as their AI leader. Share them with

your direct reports and, where appropriate, with your broader organization. This act of transparency is one of the highest-leverage trust-building moves available to a leader.

- Run a Compass review with your leadership team. Using the maturity assessment results from Days 1–30, evaluate progress across all six directions. Celebrate genuine gains. Name the directions that have not moved and commit to specific actions in the next ninety days. The practice of quarterly Compass review should not end at Day 90; it should become a standing leadership team ritual.
- Customize the next 90-day cycle. Based on what you learned in this first cycle, adjust your development priorities for the next quarter. The 90-day plan is not a one-time exercise; it is the cadence of serious AI leadership development.

Diagram 9.9: The 90-Day Milestone Tracker

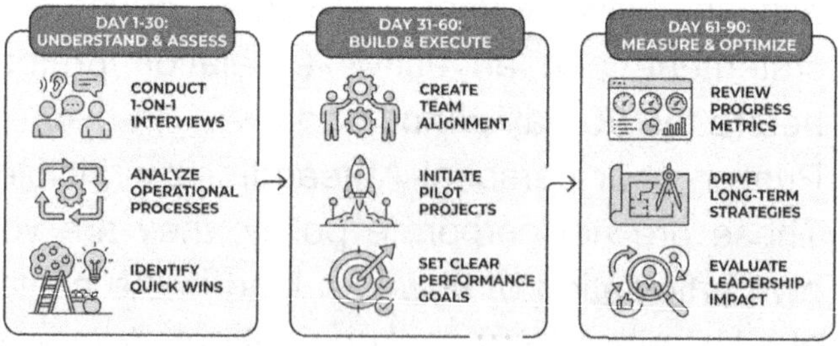

THIS 90-DAY MILESTONE TRACKER OUTLINES THE CRITICAL FOCUS AREAS AND EXPECTED KEY ACHIEVEMENTS FOR A NEW LEADER TO ESTABLISH STRONG FOOTING, BUILD TRUST, AND DELIVER RESULTS.

Customizing for C-Suite Versus Operational Manager Starting Points

The 90-day plan above is written for a senior leader, someone who has direct influence over governance structures, alignment bodies, and organizational communication. For C-suite executives, the plan largely applies as written, with the addition of external stakeholders and board communication activities that the plan's structure does not fully capture.

For operational managers and leaders who have significant influence over their own teams but limited direct authority over enterprise governance, the 90-day plan requires adaptation rather than wholesale replacement. The AI-CLEAR assessment and Trust Architecture audit are equally relevant at every leadership level. The governance body's work should be adapted to participate in or influence existing governance structures rather than create new ones. The communication calendar should focus on team-level communication. And the workforce AI readiness assessment should target the specific roles within the manager's direct span of control.

The principle that does not change regardless of seniority: the 90-day plan must produce visible organizational artifacts, documents, decisions, initiatives, and conversations that can be reviewed at Day 30, Day 60, and Day 90. Leadership development that produces only internal insight and no external behavioral change is learning, not leading. The purpose of the plan is action.

Sustaining AI Leadership Over Time

Why AI Leadership Is a Practice, Not a Credential

Every credential-based approach to AI leadership carries the same implicit promise: complete the program, earn the certification, become an AI leader. The promise is seductive and largely false. The AI landscape is changing at a pace that makes any fixed-point qualification obsolete within eighteen months. The regulatory environment is evolving across multiple jurisdictions simultaneously. New AI capabilities, particularly in agentic and multimodal systems, are creating leadership challenges that did not exist when many existing AI leadership frameworks were written.

This is not an argument against structured learning. It is an argument against treating structured learning as a destination rather than a starting point. The serious AI leader treats their capability development as a physician treats medical knowledge: a continuously updated practice that requires regular investment, peer learning, and honest self-assessment against current standards, not against the standards that existed when they first trained.

The practical implication is that the Compass review, the AI-CLEAR self-assessment, and the Trust Architecture audit are not exercises you complete once and then forget. They are quarterly rituals. The maturity levels you reached in this first 90-day cycle will look different in six months as the AI landscape around you evolves. The leader who revisits their Readiness dimension every quarter genuinely, not performatively, will rarely be caught flat-footed by a new AI development that their organization needed them to understand.

Building Personal Learning Rhythms

The information landscape for AI leadership is both vast and noisy. The serious AI leader does not try to consume everything; they build selective, high-signal learning rhythms that keep them current without creating the cognitive overload that produces reactive rather than thoughtful leadership.

A practical learning rhythm for serious AI leaders has three levels. The daily level is narrow and highly filtered: one source of curated AI leadership intelligence, not AI news generally, but specifically the intersection of AI and organizational leadership, governance, and workforce impact. Five minutes of high-signal reading is worth more than forty-five minutes of undifferentiated news consumption.

The monthly level involves deeper engagement with a single significant topic. Not skimming, reading, discussing, applying. One well-chosen paper, case study, or leadership perspective, when absorbed and discussed with a peer or direct report, does more for leadership development than a dozen articles read and forgotten.

The quarterly level is the Compass review: the structured self-assessment and team conversation that connects learning to capability development. This is the cadence that prevents learning from becoming an intellectual hobby rather than a leadership practice. The quarterly cycle asks: What did I learn over the past 90 days? How has my AI leadership maturity changed? Which direction of the Compass needs attention next quarter?

Diagram 9.10: The AI Leader's Personal Learning Rhythm

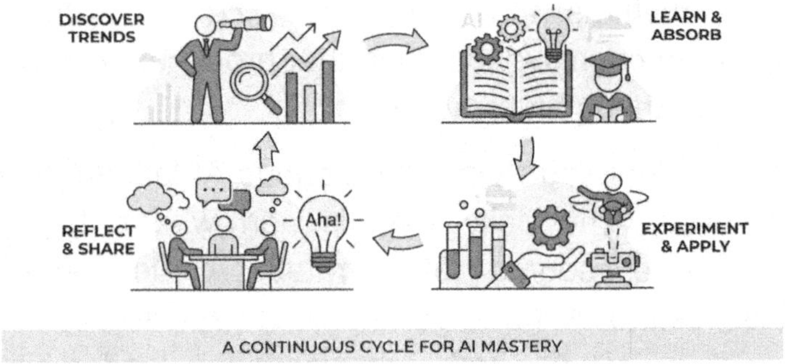

Community and Peer Learning

Individual learning has real limits. The best AI leadership learning happens in conversation with peers facing similar challenges, with practitioners in adjacent industries, and with people who hold perspectives the leader would never generate on their own. Cross-industry AI leadership dialogue is particularly valuable because it exposes leaders to AI deployment patterns, governance innovations, and workforce strategies that their own industry has not yet developed.

Formal peer learning communities, whether industry associations, executive roundtables, or internally convened leadership forums, create an accountability structure that prevents learning intentions from dissolving under operational pressure. When a peer expects you to show up with an update on your 90-day progress, you are more likely actually to make progress. The social dimension of leadership development is not soft; it is structural.

There is also a mentoring dimension that serious AI leaders cannot afford to neglect. The leaders who will navigate the next phase of AI agentic systems, hybrid workforce integration, and the emerging Chief AI Officer function are currently mid-career managers and team leaders. They are watching how the current generation of AI leaders behaves. The most important AI leadership development investment you can make in the next twelve months may not be your own AI-CLEAR score. It may be the intentional time you spend developing the AI leadership capability of a promising manager two levels below you.

Developing the Next Generation

Sponsorship in AI leadership means more than mentoring. It means using your organizational influence to put emerging AI leaders in the rooms where AI decisions are made, to credit them publicly when their thinking shapes organizational direction, and to protect the space for them to develop leadership judgment under real conditions, not just in training simulations.

The leaders who built the AI leadership capability of their organizations, who took the AI-CLEAR model seriously, who applied the Serious Decision Spectrum with discipline, who maintained the Trust Architecture with transparency, those leaders will have done something lasting if they have replicated those capabilities in the next tier of organizational leadership. A serious AI leader who retires or moves on, leaving an organization whose AI leadership capability depends entirely on their personal presence, has not built AI leadership at all. They have been the AI leadership system. Building organizational capability means building the institutional infrastructure, norms, practices, and development pathways that make the capability durable beyond any individual tenure.

Looking Forward: What Comes After the Compass

The Near-Term Leadership Challenges

Three developments in the near-term AI landscape will require serious AI leaders to extend their current capability in ways that the frameworks in this book begin to address but do not fully resolve.

Agentic AI governance is the first. As AI systems gain the ability to take multi-step autonomous actions, initiate processes, allocate resources, and communicate with external parties, the governance frameworks built for tool-based AI are no longer sufficient. The Serious Decision Spectrum will need to be applied at the system design level, not just at the individual decision level: when a leader authorizes an agentic system, they are effectively pre-authorizing every decision that system will make within its operational scope. The Trust Architecture will need a new layer, Agentic Trust, that specifically addresses the leader's calibrated confidence in autonomous AI systems acting on their behalf. These are not distant challenges. For many organizations, governance is the challenge of the next eighteen months.

The hybrid workforce is the second. Chapter 7's workforce readiness framework effectively describes the current inflection point. But the near-term horizon involves a deeper integration of human and AI labor than most organizations have designed for. Roles that were conceptually "augmented" will effectively become collaborative in a technical sense, a professional working alongside an AI agent that handles specific tasks within a shared workflow, with real-time interaction, role negotiation, and accountability ambiguity that current HR and governance frameworks do not adequately address. The leader who has built a strong workforce development capability is well-positioned to lead through this transition. The leader who has not will find that the human capital consequences of agentic AI arrive much faster than they anticipated.

The emerging Chief AI Officer role is the third. Organizations that had the foresight to create a Chief AI Officer position early are already discovering the limitations of having designed that role around AI deployment rather than AI leadership. The CAI officer for the next five years will need the full Compass capability, not just technical understanding and governance discipline, but the communication, trust architecture, and human development capabilities that make AI leadership sustainable. Leaders building that role or helping to define it in their organizations should map it against all six Compass directions, not just the technical and governance ones.

DIAGRAM 9.11: THE NEAR-TERM AI LEADERSHIP HORIZON

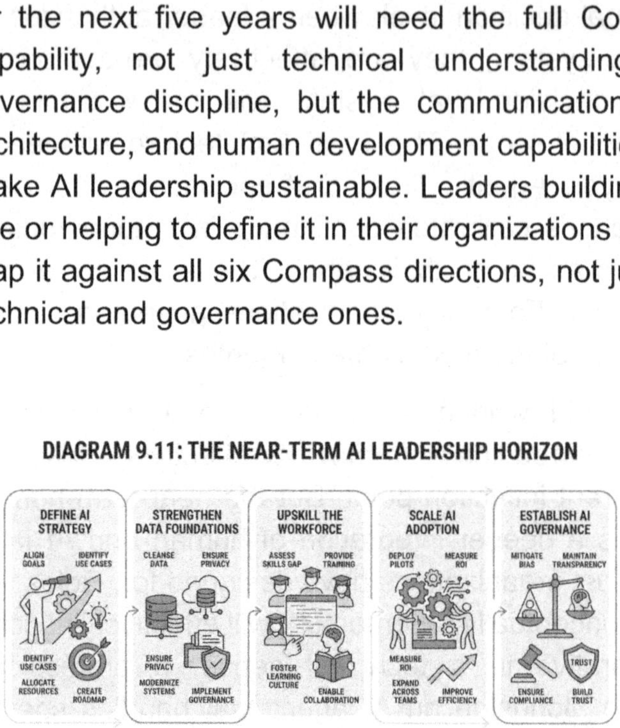

A FRAMEWORK FOR LEADERS TO NAVIGATE RESPONSIBLE AI ADOPTION AND CAPABILITY BUILDING IN THE NEAR-TERM.

The Medium-Term Horizon

Beyond the near term, serious AI leaders should be thinking about a development that will reshape the relationship between leadership and learning: AI systems that teach, coach, and evaluate leadership performance.

This is not speculative. AI coaching tools for communication, decision-making, and stakeholder management already exist. The medium-term trajectory takes them from optional add-ons to core development infrastructure: AI systems that observe leadership behavior across thousands of organizational interactions, identify patterns invisible to any individual coach or manager, and generate personalized development recommendations with a specificity that no human coach can match at scale.

This creates a specific leadership challenge that currently lacks a good answer: how does a leader maintain Self-Trust, the fourth layer of the Trust Architecture, when an AI system has better observational data on their leadership behavior than they do? The answer is not to reject AI-assisted leadership development. It is to approach it with the same calibrated trust that the Trust Architecture prescribes for all AI systems: earned incrementally, validated continuously, and held with the honest recognition that the system's outputs are information, not instruction. The leader who understands that distinction will use AI coaching tools more effectively than the leader who either dismisses them or surrenders to them.

The Leadership Constant

Across all the changes that AI will bring- the agentic systems, the hybrid workforce, the coaching tools, the regulatory evolution, and the capabilities that do not yet exist- certain things will remain true about effective organizational leadership.

People will still need to understand why decisions are made. The communication capability from Chapter 4 does not become obsolete as AI advances; it becomes more critical, because the gap between what AI can do and what most people understand about it will continue to generate organizational anxiety that only clear, honest human communication can address.

Organizations will still need trust as their operating medium. Every chapter in this book, if reduced to a single sentence, says the same thing: leadership is the management of trust relationships. AI changes the specific trust relationships that matter most and the specific behaviors that build and erode them. Still, it does not change the fundamental structure of human organizations as trust-based systems. The leader who understands this will navigate every AI development, however dramatic, with their fundamental competence intact.

Accountability will still be a human responsibility. The clearest constant in AI leadership is this: no matter how autonomous, accurate, or impressive an AI system becomes, the human leader who deployed it, governed it, and authorized its use is the one who answers for what it does. Accountability cannot be outsourced to the algorithm. This is not a legal observation; it is a leadership one. The leader who genuinely understands and genuinely accepts this accountability, in the Assert spirit of the Serious Decision Spectrum, is the leader whose organization can trust them with AI.

And people will still need leaders who see them and understand that the organization is not primarily a collection of workflows and optimizations but a community of people working with dignity and purpose.

The AI leader who keeps that in mind through every pilot, governance review, and maturity assessment is the one who earns the trust that makes all the frameworks work.

DIAGRAM 9.12: THE LEADERSHIP CONSTANTS IN THE AI ERA

CORE HUMAN LEADERSHIP COMPETENCIES ARE CRITICAL AMIDST TECHNOLOGICAL ADVANCEMENTS.

Your Role in Shaping the AI Era

This book is about developing your capability as an AI leader. But capability for its own sake is not the goal. The goal is what you do with it, the specific, consequential choices you make as a leader about how AI is built, deployed, governed, and developed within your organization.

Those choices have consequences beyond your organization. The leaders who establish responsible-by-design governance infrastructures are raising the standard for their industries. The leaders who invest seriously in workforce readiness are demonstrating that AI transition and workforce dignity are not opposite; they are complementary commitments that serious organizations can pursue simultaneously. The leaders who maintain genuine Trust Architecture, including self-trust to override AI recommendations when human judgment calls for it, are proving that AI capability and human accountability can coexist within the same organization.

These are not small contributions. The AI era will not be shaped primarily by the technology companies building the models. It will be shaped by the tens of thousands of organizational leaders who make daily decisions about how AI enters the lives of their people, customers, and communities. You are one of those leaders. The Compass you carry out of this chapter is not a theoretical instrument. It is the tool with which you will make those decisions not perfectly, but seriously, consistently, and with your eyes open.

The Serious AI Leader's Checklist for Chapter 9

Use this checklist to confirm that the integration work of this chapter has been translated into concrete leadership commitments.

- I have completed the AI-CLEAR self-assessment and identified my highest-leverage development dimension.
- I have completed a Trust Architecture audit across all four layers and taken at least one active maintenance action.
- I have mapped my organization's three most consequential current AI decisions on the

Serious Decision Spectrum and confirmed that the governance approach matches the quadrant assignment.

- I have completed the Serious AI Leadership Maturity Assessment for myself and facilitated, or plan to facilitate, a team-level assessment.
- I have written my 90-day action plan with specific actions assigned to Days 1–30, 31–60, and 61–90.
- I have identified which of the six Compass directions is currently my organization's weakest and have a specific plan to strengthen it.
- I have built, or committed to building, a personal AI learning rhythm at the daily, monthly, and quarterly levels.
- I have named at least one emerging AI leader I will actively sponsor in the next six months.
- I have drafted my personal AI leadership principles and have a plan to share them with my team.
- I understand the near-term challenges of agentic governance, hybrid workforce, and the evolving CAIO role, and have considered which of these will arrive in my organization first.

DIAGRAM 9.13: THE SERIOUS AI LEADERS COMPASS: FULL INTEGRATION VIEW

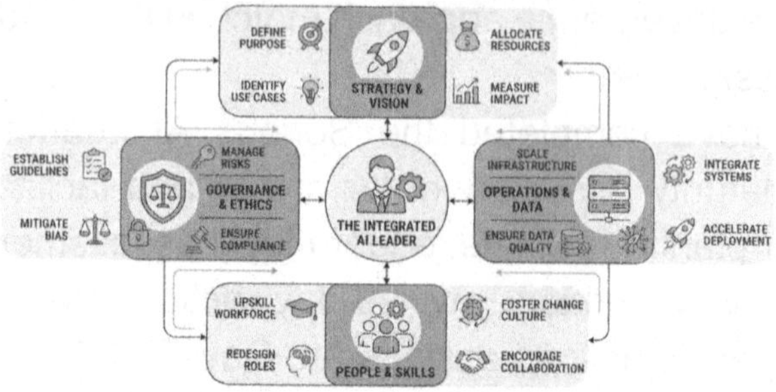

THIS DIAGRAM ILLUSTRATES THE FOUR KEY DOMAINS LEADERS MUST SYNCHRONIZE FOR SUCCESSFUL, END-TO-END AI ADOPTION AND LONG-TERM VALUE CREATION ACROSS THE ORGANIZATION.

The Serious Commitment

Nine chapters ago, this book made a claim: that serious managers can lead AI initiatives effectively, not because they master every technical dimension of the technology, but because they lead. They bring rigorous thinking, genuine human commitment, disciplined frameworks, and honest self-awareness to the hardest organizational challenge of the current era.

That claim has now been developed, tested, and integrated into a complete system. The AI-CLEAR Leadership Model tells you where to look within yourself. The Serious Decision Spectrum tells you how to assign AI authority with discipline. The Trust Architecture tells you what organizational relationships to maintain and how. Communication capability helps you make AI initiatives comprehensible and trustworthy to the people who must live with them. The alignment frameworks tell you how to build genuine organizational consensus rather than performative consensus. The workforce investment principles tell you what you owe your team. The stewardship commitment tells you what you owe everyone else. And the Compass tells you how it all works together.

The commitment that serious AI leadership requires is not the dramatic commitment of a bold strategic announcement. It is the quieter, more durable commitment of consistent practice completing the AI-CLEAR assessment every quarter even when the results are uncomfortable, maintaining the Trust Architecture even when it is easier to let a relationship drift, applying the Serious Decision Spectrum even when organizational pressure wants to default every decision to Automate, and showing up for your team as the human leader they need you to be, not the AI orchestrator that the technology narrative sometimes suggests is the ideal.

You will not make every decision right. No serious AI leader does. Technology will surprise you; the organizational dynamics will resist you, and there will be days when the gap between your current capability and what the situation requires feels discouraging. On those days, the Compass is still there. The directions have not changed. Practice has not become less important because it is hard. In fact, the practice becomes most valuable precisely when it is hardest, when the situation is most complex, and the stakes are highest. The organizational pressure to take the easy path is strongest.

That is when all the pieces, working together, are not a metaphor. It is the operational condition that separates leaders who get the best from AI and give the best to the people working alongside it from those who merely manage in its vicinity.

This is the work. You are the leader it requires. Do it.

11 Conclusion

The Leader the Moment Requires

There is a scene that plays out in organizations around the world every day. An AI system produces a recommendation. A manager has to decide what to do with it.

That single moment, the pause between the algorithm's output and the human's response, is where this entire book lives.

In that pause, everything you have built as an AI leader either shows up or it does not. Your conceptual grounding tells you whether the recommendation is plausible. Your mindset determines whether you approach it with calibrated curiosity or reactive compliance. Your decision framework tells you which quadrant this decision belongs to and how much AI authority is appropriate. Your communication skills shape how you explain your eventual choice to the people who need to understand it. Your trust architecture determines whether you and your team have the confidence to act decisively. Your alignment work means that your choice is consistent with what your leadership team has agreed to pursue. Your investment in your workforce means the people around you are equipped to engage with AI as capable partners rather than anxious bystanders. And your stewardship principles ensure that the downstream consequences for people, for data, for organizational culture are considered alongside the immediate outcome.

That is the Serious AI Leader's Compass in action, not as a checklist to complete before every decision, but as a leadership character that is present in how you show up because you have done the work to internalize it.

What the Journey Through This Book Has Built

Nine chapters. Each one is designed to deepen a specific dimension of your AI leadership capability. Together, they form something more than the sum of their parts: a complete, integrated foundation for leading in the AI era.

We began in Chapter 1 by grounding you in the actual landscape of intelligent machines, cutting through both the hype and the mystification to equip you with the vocabulary and conceptual framework that effective AI leadership requires. You learned what AI is and is not, what agentic AI means for the leadership challenge, and what the current state of enterprise adoption tells us about where the real work lies. That foundation is not merely introductory material. It is the bedrock on which everything else rests. A leader who does not understand the technology they are governing cannot govern it well, no matter how sophisticated their leadership skills are in other domains. Operational clarity about the technology is the first obligation of the serious AI leader, and Chapter 1 delivered it.

Chapter 2 moved inside into the mental models, biases, and assumptions that determine how you respond to AI in real time. The AI-CLEAR Leadership Model gave you a five-dimensional diagnostic for your own AI leadership posture, and the concept of discernment, the disciplined judgment about when AI adds value and when it diminishes, emerged as the most underrated skill in the current landscape. The "both/and" mindset replaced the false binary of human versus AI with the more productive and more accurate reality: the best outcomes come from integrating both, with human leadership providing the direction, the values, and the judgment that no algorithm can supply. Chapter 2 established that the AI era is not a technology problem to be solved. It is a leadership problem to be led.

In Chapter 3, you applied that mindset to the domain where leadership is most visibly tested: decisions. The Serious Decision Spectrum gave you a practical tool for classifying decisions along the axes of data density and human stakes, and for calibrating AI authority accordingly. You encountered the cognitive biases that AI can amplify as readily as it can reduce, and you built a personal policy about the types of decisions that belong in the Assert quadrant, where your leadership, your values, and your accountability are irreplaceable. Every consequential decision you make from this point forward can be evaluated through the Spectrum. That is workflow-level impact.

Chapter 4 turned to the skill that determines whether all the other skills produce organizational results:

communication. The most effective AI leaders are not those who know the most about the technology, but those who can translate it across audiences, navigate the trust-building and trust-maintaining demands of multi-stakeholder AI communication, and tell an honest story about AI's capabilities and limitations that survives contact with organizational reality. You built a communication toolkit for five critical AI leadership scenarios and developed a clearer sense of your role as a bridge between technical reality and organizational understanding. AI that cannot be explained cannot be trusted, and AI that cannot be trusted will not be used well.

Chapter 5 addressed the most underinvested asset in enterprise AI: trust. The Trust Architecture, with its four layers of system trust, team trust, stakeholder trust, and self-trust, gave you a map of the trust landscape that every AI leader must actively manage. The paradox of high AI adoption alongside persistent workforce anxiety revealed not a technology problem but a leadership problem: AI is being adopted faster than the governance, communication, and accountability structures that make it trustworthy. Your role in closing that gap is not peripheral; it is central to whether AI delivers on its promise in your organization. Trust is not a soft outcome. It is the infrastructure on which every AI initiative stands or falls.

Chapter 6 scaled the conversation to the organizational level with a focus on executive alignment, the capability that research consistently identifies as the single most powerful predictor of AI initiative success. You learned the critical distinction between support and alignment, built the structural tools to sustain real alignment through multi-year AI transformations, and developed a clear understanding of the AI champion role that keeps alignment alive across formal governance touchpoints. AI strategies that enjoy broad executive support still fail when the organization lacks true shared commitment. Chapter 6 gave you the tools to build the real thing.

Chapter 7 addressed one of the most consequential and most frequently neglected dimensions of AI leadership: building the team that can lead alongside AI. Workforce readiness is not a human resources function delegated below the executive suite; it is a strategic imperative that belongs in every AI leader's active portfolio. You examined what it means to reskill with intention: not just closing today's skill gaps but building the adaptive capacity that enables your team to meet the next wave of AI capability. You explored the distinctive pressures facing middle managers, the people who translate organizational AI strategy into daily operational reality and who bear the heaviest burden of managing resistance. You built frameworks to foster psychological safety that make experimentation possible and sustain honest communication. Mission-aligned workforce development is not an add-on to AI leadership. It is one of its foundations.

Chapter 8 brought the book's most human and most consequential theme to the foreground: stewardship. The leader's obligation to the people, the data, the systems, and the communities affected by their AI decisions is not a compliance burden; it is the expression of leadership at its most mature. You developed a responsible AI framework that functions as operational governance rather than a values declaration. Responsible by design is not a constraint on AI ambition; it is the condition under which AI ambition earns the right to be sustained. The reskilling covenant, the data ethics principles, the governance cadences: these are not bureaucratic additions to the AI leader's role. They are the architecture of trust that makes everything else work.

And in Chapter 9, you assembled it all into the Serious AI Leader's Compass, a living framework for AI leadership that operates as a system rather than a checklist. The nine capabilities are interdependent: conceptual grounding enables better mindset work, better mindset enables sounder decisions, sounder decisions communicated well build trust, trust enables alignment, alignment enables workforce investment, workforce investment enables stewardship, and stewardship closes the loop back to the organizational culture that determines whether AI leadership is sustainable over time. You completed a maturity assessment, built a 90-day action plan, and developed the habits that will keep your AI leadership capabilities current and relevant as the technology continues to evolve.

Diagram C.1: The Nine-Chapter Journey

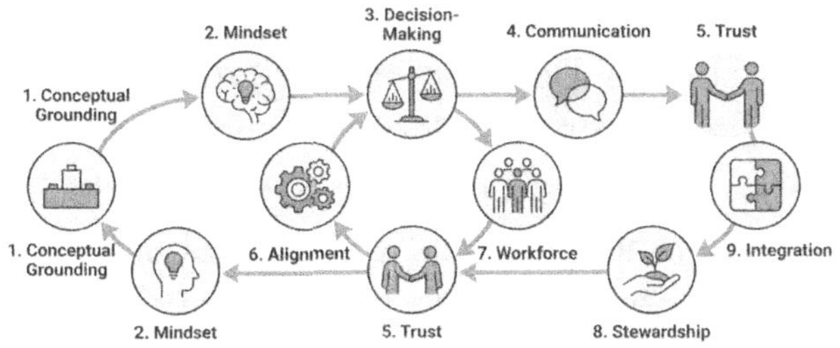

Caption: An ongoing and iterative journey to master AI leadership development.

The Frameworks as Living Tools

The three frameworks introduced in this book, the AI-CLEAR Leadership Model, the Serious Decision Spectrum, and the Trust Architecture, are not artifacts of the reading experience. They are tools designed to be used, returned, and revised as your AI leadership context evolves. What distinguishes serious AI leaders from informed bystanders is not whether they have read about these frameworks. It is whether the frameworks are present in their decisions.

Revisit your AI-CLEAR self-assessment every quarter. AI environments evolve rapidly, and the dimension that was your strength six months ago may be under new pressure today. A leader who rates themselves four on Readiness in January and assumes that score holds in October has confused a snapshot with a standing posture. Rate yourself honestly across all five dimensions: Curiosity, Leverage, Empowerment, Accountability, and Readiness, and treat your lowest score as your highest-leverage development investment. The AI-CLEAR model is most powerful not as a report card, but as a compass for where to focus next.

Apply the Serious Decision Spectrum to your most consequential current AI decisions not theoretically, but literally. Draw the quadrants. Plot the decisions your team is managing this quarter. Challenge any decision that seems to have migrated from Assert to Automate without a conscious organizational choice being made. Algorithmic authority tends to expand by default; human authority contracts by neglect. The Spectrum is your primary tool for preventing that drift and for ensuring that the pilot-to-production pathway for any new AI capability includes explicit agreement about which quadrant it belongs in and why.

Conduct the Trust Architecture audit with your leadership team at least annually, and more frequently if your AI environment is changing rapidly. Ask which layer is at risk right now: system trust, team trust, stakeholder trust, or self-trust. Ask where trust has eroded in the past 90 days and what specific actions you will take to rebuild or reinforce it. Trust Architecture is most valuable not as a retrospective diagnosis but as a prospective maintenance practice. Trust, once broken, is expensive to rebuild. Proactive maintenance is far cheaper than crisis repair and far less damaging to the workforce confidence that Chapter 7 established as the foundation of AI-ready teams.

Used together, these three frameworks form an integrated leadership system. The AI-CLEAR model assesses your posture. The Serious Decision

Spectrum governs your choices. The Trust Architecture manages your relationships. A leader who operates all three intentionally, habitually, and honestly is a leader who has internalized not just the content of this book but the practice of serious AI leadership.

Diagram C.2: The Three Frameworks as an Integrated System

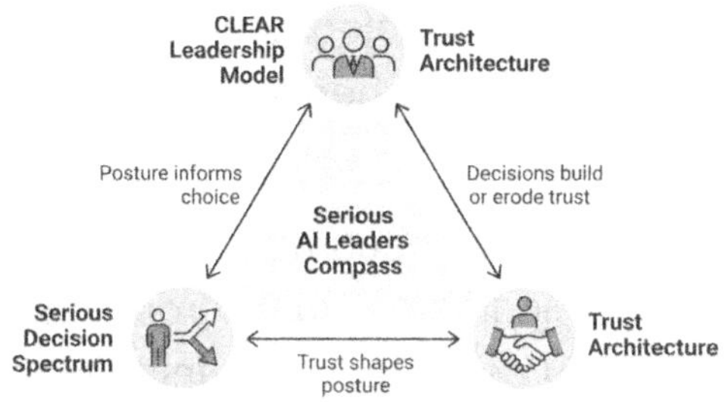

This caption 2.: infographic designes for a business leadership book, an executive and corporate tone.

The Future of AI Leadership

The landscape you will go through in the next three to five years will be significantly different from the one this book was written to address, not because the leadership principles will change, but because AI itself will evolve in ways that create new challenges for each of the nine capabilities you have built.

Agentic AI is the most immediate frontier. As autonomous systems take on more complex, multi-step tasks and major organizations commit substantial portions of their AI investment to agentic systems, the challenges of governance and stewardship will intensify. The question of who is accountable when an AI agent makes a consequential error will move from theoretical to urgent. The "agentic manager," a human whose primary job is to oversee, correct, and direct autonomous AI systems, is already emerging as a distinct organizational role, with skill requirements that current management development programs have yet to address. The leaders who will navigate this transition most effectively are those who have done exactly what this book has asked: internalized the principle that accountability cannot be delegated and built the self-trust to exercise judgment when the algorithm's answer is difficult to evaluate.

The hybrid workforce will become the default operating model. Research indicates that organizations with extensive agentic AI use expect meaningful reductions in middle management layers, not because managers are being replaced wholesale, but because AI is absorbing the information-brokering and coordination functions that historically justified many management roles. The managers who survive and thrive in this environment will be those who have shifted from information management to judgment and relationship leadership, exactly the capabilities this book has been building. Chapter 7's investment in workforce readiness and psychological safety is not preparation for a distant future. It is preparation for the next two years.

AI literacy will become a baseline organizational competency rather than a specialist skill. The leaders who invest now in team-level AI capability through the Empowerment dimension of AI-CLEAR, transparent communication, co-designed governance, and the honest reskilling conversations that Chapter 7 and

Chapter 8 made explicit will have a significant competitive advantage when the next wave of AI capability arrives. The organizations that treat AI literacy as optional today will find themselves in a permanent catch-up cycle, dependent on talent markets that cannot supply what they failed to develop internally.

The trust deficit will deepen if not actively addressed. The paradox of high AI adoption and low workforce trust in AI systems is not self-resolving. It requires deliberate leadership intervention, the kind of intervention that the Trust Architecture and the communication tools in this book are designed to support. Leaders who build trust infrastructure now are investing in organizational resilience that will determine competitive outcomes over the next three to five years. The AI leaders who get this right in the near term will inherit a compounding advantage: trust built today makes every subsequent AI initiative easier to govern, faster to scale, and more legitimate in the eyes of the workforce and stakeholders who must ultimately support it.

What will not change is the nature of the leadership challenge itself. Every AI era will require the same things it has always required of serious leaders: clarity of purpose, quality of judgment, genuine care for the people affected by organizational decisions, and the discipline to hold the line on values when the pressure to cut corners is highest. The specific content of those judgments will evolve. The frameworks for exercising them will need to be updated. But the character of the leader who exercises them well- curious, accountable, empowering, ready, and above all, human- will remain exactly what it has always been.

Diagram C.3: The AI Leadership Horizon: Near-Term Challenges

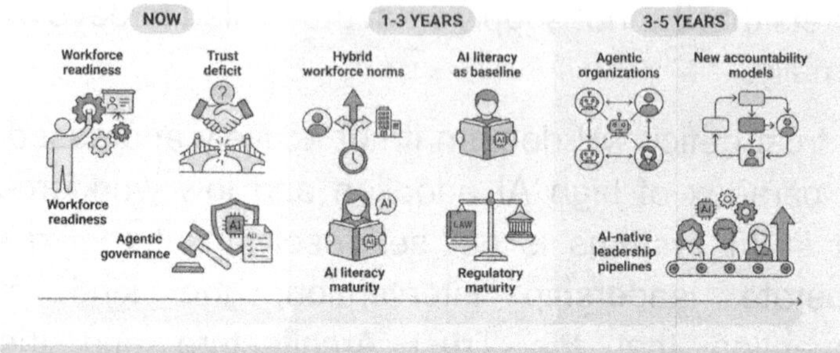

Diagram C.3: The AI Leadership Horizon to lenting mannata and adcerhip Horizon: Near-Term Challenges

Your Role in the AI Era

You picked up this book because you are serious about leading well in a moment that demands it. Not performing AI leadership for the quarterly earnings call or the all-hands meeting. Not outsourcing AI strategy to a technology team that lacks the organizational authority to execute it. Not treating workforce anxiety as someone else's problem or data ethics as a legal department concern. Leading with the clarity, the accountability, the humanity, and the discipline that the word has always required, applied to the most consequential technology shift of our professional lifetimes.

The Serious AI Leader is not defined by their technical expertise. The quality of their judgment defines them. They are defined by the trust their teams and stakeholders place in how they govern AI, not just whether the AI works, but also whether it is used well, honestly, and in ways that reflect the values of the organization and the people it serves. They are defined by whether, when the algorithm and the human disagree, they have the self-trust to know which one to listen to.

They are also defined by how they treat people as they navigate the disruption that AI creates. The reskilling covenant is not a human resources nicety; it is a leadership obligation. The psychological safety that enables honest conversations about AI's risks is not a culture program; it is the operational condition for good governance. The middle manager who is simultaneously expected to deploy AI, manage resistant teams, and demonstrate AI-era relevance deserves a leader who has thought through their burden and built the organizational structures to reduce it. Serious AI leadership is, at its core, leadership on behalf of people, not despite the technology, but through it.

That is a high bar. It is also an achievable one. And the work this book represents the thinking, the frameworks, the honest self-assessment, and the 90-day action plan you now carry is the foundation on which that leadership is built. You have not reached the end of the AI leadership journey. You have built the foundation from which to navigate it with confidence, with intention, and with the kind of steadiness that serious moments require.

A Call to Continued Learning

This book is one volume in the Serious Managers' Guide to AI series, a collection designed to build comprehensive AI leadership capability across the full range of functions and challenges that serious managers face. Each volume goes deeper into a specific domain: AI strategy and investment, AI and organizational culture, AI in product development, AI ethics and governance, the AI-enabled supply chain, the AI-ready finance function, and more. The series is designed to be read as a curriculum or consulted as a reference, whichever serves your learning style and professional context.

If the Serious Managers' Guide to AI Leadership has given you the orientation and the frameworks, the series will give you the depth. The principles you have built here- the AI-CLEAR mindset, the Serious Decision Spectrum, the Trust Architecture, the workforce readiness commitment, the stewardship ethic, and the full Compass- are the through-line of every subsequent volume. You will recognize them, apply them in new contexts, and find them more powerful with each application. A framework understood in one domain and applied in five becomes leadership instinct.

The AI era does not need more leaders who know about AI. It needs more leaders who lead with AI thoughtfully, accountably, and with genuine care for the people and organizations they serve. The distinction matters. Knowing about AI makes you conversant.

Leading with AI governing it, shaping its use, building the human structures around it that determine whether it creates value or erodes it- makes you responsible for outcomes that extend well beyond any single initiative or quarterly result.

The work of becoming that leader is never finished. Technology will evolve. Your organization will change. The governance challenges will deepen and multiply. The people looking to you for direction will need more from you tomorrow than they needed today. The nine chapters behind you have built the foundation. What you do with that foundation, the choices you make, the standards you hold, the trust you build and protect, is the work that remains. It is serious work. It is necessary work.

And It Is Yours To Do.

You Are That Leader.

Now Lead.

12 Works Referenced

Alaassar, Ahmed, et al. "Human-in-the-Loop Governance for High-Stakes AI Systems." *AI and Ethics*, vol. 4, no. 3, 2024, pp. 211–232. (CH3)

Al Harrasi, Nasser, and Abir Al Mujaini. "Leadership Governance under Algorithmic Mediation: Reconceptualizing Transformative Leadership through an Integrative Review." *Leadership & Organization Development Journal*, 2026, pp. 1–21. (CH5)

Amershi, Saleema, et al. "Guidelines for Human–AI Decision-Making in Enterprise Workflows." *Communications of the ACM*, vol. 67, no. 10, 2024, pp. 54–63. (CH3)

Binns, Reuben, and Michael Veale. "Is That Your Final Decision? Multi-Stage Decision-Making and Contestability in AI Systems." *Computer Law & Security Review*, vol. 52, 2024, article 105903. (CH3)

Brock, David C., and Margaret O'Mara, editors. *AI in the Age of Responsibility: Governance, Risk, and Accountability*. MIT Press, 2025. (CH8)

Brynjolfsson, Erik, et al. "Generative AI at Work." *National Bureau of Economic Research Working Paper*, no. 31682, 2024. (CH1)

Bughin, Jacques, et al. "The Economic Potential of Generative AI: The Next Productivity Frontier." McKinsey Global Institute, 2023. (CH1)

Calo, Ryan, et al., editors. *The Oxford Handbook of AI Governance*. Oxford UP, 2025. (CH8)

Carter, Sarah, and Daniel Susskind. "Managing the Organizational Consequences of Generative AI." *California Management Review*, vol. 66, no. 2, 2024, pp. 5–28. (CH2)

Cascio, Wayne F., and John W. Boudreau. "AI, Work, and the Future of Talent Management." *Human Resource Management*, vol. 63, no. 1, 2024, pp. 3–18. (CH7)

Cath, Corinne. "Governing Artificial Intelligence: Upholding Human Rights and Democratic Values." *International and Comparative Law Quarterly*, vol. 73, no. 4, 2024, pp. 901–928. (CH8)

Center for Security and Emerging Technology. *Measuring AI Adoption and Risk in Large Organizations: 2024 Survey Report*. Georgetown University, 2024. (CH1)

CIO Council. *Playbook for the Responsible Use of Generative AI in the Federal Government*. Executive Office of the President, 2024. (CH8)

Daugherty, Paul R., and H. James Wilson. *Radically Human: How New Technology Is Transforming Business and Shaping the Future of Work*. Updated ed., Harvard Business Review Press, 2023. (CH2)

Deloitte. *State of AI in the Enterprise, 6th Edition: From Ambition to Accountability*. Deloitte Insights, 2024. (CH6)

European Commission. *Artificial Intelligence Act: Provisional Agreement Text*. Publications Office of the European Union, 2024. (CH8)

Floridi, Luciano, and Josh Cowls. "A Unified Framework of Five Principles for AI in Society." *Philosophy & Technology*, vol. 37, 2024, article 12. (CH8)

Gallagher. *AI Adoption and Risk Survey 2025: Governance, Talent, and Trust Gaps*. Gallagher Research & Insights, 2025. (CH5)

Gartner. *Top Strategic Technology Trends for 2025: Agentic AI and the Future of Work*. Gartner Research, 2025. (CH1)

Google DeepMind. *Frontier AI Safety and Governance: Technical and Organizational Approaches*. Google DeepMind, 2024. (CH8)

Harvard Business Review Analytic Services. *Leading with AI: How Executives Turn Experimentation into Enterprise Value*. Harvard Business Publishing, 2023. (CH6)

IBM Institute for Business Value. *AI Governance in Practice: From Principles to Operating Models*. IBM, 2024. (CH5)

IEEE. *IEEE 7000-2024: Standard for Addressing Ethical Concerns during System Design*. IEEE Standards Association, 2024. (CH8)

Kellogg, Katherine C., et al. "Algorithmic Management and the Future of Leadership." *Academy of Management Annals*, vol. 18, no. 1, 2024, pp. 1–39. (CH2)

KPMG. *Trust in Artificial Intelligence: Building Confidence in Enterprise AI Systems*. KPMG International, 2023. (CH5)

Lee, Kai-Fu, and Chen Qiufan. *AI 2045: Leadership, Power, and the New Work Order*. Currency, 2025. (CH2)

McKinsey & Company. *The State of AI in 2024: Generative AI's Second Year*. McKinsey Global Survey, 2024. (CH1)

Microsoft. *Responsible AI Standard, v2: Enabling Trustworthy AI Systems*. Microsoft Corporation, 2023. (CH8)

Mollick, Ethan. *Co-Intelligence: Living and Working with AI*. Portfolio, 2024. (CH2)

NIST. *Artificial Intelligence Risk Management Framework (AI RMF 1.0)*. National Institute of Standards and Technology, 2023. (CH5)

OECD. *OECD Framework for the Classification of AI Systems*. OECD Publishing, 2023. (CH1)

OpenAI. *Model Spec for Frontier AI Systems: Safety, Alignment, and Deployment*. OpenAI, 2024. (CH8)

PwC. *AI Business Maturity 2025: From Pilots to P&L Impact*. PwC Research, 2025. (CH6)

Sacavém, António, et al. "AI-Driven Leadership: Decision-Making, Competencies, and Ethical Challenges—A Systematic Review." *Administrative Sciences*, vol. 16, no. 4, 2026, article 173. (CH3)

Saxena, Anurag, and Mary Uhl-Bien. "Relational Leadership in the Age of AI: Rethinking Followership, Agency, and Control." *The Leadership Quarterly*, vol. 35, no. 2, 2024, article 101746. (CH4)

Shneiderman, Ben. "Human-Centered AI: A Governance Agenda for Reliable, Safe, and Trustworthy Systems." *AI and Society*, vol. 39, no. 3, 2024, pp. 765–781. (CH5)

Stanford Institute for Human-Centered AI. *AI Index Report 2025: Tracking Global AI Development*. Stanford University, 2025. (CH1)

Suleyman, Mustafa, with Michael Bhaskar. *The Coming Wave: Technology, Power, and the Twenty-First Century's Greatest Dilemma*. Crown, 2023. (CH8)

Tambe, Prasanna, et al. "AI, Management Practices, and Organizational Performance." *Management Science*, vol. 70, no. 1, 2024, pp. 1–23. (CH6)

UK Information Commissioner's Office. *Explaining Decisions Made with AI: Guidance for Organizations*. ICO, updated 2023. (CH3)

UNESCO. *Recommendation on the Ethics of Artificial Intelligence: Implementation Guidelines*. UNESCO, 2023. (CH8)

U.S. Department of Labor. *Artificial Intelligence and the Workforce: Policy Considerations for Employers and Workers*. Office of the Assistant Secretary for Policy, 2024. (CH7)

U.S. Government Accountability Office. *Artificial Intelligence: Key Practices to Help Ensure Accountability and Responsible Use in Federal Agencies*. GAO-24-106543, 2024. (CH8)

World Economic Forum. *Empowering AI Leadership: A Boardroom Guide to Risk, Strategy, and Governance*. World Economic Forum, 2023. (CH6)

World Economic Forum. *Jobs of Tomorrow: Large Language Models and the Future of Work*. World Economic Forum, 2024. (CH7)

World Health Organization. *Ethics and Governance of AI for Health: Policy Guidance for Decision-Makers*. WHO, 2023. (CH8)

Made in United States
North Haven, CT
04 November 2026

21760243R00232